TECHNICAL WRITING, SIMPLIFIED

NELL JOHNSON | MARY SYLWESTER

FOURTH EDITION

Cover design by Finn Sylwester

Second Printing

ISBN 13: 978-1543268485
ISBN 10: 154326848X

Introduction

This book focuses on the essentials. It is designed for the advanced community college student or lower-level university student as an introduction to professional and technical writing. Our goal is to help students learn about the writing that may be expected of them in the workplace.

We wrote this textbook because we were frustrated at the textbook options available for our students. Most are expensive, and many are overwhelmingly complex. We wanted to create an affordable textbook that offered instructions about the writing process and the ethics associated with professional writing, along with specific, practical advice for constructing common workplace documents.

Our textbook offers easily understood models and instruction, with a straightforward structure that makes it easy for the student to work through the book, adding knowledge while practicing different forms and skills.

Unless otherwise specified, the text and graphics in this textbook are products of the authors. No part of this textbook may be reproduced without the written consent of the authors.

To Students:

We know that you are challenged by busy lives and thin wallets. We know that when we order an expensive textbook, you sometimes try to get along without it, trying to learn as much as possible from lectures and discussions. Books that include much more information than we can cover in class have begun to seem an unreasonable requirement, as well as much more complicated than is necessary. We hope that you will find this book easy to read, well organized, and useful, as well as fairly priced.

We have designed this book so that you can learn by doing. Exercises at the end of each chapter prompt you to create documents to practice the skills and knowledge learned. Examples within each chapter give you models of professional documents, and checklists at the ends of the chapters help you make sure that your assignments are complete and that they correspond to professional standards. Sidebars about professionalism and ethics, international considerations, and other helpful tips appear throughout the book to enrich your understanding. A Professional Vocabulary section at the end of the book provides a quick reference for key words and acronyms commonly used in business writing that may be mysterious, such as "bitmap graphic," "Gantt chart," or "deliverable."

Because many of you are already working in professional careers or preparing for entrance into competitive vocational programs, Professional & Technical Writing can be one of the most useful courses in your schedule. We hope this book will be a practical resource for you even after you finish the course.

To Instructors:

We know that some students learn best by following examples and inferring the rules, much as they originally learned their native language. Other students will want to read or hear explanations or instructions about how documents are made before creating one for themselves. We offer both the "how" (instructions) and the "what" (examples) with discussion topics and exercises designed to make instruction straightforward for both groups. We imagine our audience to be not only the student new to this type of writing, but also the student/worker, who may be asked to put together a report, write instructions, or respond to a client.

We have organized this book in the same way we normally organize our syllabi for a professional and technical writing course. We start with information about what it means to write professionally and ethically, and we share our knowledge of the writing process as it exists in a business setting. The chapters devoted to specific forms, such as short reports or user instructions, are organized so that students add skills in page design as they move through, with graphics just before the forms that absolutely require them, such as user instructions. We have placed the Job Application Materials chapter at the end, to send students into the world symbolically, if not in fact.

We welcome feedback about this textbook, as we continue to revise and update content. Write to Mary Sylwester at *mary.sylwester@pcc.edu* or Nell Johnson at *nell.johnson@pcc.edu*.

Table of Contents

Resources

Sample Documents

Checklists

Decision Aids

Worksheets

1 - Professionalism and Ethics

This chapter focuses on **you**. When you sit down to your laptop to draft an email, your personality, perspective, and character all come into play. Even in "technical communication," which theoretically erases all subjectivity, the "you" will always emerge. You establish your credibility by citing sources and thinking logically. You demonstrate your ability to write clearly, without pretense or offense. You learn to negotiate the area of non-verbal communication so that your professional stance is noticed and appreciated.

THINKING LOGICALLY

Logic is your friend. Logic helps you to weigh consequences, check criteria, analyze data, investigate alternatives, and avoid assumptions. The combination of the steady use of logic and knowledge is wisdom. A wise and logical colleague is a valuable asset, a person you will consult again and again.

One of the best ways to gain credibility is to demonstrate that you are a logical thinker. Logic is held in high regard in the US workplace, so it is important to think critically and use logic to guide actions and beliefs. "Logical fallacies," or logical blunders disguised as sound thinking, are ways that people fool themselves and others.

Some of the more common logical fallacies are:

- **Ignorance**: Claiming something is true because it has never been proven false, or vice versa. "Nobody can prove that the universe is infinite. Therefore, the universe is finite." Just because it hadn't been proven doesn't mean it isn't probable or true.

- **Appeal to emotion**: Basing your argument on pity, love, sex, or pride rather than reason. "We've always been proud of our square-shaped widgets, and don't want to change them." Being proud of something doesn't make it good. Or, "it would be a shame if I don't get a red Camaro when I graduate from high school; I made good grades." "If you buy this cologne, you will feel free and happy."

- **Authority**: Saying that something is true because somebody else, even a respected authority, said it is true. Evidence must be presented. "We need to build parking garages because Mayor Biggenbottom says that our town needs more parking spaces."

- **Circular argument**: Saying that something is true by restating it in a different way rather than giving a reason. "Political party X is popular because most people belong to it."

- **Either-or argument:** Saying that there are only two alternatives. "America—love it or leave it." This type of argument can be used to bully people into strange behavior. Jim Jones of the People's Temple in Guyana told his followers that they had two choices: to drink the poisoned Kool-aid, or die at the hands of the US government. They drank the Kool-aid. Be extra cautious when someone offers you an either-or choice. There are usually many more options.

- **Bandwagon argument**: Saying that because an idea is popular, it is true. "Of course the earth is flat. Ask anybody!"

- **Hasty generalization**: Saying that from just one or two examples, conclusions can be drawn on a large scale. "No pit bull can be trusted; my neighbor had one that ate his cat."

- **Post hoc reasoning**: Saying that because something follows a previous event that it was caused by the event. "Our cafeteria has a new manager. That explains why three people are out sick with stomach viruses."

- **Oversimplification**: Taking out important information in order to show cause and effect. "We can solve all the personal problems in this country by sending more greeting cards."

- **Ad hominem (personal attack):** Criticizing the person or people whose ideas you disagree with and often using derogatory names to describe them. Personal attacks often occur when emotions override logical thought processes. "You're just an idiot if you don't believe what I believe." "Members of political party X are cold-hearted and greedy." "Members of political party Y are stupid tree-huggers who can't face reality."

- **Straw man**: Focusing on a lesser, more winnable point rather than the main point. "Opposition to raising the minimum wage amounts to support of slavery." Since everyone is against slavery, the writer is trying to use that agreement to gain acceptance of a less winnable point.

- **Red herring** (yes, it stinks): Diverting attention from the main points of an argument to an unrelated point. When asked what specific changes a political candidate intends on making when elected, the candidate might respond with a focus on other's shortcomings: "The other candidate doesn't have any good ideas for change."

Avoid these logical fallacies and learn how to recognize them in the media and in speeches and conversations.

CITING SOURCES AND AVOIDING PLAGIARISM

In a world where information and images are readily available in multiple formats, writers are often tempted to copy what others have written and claim it, implicitly or explicitly, as their own. This copying is a form of stealing, called "plagiarism." Copying or summarizing even small bits of text or graphics without acknowledgment is considered plagiarism, and writers must be scrupulously careful that their writing is original.

To avoid plagiarism, keep careful notes about your reading and the sources you have read or sites you have visited so that you can return to them when necessary to find a quotation or get specific citation information. Never try to paraphrase or summarize while looking at the source itself, as it is easy to echo the wording or phrases of the writer inadvertently. Journalists have lost their jobs for plagiarism; other writers, artists, and politicians have been shamed or have lost their professional credibility.

It is important to understand that words, images, and figures, even those that do not have an individual's by-line, are products of someone's intellectual and creative labor and are owned by a person or company. Technical writers are paid instruments of the company they work for, and the products of their labor belong to the employer, not the individual.

On the Internet, information tends to be copied and pasted in flagrant violation of ownership and copyright, making it difficult to determine who deserves credit, or which version is the original. Use the most reliable sources you can: websites that have a commercial motive are less reliable than educational or government sites. For instance, the *Army Field Manual* is probably a much better source than a wilderness outfitter website for survival instruction because its purpose is specifically to help soldiers survive, as opposed to selling survival gear.

To cite sources properly, you must **acknowledge each source** in **both of these ways**:

- In-text citation near the point(s) in your text where the source is used, **and**
- End of document citation in a list at the end of your document, which may be called "Works Cited" or "References" depending on the documentation format you are using.

A few different documentation styles are in common use today, and two are favored in academic writing: MLA (Modern Language Association) and APA (American Psychological Association) styles. The Chicago style, based on rules developed by the University of Chicago Press, is another. The Associated Press (AP) has a particular stylebook for journalists. Citation makers such as EasyBib.com can help you easily format citations in the particular style used in your industry.

The following example demonstrates a scenario that requires citation, and shows a proper citation of the source in MLA format:

Example:

You are given the task of reporting on organisms living in the Great Salt Lake in Utah. Your instructor has asked you to use MLA style.

1. You Google "fish in Salt Lake," and see a list of websites.
2. You go to a research website, oceanlife.edu, and find the following fact in an article called "Marine Life in Inland Salt Seas," by biologist Jerome Taxman:

   Twenty thousand fish live in Utah's Great Salt Lake.

3. You want to use this fact in your report. In the text, you must have a parenthetical citation, which is the information within the parentheses.

   It's often assumed that there are no fish in the Great Salt Lake. However, at least one research biologist has stated that there are as many as 20,000 fish inhabiting the body of water (Taxman).

4. In a Works Cited list at the end of the document, you must also give the entire source information:

   Taxman, Jerome. "Marine Life in Inland Salt Seas." OceanLife.edu, Ocean Life Foundation, 24 Feb. 2016, www.oceanlife.edu/inlandsaltsea.

This is an example of just one kind of source in one type of documentation style. In citing your sources, you should consult a documentation handbook for the style used in your field.

There is an exception to the mandate to document your sources. In a business setting, you may be presented with a document that has a history within the company and asked to revise it. In this case, the company is the owner of the material and so you may use and shape the existing text without worrying about citing the individual who drafted the last version. However, if outside sources are cited, they must remain in the document.

Copyright

Websites, books, periodicals, sound recordings, films, and other published material often display a copyright symbol (©) or even just the word "copyright." In a book, that word or symbol is shown on the reverse of the title page; on a website, it is normally found at the bottom of the home page. This symbol is a reminder of ownership; even if no copyright symbol is shown, you should always respect the source and cite any borrowings correctly. Copyright laws guard against unauthorized copying and give owners of intellectual or creative material the right to profit from their own work, either financially or through recognition of their achievements.

If you plan to use a significant portion of a copyrighted work, or use even a small piece in a significant way, you should contact the publisher or owner to ask for permission. Even if you give credit to the original creators, sometimes the ways you plan to use the material may violate the owner's interests. For example, it would not be acceptable to rent a movie, set up a screen in your backyard, and charge neighbors to view it. But it is fine to rent a movie and show it to a handful of children in your living room at your nine-year-old's birthday party. The difference is that the first example infringes upon the copyright owners' ability to profit from the product of their labor. Similarly, it is not acceptable to photocopy half a book without permission from the publisher and hand it out to a class, nor make a software company's published manual the basis for your own set of user instructions. The publisher, quite reasonably, wants to make money from its investment and is not interested in giving away its product.

There are federal laws about using copyrighted material. In general, uses that are related to research or academic purposes, and that involve small portions of the original product, are considered "fair" and do not require special permission. Sections 107-118 of the U.S. Copyright Law give guidelines for "fair use." These Fair Use Guidelines require some thought about what, exactly, is being copied and why:

- What type of published material is in question? (Quoting a paragraph from an academic article may be "fairer" than playing a catchy song chorus.)
- Will it be used in an educational, nonprofit setting, or will it be used to create profit? (Use for teaching is "fairer" than for selling.)
- What fraction of the original material will be used? (A small fraction will be "fairer" than a larger one.)
- Will using this piece of the material decrease the demand for the whole? (One image from a photo gallery is "fairer" than a set of representative images that seem to cover the whole show.)

For a full discussion of Fair Use under U.S. Copyright Law, see http://www.copyright.gov/fls/fl102.html.

To read the entire U.S. Copyright Law (Title 17 of the U.S. Code), see http://www.copyright.gov/title17/.

Creative Commons ⓒⓒ

Creative Commons is a nonprofit organization (***CreativeCommons.org***) that has invented a new kind of copyright license. While copyright laws protect creators of original content, creative commons licenses allow researchers, writers, and artists to give consent to certain kinds of copying, thereby circumventing the complex permissions process but preserving attribution.

You can search for works covered by Creative Commons licensing through the Creative Commons.org website: **httpps://search.creativecommons.org.**

A creative commons license does not replace traditional copyright, but instead provides a method for sharing content in specifically-approved ways, or, if the author desires, for putting a work into the public domain. For example, some CC licenses allow for use and sharing but not commercial use; others allow sharing but no changing of the original form and content; some allow commercial use, changes, and mixing with other content. When using work with a CC license, you must be very careful that your use falls under the particular license restrictions.

All work licensed through Creative Commons must provide attribution to the author or site, even if the work is intended for the public domain. Check the *CreativeCommons.org* website for examples of best ways to cite these sources and give proper credit to the author.

All Creative Commons-licensed works used in this textbook are attributed in the figure caption

USING PLAIN LANGUAGE

The Plain Language movement began in the late twentieth century with a group of federal employees who believed that the US public deserved clear documents. According to their website, plainlanguage.gov, plain language "… is communication your audience can understand the first time they read or hear it." The Plain Language website continues to be the most up-to-date and helpful source for eliminating foggy, pompous, wordy, inflated, and unacceptably complex language.

With the Plain Writing Act of 2010, the use of plain language in federal government agencies became mandatory. Using plain language in all workplaces has not become mandatory—yet—but it is a very good idea. Why? Because your goal as a communicator is to reach your audience, not impress them at the expense of understandability. Clear communication is successful communication. Much like cell phone service, the message depends on the strength of the signal. As a general rule, the fewer the words, and the smaller the words, the better.

The following table will give you an idea of how plain language can be used:

Table 1-1 Examples of Inflated Language and Plain Language Alternatives

Original	Plain Language
Did not meet minimum requirements	Failed
A number of	Some
Assistance	Help
Expeditious	Quick
In the event of	If
Remuneration	Payment
Is applicable to	Applies to

Plain language can be used to simplify communication. To become more familiar with guidelines and resources, visit the Plain Language website at plainlanguage.gov.

Avoiding Doublespeak

A sub-category of inflated language is called "doublespeak," a term that George Orwell originated in his landmark science fiction novel, *1984*. Doublespeak attempts to confuse or cover up a negative reality by superimposing it with a neutral or positive-seeming term. Some examples from twenty-first century political, corporate, and professional jargon include:

Table 1-2 Examples of Doublespeak and Plain Language Alternative

Doublespeak	Plain Language
Human intelligence	Spies
Failed to meet wellness potential	Died
Neutralize	Kill
Defense	War
Unclassified	Not secret
Downsize	Fire employees
Collateral damage	Bystander deaths
Escalate the issue to management	Tell the manager
Misrepresentation	Lie
Enhanced interrogation	Torture
Pre-owned vehicle	Used car

Then there are the over-used clichés (Table 1-3) in business that one can hear over and over in the average business meeting. This type of language should be avoided because it has been used so often that it fails to carry much meaning.

Table 1-3 Examples of Business Clichés

Business Clichés		
Result-driven	Value-added	Incentivize
Synergy	Revisit	Out of the loop
Think outside the box	Touch base	Benchmark
Optimize	Take this offline	Paradigm shift
Strive for excellence	Wrap this up	Run up the flag pole

You may have gotten used to hearing clichés, doublespeak, inflated language, and wordiness on television, in company meetings and documents, and in public speeches—maybe even in your company's mission statement. But as professional writers, **you have to avoid this pitfall**. Why? Your goal is to communicate information as clearly and simply as possible.

Avoiding Exclusionary Language

Using words that assume your audience is homogenous when it may not be is considered exclusionary because you are excluding some members of the group. One of the most common types of exclusionary language is sexist language, also referred to as "gender-biased" language.

Examples of sexist language:

- **Using "he" when referring to both male and female**, even if the females are a significant minority in your audience. Example: "Every student should bring his book."
- **Assuming that certain jobs have genders**: for example, assuming that doctors are males and nurses are females. It is irksome to hear "woman doctor" and "male nurse."
- **Using sexist job titles**: "stewardess" ("flight attendant" covers both male and female)

Make sure that your words do not exclude any potential member of your audience. Do not assume that your readers are the same in gender, sexual orientation, religion, race, or any other characteristic unless your audience is specifically of that group. For example, if you are writing a newsletter for the members of a Methodist church, it's safe to assume that your audience is Christian and Methodist.

International Note:
Sexist language is not the same thing as using nouns with gender as in Spanish and some other languages. For example: "el lápiz" (pencil, masculine) or "la pelicula" (film, feminine) is not sexist. However, if you assume that a film director is always male, that is a sexist assumption.

DEFINING COMMUNICATION

What is communication? The shortest answer is "*any message (verbal or non-verbal) sent or received (intentionally or unintentionally).*"

Communication is usually broken into two broad areas: verbal (using words) and non-verbal (all the other ways). Verbal communication can be broken down into two types, spoken and written. A simplified outline of communication would look like this:

- Verbal
  - Spoken
  - Written
- Non-verbal
  - Appearance
  - Actions

The other chapters in this textbook address ways to communicate in written form. Therefore, that topic won't be discussed further in this chapter. However, spoken and non-verbal communication are very important to your success and deserve your attention.

Spoken Communication

For the purposes of this section we will refer to "verbal" to indicate what is spoken rather than what is written. In different fields the definition changes (remember the verbal section of the SAT?), but "verbal" usually refers to "spoken" in most contexts.

The best speakers are those who believe their words are important. Believing in what you have to say makes the listener want to listen. The electric charge is present that gives your words energy that they would not have if you are just repeating what someone else said or believes.

Moderation is the key for effective everyday speaking. Match your visual cues to your words and delivery. Speak in an even tone, but not a monotone. Avoid "uh's" and "whatever's." You should go up and down in your tones, but try not to increase or decrease your volume significantly. Increasing your volume can be perceived as anger and will cause some listeners to stop listening or even leave. Speaking too softly may give the impression that you don't fully believe what you're saying or that you don't want too many people to hear it.

As you maintain eye contact and speak clearly using words your audience (the listener) can understand, look for cues from the listener that he or she is understanding you.

Positive Cues

Positive cues include

- Listener makes eye contact with you.
- Listener nods their head.
- Listener mimics your body language (really interesting area of research!).
- Listener smiles.
- Listener asks questions.
- Listener responds with additional information that demonstrates that he or she understands and furthers the conversation.

Negative Cues

Some cues that you may not be reaching your audience are

- Listener doesn't look at you.
- Listener doesn't nod their head.
- Listener answers their cell phone or checks a text message (if the listener sends a text message, forget it!).
- Listener frowns or yawns.
- Listener doesn't ask questions.
- Listener doesn't respond.
- Listener leaves quickly after you've finished or leaves before you're finished.

As soon as you attentively pick up on any cues that your listener is not engaged, ask him or her a question to get them actively involved. Then listen well, respond positively, and you'll probably have a good listener when you're ready to speak.

Non-Verbal Communication

It's often not what you say so much as how you say it. Humans are hard-wired to perceive other humans' general appearance, gestures, expressions, tone of voice, and perhaps even hormones, to understand the true meaning of the message. While you speak, others are sniffing out clues.

If you are sending a non-verbal message, which we all do every waking minute of every day, try to make your non-verbal communication match the message that you are trying to send. For example, telling someone you think his or her idea is marvelous while you roll your eyes will likely result in the listener (and observer) believing that you think the idea is rubbish. It isn't what you said, it's how you said it.

What implications does this have for the workplace? Plenty. Below is a table (Table 1-4) that shows a few negative non-verbal actions and how they may be perceived in the workplace.

Table 1-4 Negative Non-Verbal Actions and Possible Perceptions

Negative Non-Verbal Actions	Perception
Arms crossed on chest	Resistance, negativity
Rolling of eyes	Disbelief, disrespect
Texting during meeting	Lack of interest, unprofessionalism
Refusal to make eye contact	Sneakiness, shyness
Fidgeting	Discomfort, may be hiding something
Putting hands to face, covering mouth	Insecurity
Stern or frowning face	Unhappiness, anger
Emotionless face	Observer projects whatever emotion they themselves are feeling

On the other hand, there are many ways to send positive non-verbal messages, some of which are shown in Table 1-5:

Table 1-5 Positive Non-Verbal Actions and Possible Perceptions

Positive Non-Verbal Actions	Perception
Arms at side	Confidence
Eye contact	Good listener, honesty
Taking notes	Interest, intelligence
Asking non-confrontational questions	Interest, understanding, respect
Remaining still while listening	Focus, respect
Limiting hand movements	Confidence
Pleasant expression on face	Happiness, approachability

From this introductory lesson on non-verbal communication, you can see how your actions are extremely important in the workplace. There are many sources to use if you want to read up on how you can best communicate non-verbally in the workplace. A couple of non-technical sources you may want to investigate are:

Contreras Schwartz, L. (n.d.). Nonverbal communication with workplace interactions. *Houston Chronicle*. http://smallbusiness.chron.com/nonverbal-communication-workplace-interactions-844.html

Smith, Jacqueline. (2013, March 11). 10 Nonverbal cues that convey confidence at work. *Forbes*. http://www.forbes.com/sites/jacquelynsmith/2013/03/11/10-nonverbal-cues-that-convey-confidence-at-work/#7635e37f7ac5

Workplace Politics

Politics in the workplace has gotten a bad reputation. It's usually thought of as a quagmire of self-interest mixed with gossip, buddy-buddying, and treachery. Although politics can certainly have these results if used improperly, you should think about workplace politics in a different way and be able to use it beneficially.

Politics occurs whenever and wherever two or more people interact. It's part of human nature. Almost all of us want others to like them, and we want to be able to promote our wonderful ideas. This is normal and natural and good.

Because you want others to like you and your ideas, try to position yourself for these things to occur. This "stance" gives you an optimal chance for success.

The "up" side of politics, as shown in Table 1-6, can benefit both ourselves and our employer. Some examples are:

Table 1-6 Positive Political Actions and Possible Results

Positive Political Action	Positive Result
Explaining your idea for improvement	Provides a possible way to improve
Building a project team	Gets work done
Complimenting a coworker on their work	Builds trust and willingness to cooperate
Complimenting your boss on their management skills (not excessively or without cause)	Makes your boss realize that you are attentive and willing to recognize achievement
Trying to get a promotion	Rewards you monetarily for your exceptional work
Working late (occasionally)	Shows that you are committed to the greater good
Writing a proposal for change	Shows that you are a serious employee who is trying to improve the status quo
Speaking well of others	Makes others feel good and engenders trust and openness
Refraining from gossip	Shows gossipers that you're not talking about them behind their backs

And now for the downside of politics. These are the items that have given politics a bad reputation. Table 1-7 shows some examples.

Table 1-7 Negative Political Actions and Possible Results

Negative Political Action	Negative Result
Promoting an idea that will only benefit you or your workgroup at the expense of others	Causes mistrust, perhaps even among your own workgroup
Criticizing a coworker	Makes the coworker distrust and even dislike you
Complimenting your superiors excessively	Makes your superiors question your motives
Complaining to other employees about your salary	Makes you appear to be unprofessional and perhaps even a whiner
Being a workaholic	Makes you less and less effective with each extra hour. Your efforts may even damage the team's hard work.
Complaining to others about the way things are done and trying to build support for more complaining	Shows that you are a troublemaker
Talking about coworkers behind their backs or trying to make an "us versus them" conflict	Wastes time, causes problems with coworkers' perceptions of each other, makes you look untrustworthy
Spreading gossip	Wastes time, can cause huge personal distress, shows that you are willing to believe rumors and may not be dealing with the facts in all cases

Recognize any of these situations? Avoid these pitfalls. If you don't, you may not feel the implications immediately, but they will catch up with you. If you see these things in your peers, do not tattle because it can backfire. People who misuse politics are usually "hoisted by their own petard," to quote Shakespeare loosely. (A petard was an explosive device used to break open a gate or door.) In other words, the methods people use to cause harm to others usually cause harm to themselves instead.

CRITERIA FOR WRITING IN A PROFESSIONAL AND ETHICAL MANNER

The following eight criteria are frequently used to judge the quality of a document or web page. To the right is your ethical and professional mandate.

- **Honesty** – You must be honest, factual, and give credit to sources.
- **Clarity** – You must be clear.
- **Accuracy** – You must be accurate.
- **Comprehensiveness** (completeness) – You must provide complete information.
- **Accessibility** – You must communicate in a way that the audience can easily find and use what they need.
- **Conciseness** – You must avoid wordiness.
- **Professional Appearance** – Your communication (and you) must look professional.
- **Correctness** – You must use correct grammar, spelling, and punctuation.

Using communication effectively in the workplace is a practiced skill. Whether speaking, writing, or listening, you leave impressions on others that can be positive or negative. To be professional, use methods of communication that will enhance your image and the workplace goals. When you use an ethical and professional approach, everyone in the organization benefits.

DISCUSSIONS

1. Why is it important to avoid sexist language in the workplace?

2. Have you ever been the recipient of exclusionary language bias? What were the circumstances? How did you feel? What is your opinion of the person who excluded you?

3. Discuss an example that you have witnessed of negative and positive workplace (or classroom) politics. What were the actual or likely results of each?

4. Discuss the ethics of using plain language. How does the use of plain language help the reader? Why should the writer care?

5. Start a list of inflated terms and their plain language equivalent and pass it around the class or discussion board. See how many you can come up with. Start another list of doublespeak terms. If you have a workplace, you can start a list of worn-out clichés that you hear all too often.

6. Imagine that you spent several years doing very specific research in your area of expertise. You published your ground-breaking results in an extensive report in a trade journal. Six months later, you read an article in another journal in which the writer claims to have undertaken the same research with the same results, using phrasing and even whole paragraphs from your report, without giving you any credit—doesn't mention you, your research project, or the extensive report you published. Is this a problem? Discuss.

EXERCISES

1. Read about logical fallacies on the Internet. Choose three fallacies and give an example of each that you may have heard or read. You can invent the example if you prefer. However, if you know the source, give the source. Discuss why each example defies sound reasoning. How does it fail the logic test? **Write your results in a short memo report (about 2 pages) to your instructor.** The bracketed items must be replaced with actual names and today's date.

> MEMO
> To: [Your Instructor's Name], Instructor
> From: [Your Name], Student
> Date: [Today's Date]
> Subject: Examples of Three Logical Fallacies
>
> As you have asked, I present three examples of different types of logical fallacies. My results are in this report. If you have any questions, please let me know.
>
> [Make sure your paragraphs start at the left margin. Single space all the lines in your paragraphs and add a double space between paragraphs.]

2. Search the internet and find an article about someone who is being accused of plagiarizing. **Write a one-paragraph description of the article** and specify who is involved, what the charge is, what the penalty was, and any other pertinent information. Give your internet source.

3. **Rewrite one paragraph from this textbook** using inflated, pompous, confusing, and difficult language and sentence structure. Make it grammatically correct, but otherwise ineffective. Use lots of "thesaurus words," complex sentences, and highly formal language. Exchange the rewritten paragraph with other students and ask them to **translate it into plain language**. Read the original, your rewritten version, and the "translated" version aloud. Hint: this isn't a test to see how close the translated paragraph comes to the original. In fact, you will probably see that the translated versions and the original versions are vastly different.

4. Be aware of body language, tone of voice, and other non-verbal clues during the week. **Make a list of some that you witnessed** and what assumptions you made about the message because of the non-verbal communication. For example, did your friend roll her eyes when you were telling a story? Did your boss talk to you in a loud voice? Did somebody make a gesture to you in traffic?

5. Find a short report online that pertains to your field of interest or your major. **Evaluate the online report** using the eight criteria on page 15. Use the memo report format described in Exercise 1 and write a memo to your instructor. Make sure you give the name of the report, the link where you found it, when you accessed it, and who wrote it.

6. Use this page of your textbook to **start your own list** of doublespeak, wordiness, clichés, and bureaucratese in the left column, with plain English alternatives at the right. Your first entries might be notes from Discussion question 5 on page 16.

Doublespeak **Wordy Expressions** **Clichés**	**Plain English**

7. The following 12 sentences (pages 19-20) contain sexist language. **Rewrite the sentences to remove gender bias**.

   a. A medical student applying to this University should have completed all high school science courses, and his average grade should be a “C” or higher.

   b. When a woman decides to become a nurse, she must realize that she is entering into a noble profession.

   c. Throughout the history of mankind, we have sought to control the weather.

   d. When I ask a student for his assignment, I expect him to submit it.

   e. I was pulled over by a policewoman, who gave me a ticket.

   f. The court assigned me a lady lawyer.

   g. Every workman on the highway must wear his helmet.

h. A pilot can use his microphone to communicate with the stewardesses.

i. Executives and their wives are invited to the banquet.

j. A good secretary must pay close attention to her boss's schedule and never double-book him.

k. George has decided to become a male nurse.

l. We were told it takes 6 man-hours to complete the kitchen wiring.

2 - The Writing Process

The process of writing may seem mysterious. Indeed, you may have thought that writers somehow get "inspired by muses" and that creativity and self-expression are the main goals of writing. Perhaps you even believe that some people are born good writers and that writing skill cannot be learned.

However, current research on the process of writing—how a human being decides when, how, and what to write—reveals quite another picture. Writing is just another skill that can be learned with knowledge and practice. It is the unglamorous act of applying pen to paper, or tapping on a keyboard, that creates a first draft. Some writers face writer's block before they can even put a single word on the page because they believe that the first draft must be close to perfection. The opposite is true; the magic happens in the rewriting. Documents almost never come out the way you want them the first time. Like a sculpture, a document usually undergoes a very rough initial phase and is gradually molded into the final product.

One of the most influential scientists who studied writing was James Kinneavy (1920-1999). He set up a framework to show the basic structure of writing, which he called the "Communication Triangle"(Kinneavy, 1969):

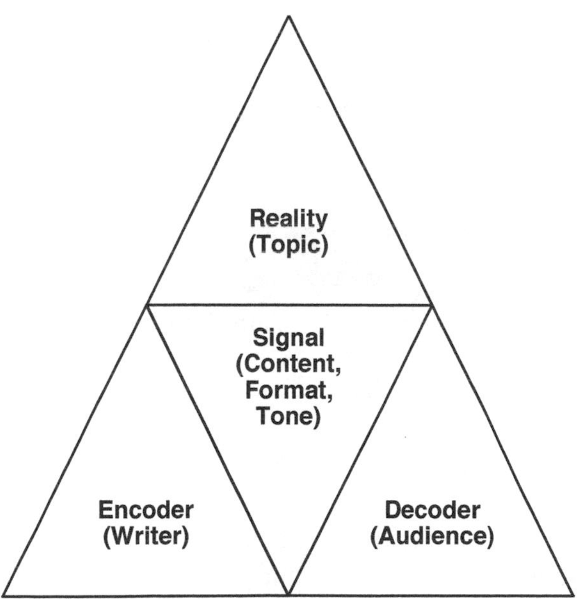

Figure 2-1 Kinneavy's Communication Triangle

The "encoder" is the writer; the "decoder" the reader, reality is the topic, and the "signal" is the written text, including not just the content, but also the ways in which the content can be presented and understood. Kinneavy's terminology is somewhat academic, but the idea is that the "signal" or text is changeable, not an inspired gift or an automated product: constructing a text involves an interpretation of reality specific to the relationship between writer and reader: the writer's point of view, his or her consideration of the reader's assumptions, and even the format and style of the writing itself may change the ultimate written document. You will see the triangle icon appear throughout this textbook as a visual reminder of the relationship among the technical writer, the audience for his or her writing, the elements of the real world that concern both, and the resulting product.

DEFINING YOUR PURPOSE

Before writing anything, consider why you are doing it—in other words, the *purpose* you want this document to accomplish. Do you want to get that report crossed off your list? to get the boss off your back? to impress your colleagues? to get a start on that novel? These motives might be part of your personal reality, but as a technical writer, the reality you are concerned with is not personal, but professional. Think harder. Adjust your perspective. You can find your purpose in considering the topic that needs to be addressed and the audience that you want to reach, as demonstrated in Figure 2-2, below:

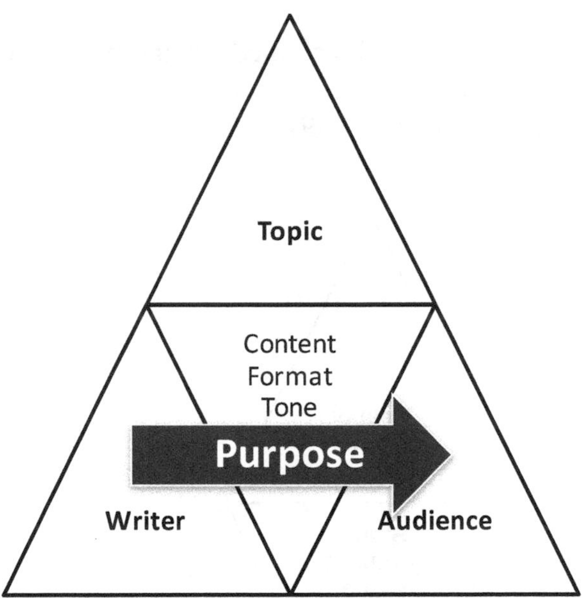

Figure 2-2 Communication Triangle - Purpose

In most technical writing formats, your writing reflects on your employer rather than on yourself. Technical writing does not have bylines and will not bring you fame. Good technical writers keep themselves invisible. If the writing has punch or attitude, that style is credited to the business, not to the writer. Even in professional communication such as emails or memos, personal bias and emotion have no place. So, the first step in defining the purpose of a document is to readjust your point of view. Whatever your personal objectives in writing the piece, they are secondary to the goals of the business, organization, or product.

More than One Purpose

There is usually a primary purpose *and* an underlying goal, even in the most ethical and straightforward documentation. For example, a new job procedure may streamline production, *and* it may also enable the company to phase out machinery that is becoming expensive. A manager may write a memo to all employees about the vacation policy, but he or she may *also* aim to curtail abuses by one or two people. A new user manual may showcase a new and useful product feature, *and* discourage users from using a third-party product. Writing is a powerful tool, and as a technical writer you need to be aware that there may be multiple goals for even the simplest writing that you do.

The purpose of your document probably falls into at least one of the categories below. Some pieces of writing may do all three of these at once, so the items in the list below may appear in more than one category:

- **inform:** reports of all kinds; newsletters; labels; some memos; some letters; process descriptions; proposals.
- **instruct:** some letters; some memos; manuals; user instructions.
- **persuade:** advertising; some letters; some memos; recommendation reports; proposals; job application materials.

Research

To understand the true role of the document you are being asked to create, ask questions and read existing company documents. If you do not understand the underlying background, controversies, and goals, the document you produce will not address its true purpose.

- Does this document **respond** to an existing controversy or problem? Review the writing available to you about this topic and, if possible, interview people who are familiar with the issue to give yourself a sense of background.
- Does this document **replace** an existing piece of writing that has been judged outdated or inadequate? Obtain the prior document and read committee minutes or notes from involved parties about it. Try to understand the failings of the older document.
- Does this document **introduce** a new product or company? Take time to read all relevant information about the new developments to understand them. Try out the product yourself to make sure you know how it is used.
- Does this document **present** a lot of complex and detailed information? Part of your role will be to structure, synthesize, and restate for your audience. Spend time reading and organizing information for a presentation that is relatively easy to understand. If you encounter information that you do not understand, **ask the person who provided the information to explain it.** Often, people can speak about their work in straightforward terms, but are unable to write clearly about it.

- Does this document **instruct workers** about a job procedure? Ask for a run-through, and watch. Go through the procedure yourself, or, if that is not possible, have a specialist in the procedure go through it step by step with you while you take notes. Ask about previous problems and common misunderstandings.
- Does this document **instruct users** about how to use or assemble a product? Ask for someone who is familiar with the product to instruct you in its assembly and/or use. Ask questions and take notes. Go through the process on your own, without a guide, and note the questions that come up.

For any document, ask others in the company or organization what they hope the effects of this piece of writing will be.

DEFINING THE TARGET AUDIENCE

Now that you understand exactly **why** you are creating a document, you must decide **who** you want to reach. To be effective, you must connect with your target audience. Knowing who your audience is will affect your approach to important elements such as topic, format, tone, page layout/design, and content.

"Audience" is a general term that communication specialists use to refer to whoever is going to read, see, or hear a particular product. The "target audience" is a very specific group of people—or even just one person—who we hope will be receptive to our message. "Product" can refer to a document, a magazine article, a TV ad, a movie, a web site, or almost any other presentation. For the purposes of this textbook, we'll use the term "document" to refer to our particular product.

If you describe your audience as "anyone who…", you haven't identified a target audience. Think carefully about the "anyones" you want to reach.

Figure 2-3 below shows the communication triangle with the target audience emphasized to signify its importance.

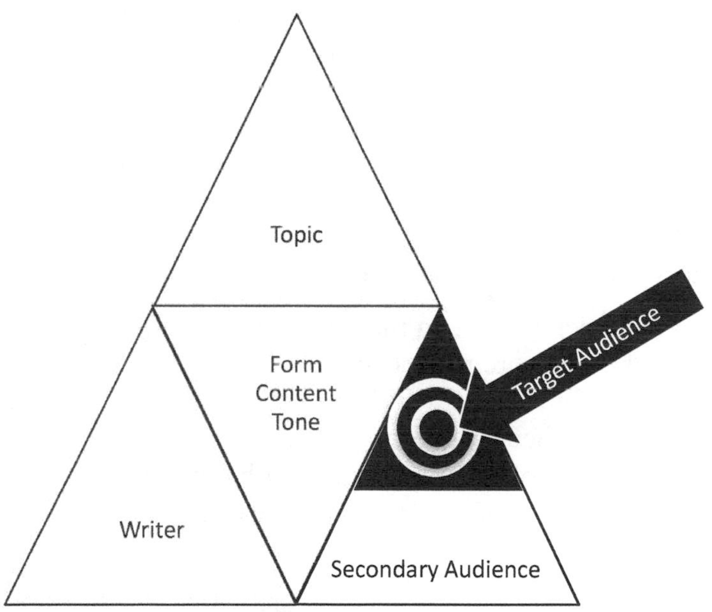

Figure 2-3 Communication Triangle - Audience

Determining the audience is an extremely important and sometimes complicated step. For example, the target audience for this textbook is you. Most likely you are either a first or second year college student at a community college or public university. This textbook has been written with your particular needs and concerns in mind.

Secondary Audiences

After you have thoroughly analyzed your target, or primary, audience, you will have to determine if there are any other, less direct, audiences. For example, if you work in XYZ Cable Company and you are going to write a set of instructions for Cable Installation Technicians, your primary audience would be the employees who install cable TV. However, if Cable Installation Supervisors sometimes fill in for as installers, they would be considered a secondary audience. Another example would be a memo sent to your work group (primary audience) announcing a process change with a copy sent to your supervisor, who would be the secondary audience. He or she might already know about the change but want to oversee how you related the information to the work group.

Why should you care about the secondary audience? Even though you may not be primarily focused on this audience, those readers may also use your document. Your work must still make sense to them, be usable for them, and consider their concerns.

Internal and External Audiences

Your target audience can be internal or external. An internal audience is made up of readers within your organization or well-defined group, such as co-workers, supervisors, or club members. An external audience consists of readers outside the organization, such as customers or the general public. Whether you are writing for an external or internal audience, you will need to target your readers' needs and expectations carefully in order to communicate effectively with them. One effective method of informal audience analysis is to use a checklist. Use the External Audience Worksheet at the end of this chapter (page 44) to help analyze an audience outside of your immediate workplace—for example, if you are writing a flyer to be distributed to the public or a letter to customers.

Most often, your audience will be an internal one—within your own organization. Emails, memos, and reports are produced daily in every workplace. When you are preparing to write a document that will be seen by your employees, co-workers, or supervisors, consider the factors affecting the way they will read your document, such as attitudes toward the topic, job function, and their hierarchical relationship to you. Use the Internal Audience Worksheet at the end of this chapter (page 45) to help you remember these factors.

In an organizational culture such as the workplace, writers often neglect to consider audience. Missing the mark in writing workplace documents can have severe consequences. For example, if you neglect to explain important but obscure vocabulary, people will not understand what you mean and may be embarrassed to ask. Or, if you ignore existing controversies within the company about the issue, your memo may be viewed as irrelevant. No matter which audience you target, you must identify assumptions, preferences, and expectations in order to communicate effectively.

The following memo is an example of effective audience analysis. The writer is writing to an internal audience (the owner of the company). However, he is analyzing the external audience (customers of the company).

Sample 2-1 Audience Analysis in Hard Copy Memo Format, Page 1

Shorty's Skateboards

Memo

To: Fred "Shorty" McBride, Owner

From: Jason Wheeltype, Store Manager

Date: October 2, 2015

Subject: Audience Analysis of Shorty's Skateboards Customers

This memo is a response to your request that I provide an overview of our customer base so that we can reach our target audience effectively with advertising. Since I've been working here for 12 years, I have a thorough knowledge of the people who come through our door. Please let me know if you have any questions.

Note: Our customers are the audience for our advertisements and promotions. When I use the word "audience" in this memo, I'm referring to our current and future customers.

- Our target audience is overwhelmingly **male between the ages of 12 and 20**. They **live in our immediate vicinity**, within twenty blocks in all directions. However, some travel on bus to reach us for special offers or items. Since there are many skateboard shops in our city, we are considered a neighborhood store, conveniently located where our skateboarding friends can reach us.
- Our audience income varies from very little (<$2,000 year) to $20,000. Generally, our audience has a very **low income**, and has other means of support, such as parents.
- Their education and reading level is **high school senior**. They are **very computer savvy**, and surf the Internet frequently. They also use smart phones for social communication.
- They are **single**.
- They are **students** and/or **hourly employees** in food service or sales.
- Their ethnic background is mostly **Caucasian** and **African-American**.

Sample 2-1 Audience Analysis in Hard Copy Memo Format, Page 2

- They **love skateboards** and skateboard equipment. They believe that **skateboarding is an exciting and challenging pastime**.

- Their general needs are few. They need a **smart phone, a skateboard, spending money, and friends.**

- Their wants are also few. This group tends to be a simple, but very intelligent, group of young men who dedicate a large part of their day to improving their skateboarding skills and socializing with other skateboarders. They **want to feel a part of a group** of like-minded people. They don't seek popularity or status necessarily. They want to **appear "cool" and competent**. They enjoy **trying difficult moves** and **practicing with their friends**. They enjoy **watching and learning from each other**. They want access to a **wide variety of skateboards and skateboarding products**. They want to be able to see and buy the **latest skateboard equipment**.

- Their lifestyle is simple. If they still live at home, they are not the primary breadwinner and have **extra time, but not income**. If they are living independently, they don't have a large income, but they are willing to **spend a good portion** on their skateboarding lifestyle.

- Their typical behaviors include **gathering after school at the city skatepark, playing video games, working, socializing**.

- Their interests and hobbies (besides skateboarding) include **video games, movies, dating, sports, and school.**

- They are very **fluent in standard English**, but also have a **jargon** of their own, such as "casper slide" and "crooked grind."

- The audience's most comfortable language is **English**.

I hope this analysis is helpful to our advertising agency. If you need any more input, don't hesitate to ask.

Web communication offers a unique writing environment for both internal and external audiences. Factors such as ease of access and the length of time readers are willing or able to spend on the computer affect readability. Use the Web Audience Worksheet on page 46 when considering factors that affect an audience that will read your document online.

Cultural Considerations of Audience

Take into account your audience's heritage, language, and culture. You want your audience to trust you and your message. Therefore, present the material in a manner that is inclusive of cultural differences. For example, the Home Depot management has realized that its audience consists of English and Spanish speakers. The store signs and products have Spanish translations. The bilingual labeling and signage make it easy for Spanish-speaking customers to be able to find what they want—and thus attract paying customers to the store.

If you are writing a document to be read and used internationally, it is important to know the norms for business communication in the destination country. Some languages, for example, differentiate between formal and casual forms of address, and using the wrong form can be awkward or rude. Work communication in different countries may need to follow specific, established protocols.

If your target audience includes members of a specific culture or speakers of a language that is not your own, it is very important to have a member of the ethnicity or a native speaker read over your work. The dictionary definition of a word, for example, might not include its colloquial connotations, and it is unfortunately easy to offend or inadvertently mark yourself as uneducated.

Just remember that not everyone shares your particular style, worldview, or assumptions about social or business relationships, and consider how your words, and the way you present those words, may affect audiences who are not exactly like you.

FINDING THE TOPIC

The topic or subject of your document is probably the easiest piece of the communication triangle to identify:

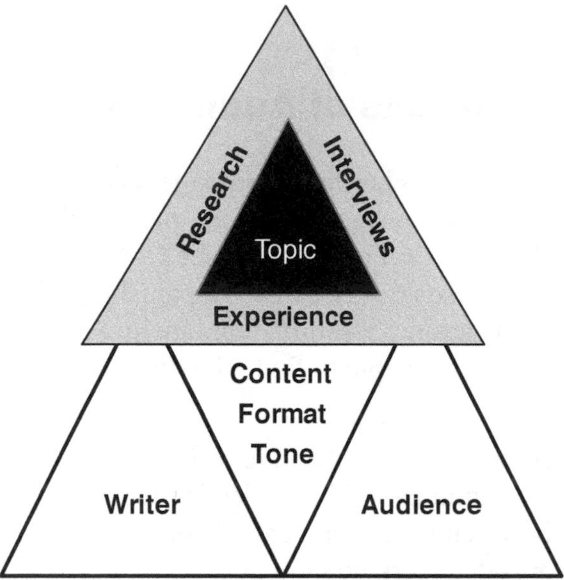

Figure 2-4 Communication Triangle - Topic

Your topic will often be a subject that you know very well. That's why you are telling others. However, it may sometimes be a subject that is not in your area of expertise. Frequently, technical writers must research a topic before writing. For example, a writer might be required to explain how to reformat a hard drive, even if he or she does not know how to do so at the beginning of the project. This might require some instruction from a knowledgeable person, practice, or access to existing documents that explain the process. The writer needs to learn *enough* about the topic to be able to fulfill the document's purpose for its audience.

Technical writers use several methods to gain knowledge about the topic:

- Searching the Internet for a general information surrounding the topic and current events relating to the topic
- Interviewing subject-matter experts (SMEs)
- Trying the product or process
- Reading literature about the product or process
- Interviewing users of the product or process

UNDERSTANDING TONE

Tone can open or block the path to effective communication. Maintaining a professional and positive tone in all professional writing encourages respect and cooperation, but allowing inappropriate tones such as anger to creep into your writing can be deadly to personal and professional relationships.

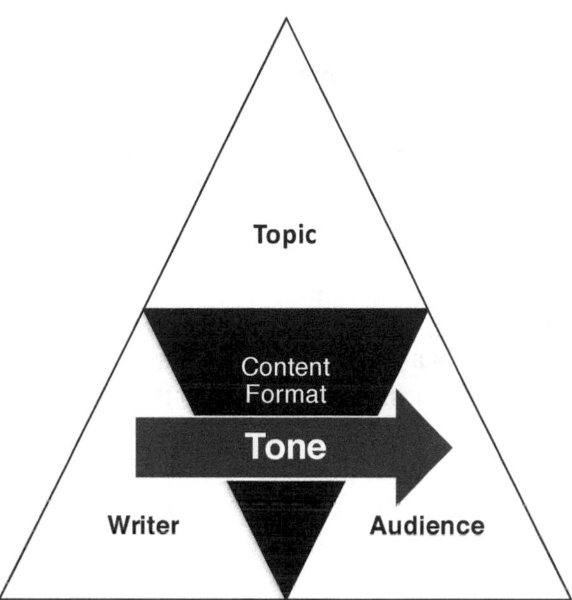

Figure 2-5 Communication Triangle - Tone

Tone of Voice

Tone helps communicate the writer's stance toward their subject and audience. The best way to think about tone is to imagine "tone of voice." As a listener, you understand immediately whether a speaker is serious or joking, friendly or sarcastic, from such clues as whether their voice rises at the end of a sentence. If you happen to be watching as well as listening, body language adds to your understanding of the speakers' attitude: are they smiling? tearful? scowling?

Tone in Written Work

Tone, matched with topic, cues the reader about how to respond. For example, when humorist Groucho Marx says, "Go, and never darken my towels again!" (*Duck Soup*, 1933), viewers laugh because he takes a dramatic but clichéd declaration ("never darken my door again") and makes it ridiculous by undermining its highly dramatic tone with a trivial topic (dirty towels).

A serious tone, paired with a serious topic, signals the audience to take each word seriously. The crowd assembled at the Lincoln Memorial in 1963 expected a history-making event even before King rose to the microphone. When Martin Luther King, Jr. announced, "Five score years ago, a great American, in whose symbolic shadow we stand today, signed the Emancipation Proclamation" (King, 1963), his solemn echoes of Lincoln's Gettysburg Address signaled a momentous occasion. More than fifty years later, we can sense the monumental nature of his speech even though we are reading his words rather than listening to his voice. Not only the reference to Lincoln, but also his word choice ("great American," "symbolic shadow") and many pauses help create his serious tone.

Tone in technical writing is more sensitive than Marx's humor or King's thunder. Technical writers cannot afford to be ironic and very seldom have the opportunity to be monumental. Your writing must be clear and serviceable, without jokes or emotional content. In technical writing, only ad copy is aimed at the heart, and then very carefully.

Positive Tone

Staying positive is a good strategy, even if there is something negative to communicate. Within a "positive" tone, there is a spectrum, and technical writers need to avoid certain too-intimate, ironic, or jocular tones. Tone indicates the writer's stance, and thus the attitude of the company that the writer represents, so it is important to find a tone that meets readers' expectations and builds positive feelings. In professional person-to-person communication, "**cordial**" is a good tone: courteous and respectful. Technical writers of user instructions generally cultivate a **neutral** tone, since they are writing to a wide range of people and it is important to be absolutely clear.

All textual elements must be considered for their effect on tone when communicating professionally. For instance, in technical writing and business communication, all caps (ex: DEAR MS. HINTON) are rare, exclamation points (ex: Please hurry!) are extremely rare, and emoticons (ex: ☺) are not used. Here are some reasons for avoiding these three elements:

- **All caps** (using all capital letters) are easily interpreted as shouting (negative tone) and should only be used when necessary, as in some headings and titles (ex: TABLE OF CONTENTS), acronyms (ex: USA), or differentiation from the previous text (ex: Press the START button.) Plus, all caps are very hard to read.
- **Exclamation points** can easily be interpreted as too emotional, whether anger, joyfulness, or ardent enthusiasm. Used frequently, they can make the writer seem flighty, juvenile, or easily excited. Use exclamation points with care, and only when absolutely necessary (which is almost never).
- **Emojis or emoticons** are very casual and should be reserved for informal communications, such as texting. If you have to add a smiley face to indicate tone, that is a sign that you need to rewrite the sentence to make it appropriately positive without the extra hint.

In the table on the next page, tones appropriate for technical writing are marked YES; tones to be avoided are shaded and marked NO.

Table 2-1 Determining Appropriate Tone

Determining Appropriate Tone
YES - Neutral - avoiding emotional statements, factual
YES - Cordial - showing respect for audience, using standards of courtesy
YES - Friendly - displaying camaraderie but respecting personal boundaries
YES - Authoritative - taking responsibility calmly and directing others
NO - Overly Friendly - referencing personal issues
NO - Intimate - cultivating close friendship and confidence
NO - Erotic - cultivating sexual connections or arousal
NO - Ironic, Sarcastic - requiring reader to interpret hidden meaning
NO - Defensive - shifting blame to avoid responsibility
NO - Accusatory - assigning blame to shame reader
NO - Angry - venting negative emotion

Strategies for Creating Positive Tone

One way to make sure your tone is in the "YES" zone is to use a **cooling off period** after writing and before sending. This period may be as short as a few minutes, or as long as a few hours or even days. The key is to let out your negative or unprofessional emotion so that you can see your way to a positive, or at least neutral, tone. If you are writing an email about something that makes you angry, consider your first draft a way to get out the emotional content. Write in a word processing document but *don't save and don't send.* Here's a draft with a negative tone that serves the writer, not the reader. The tone is not only negative, but also inflammatory—likely to cause problems, not solve them:

Example 1 - Tone: accusatory, angry

> I can't believe you were so stupid as to send out the samples without documentation. How will the client know what to do with them? ARRRGGGHHHH. This makes the company look INCOMPETENT and reflects badly on EVERYONE!

Clearly, this draft should not be sent, as it serves merely to allow the writer to vent. It is accusatory; it contains a personal attack and even an emotional outburst. The parts written in all caps "shout" with anger. This message probably made the writer feel better, but massaging the writer's ego or crushing the self-esteem of the recipient should never be the goal of professional communication. This writer needs to set the message aside for a minute, cool down, and imagine a more professional approach. How can this message be communicated in a less emotional and more productive way? The second draft of the communication, reviewed and rewritten after a cool-down period, can become at least neutral:

Example 2 - Tone: neutral, authoritative, cordial

> I understand that the ABC samples were inadvertently sent out to Comp.Labs without documentation. As the fact sheets and user instructions are an integral part of any order, I would like you to send those documents today by overnight mail to Ali McNeely at Comp.Labs. Pam will write a cover letter to go with them and will follow up with Ms. McNeely to make sure that all products are received.
>
> Thank you for attending to this quickly.

In this draft, the focus has shifted from negativity and blaming to a neutral tone that allows the writer to manage the problem that has been created. This polite but authoritative email can be sent to the employee who forgot to add the paperwork, and also to Pam, his or her supervisor. Rather than venting and blaming, the writer initiates action and assigns oversight.

Professionalism & Ethics

Note that a "thank you" is included at the end in Example 2 because the writer has asked the reader to do something. Manners are important, and words associated with polite courtesy signal respect for the audience, which generates positive feelings. Always say please and thank you, particularly if you are making a request or giving direction.

Avoiding Inflated Tone

When sending an email or other communication, avoid taking on more authority than you actually have. One of the ways writers get into trouble with this is to use the “royal we.” The expression “royal we” refers to the stilted use of the first person plural (“we”) when “I” is the appropriate pronoun. Using “we” instead of “I” distances the writer from the audience and also implies that the message comes from a higher source than the writer, or that the writer is speaking for a group.

Using “we” instead of “I” when it is not appropriate results in awkward and oddly lofty sentences such as these:

- We should all remain at our desks unless we are on break.
- We must inform you that your job has been terminated. We are sorry.
- We here at Atlas Products appreciate your hard work.

Consider the following tips for **adjusting perspective:**

- When you are the source of the information or request, use "I."

  Example: **I** would like to examine another sample.

- When you are explaining what someone else did, use third person.

  Example: **Joan** sent the sample.

- When you are telling someone what to do, use second person ("you").

  Example: When **you** have sent the sample, please log the shipment.

- When you are emphasizing the object (the sample) rather than the subject (Joan), use passive voice.

  Example: **The sample** was sent.

- When you are a designated spokesperson for a specific group, use "we."

  Example: This committee has decided that **we** would like to see a sample

CHOOSING FORMAT

The format of your document is critical to its function. What does it look like? How does it work? Your format may be anything from a web page to a quick email and is decided based on many factors. One deciding factor is whether or not your supervisor has asked you to create a certain type of document. If so, accept the format and do the best job possible. If you have the freedom to choose the format, either because the document is your idea, or you have been given some latitude with making the choice, you can use a flow chart to determine the best format for your audience and purpose (See Figure 2-6, on the next page).

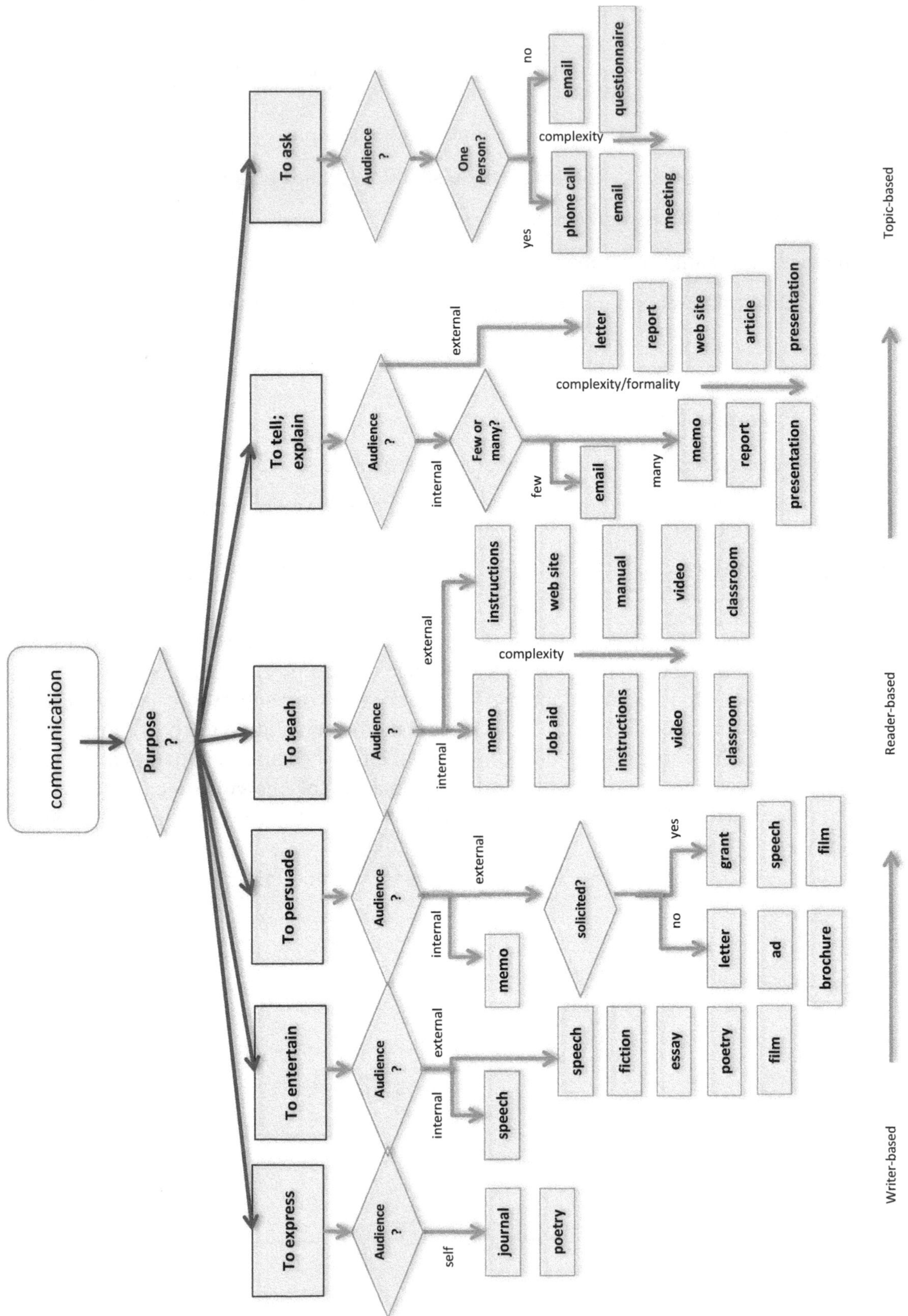

Figure 2-6 Choosing Format

THE DOCUMENT CYCLE

If a document is produced hurriedly to meet a deadline, there is a good chance something in it is not quite right, and that someone will be embarrassed later. Professional writing is real work that requires review, revision, and attention to detail.

Notice that the review and revision arrows in Figure 2-7, below, are curved to indicate a repetitive cycle. The review and revision process often repeats several times before the document is complete. Since deadlines usually demand that the review process end at some point, it will be to your advantage to plan the document cycle well and direct your reviewers' attention productively.

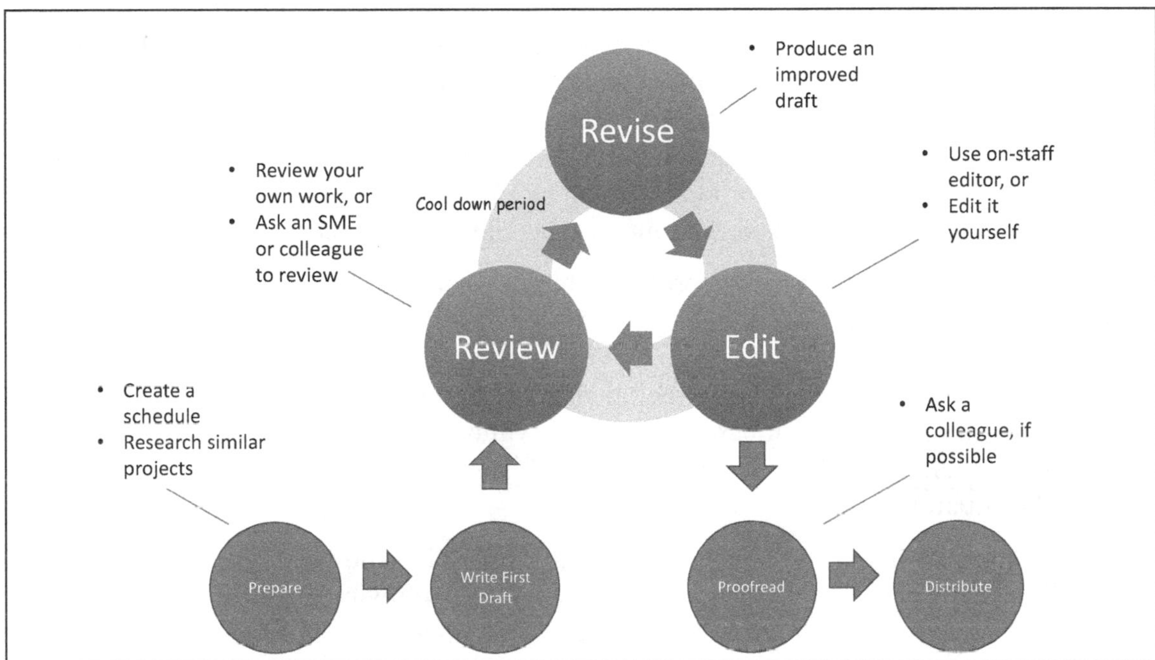

Figure 2-7 Basic Document Cycle

Preparation

The first stage of writing isn't writing at all, but thinking. In the preparation stage, you should ask questions and take notes. Read previous documents produced by the company on the same topic; investigate the history of the topic, if it is unfamiliar. If you are uncertain about what format the document should take, use the flow chart provided in this chapter (Figure 2-6). If you are uncertain about vocabulary used in people's answers to your questions, look up unfamiliar words. Check the Professional Vocabulary section at the end of this book.

Drafting

Starting at the beginning of the document is sometimes not the best strategy. Start with the piece that makes you feel most confident. After research and fact-gathering, some parts will be easier to write than others. For example, it may be fairly easy to make a table of cost estimates, but a little stickier to decide how to present the need for the expenditures in a budget report. In the end, it all needs to get done, and there is no special magic in writing the parts in the order they will eventually be read. Introductions are actually best written last, after you know what you have written.

Review

Just as technical writing is not an instant or inspired process, it is also not a solitary one. As you write, you will probably think of questions you need to ask other people, or facts you need to look up. You may be collaborating with other writers. Remember to share your work with appropriate people and invite questions and comment. Sometimes another person's point of view can cut through writer's block and provide inspiration and clarity. The review process should be worked into a schedule for completion of the document.

Outside input can sometimes solve problems almost instantly. For example, recently a writer we know felt stuck about how to present several very different projects in the same grant proposal. An informal conversation with a few people involved in those projects revealed that one of them was being included in a different grant. In five minutes, writing the proposal became much easier. Also, without that conversation, the organization could be in the awkward position of having to turn down part of an award or explain the situation to two separate grantors.

When you have a rough draft of the document, you should send it (clearly marked as DRAFT) to a few people who can offer feedback. Let the reviewers know which parts you hope they will read most carefully. For example, in a report about a new software program, you may need a programmer to examine statements about the function of the product in detail but need an accountant to check the information about the company's financial investment and expected rewards. You will save yourself and your reviewers precious time if you can direct them to the appropriate sections of the document.

Your supervisor will want to read the entire document, and he or she may also have ideas about other people to ask for information or clarification. If the document involves user instructions or job procedures, testing is a necessary step as well: ask people who represent the desired audience to read it and perform any tasks it describes, and then give you feedback about any changes that are needed.

If you have an on-staff editor, he or she may want to have input at this stage, or wait until the final editing and proofreading stage.

Cool Down Period

One of the benefits of sending a draft to other people for comment is that you can let the writing process pause. In the heat of composition, your brain may get a couple steps ahead of what is on the page, and you may sometimes confuse what you meant to say with what you have actually written. It is common, for example, to leave out small words, put in extra words, or forget that your audience is unaware of key facts. Giving your brain a rest allows the document to exist apart from your own mind.

Use this downtime to readjust your point of view. Subtract your emotional involvement, and prepare to see the document as others do: as a constructed *product* that represents the company or organization. If you feel as though the document is your baby at this point, that is a danger sign—an indication that you are personally invested. Let go.

Revision

After others have reviewed your writing and made suggestions, go back to your original draft and prepare to revise. Comments people have made will range from the minor (adding a comma, changing a number) to major (deleting a section, or questioning the approach or structure). If a comment is unclear or if you disagree with a reviewer, get clarification: have a conversation with that person. Some people are better communicators in person than in email or on paper. Ask questions. Then, revise.

Revision often involves rethinking. Now that you can see the document as others do, you can take it apart without feeling torn, yourself. You may have to discard sentences that you love, or take out sections that you enjoyed writing, in order to achieve your purpose. Some drawings or graphics may need to be removed if they don't illustrate the information well. Documents may go through many review/revision processes before they are approved for sending, or for publication. Some, such as job procedures, are constantly being revised as processes are streamlined, new machinery is purchased, and legal considerations arise. Other documents, such as investment reports, are written and revised on a regular monthly or quarterly schedule.

For revision checklists specific to special format types, see the checklist for that particular document provided in this book.

Final Editing & Proofreading

If you are editing and proofreading, do not make the changes yourself; just point out problem areas. The writer usually makes the final changes. You should be looking for details that may have been missed in the earlier reviews, or errors that may have been created by the revisions themselves. Are the page numbers sequential? Do the headings correspond to the text below them? Are sections and figures numbered correctly? Are illustrations in the right place? Do you see any extra words or missing words? Sometimes a document can make its way through several people, for example, without anyone noticing that section B has disappeared and the text now jumps from A to C, or that the graphic illustrating the budget pie has migrated to a different section. Check the math; make sure people's names are spelled correctly. Even minor errors will stand out as marks of poor attention to detail in the final product. For more information about editing, see Editing, page 277.

CREATING A SCHEDULE

Reviewing and revising are important, but at some point, you have to call *stop.* The stop-date is usually non-negotiable: a day when grants need to be submitted, when a user manual needs to go to press. To make sure the project will be finished when due, you will need to make a schedule of tasks with checkpoints for the various stages of completion. Below are examples of a special task chart, called a "Gantt chart" showing a task schedule. The first shows the proposed schedule at the start of the project; the second shows the project at midpoint, when some jobs are done and others are in process. For more examples of Gantt charts, see pages 158-159.

Table 2-2 Simple Gantt chart, beginning of project

Plan for Completion of New Job Manual by May 19							
Complete by:	**Apr. 7**	**Apr.14**	**Apr. 21**	**Apr. 28**	**May 5**	**May 12**	**May 19**
Read existing company material							
Outline; edit; plan new sections							
Identify art needed & request							
Complete first full draft							
Review & revise							
Second draft: add in artwork							
Edit & proofread; finalize art							
Final proofread; deliver to printer							◆

For a project not yet started, all bars are the same shade

Table 2-3 Simple Gantt chart, mid-project (for progress report April 14)

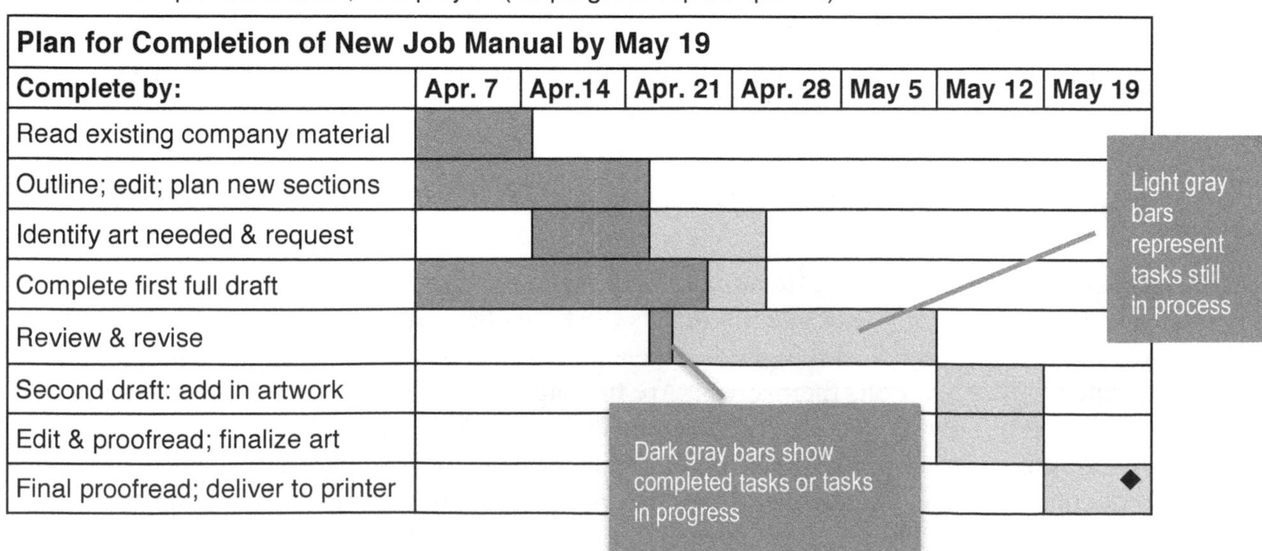

Plan for Completion of New Job Manual by May 19							
Complete by:	**Apr. 7**	**Apr.14**	**Apr. 21**	**Apr. 28**	**May 5**	**May 12**	**May 19**
Read existing company material							
Outline; edit; plan new sections							
Identify art needed & request							
Complete first full draft							
Review & revise							
Second draft: add in artwork							
Edit & proofread; finalize art							
Final proofread; deliver to printer							◆

Light gray bars represent tasks still in process
Dark gray bars show completed tasks or tasks in progress

Gantt charts can be very helpful for planning and gauging the progress of the project. They are essentially flow charts to show the layers of work on a project all moving toward the goal. The beginning and ending of each task is represented by an individual horizontal bar. Tasks are listed in process order so the chart "flows" from top left to bottom right. Gantt charts are widely used for progress reports. They can be quite simple, as in the example above, or extremely complex, showing not only multiple tasks but also project managers and resources, with different symbols representing particular stages of the work.

COLLABORATION

In the workplace, nearly all documents are produced with the help of more than one person, as businesses need to take advantage of a variety of talents and expertise. For example, a team of writers and editors may work on a document together: some might write the introduction and conclusion and others work on separate discussions, tables, or charts. Collaboration can also happen in the review and revision process: a technical writer might draft user instructions and send the document to an in-house expert for review to make sure terms and explanations are correct. A lawyer might review the instructions to recommend warnings about potential dangers to the user, or to find areas of proprietary knowledge that need to be protected. Then, the instructions might be presented to a user group to see if they are understandable.

Problems in Collaboration

When people work together, two kinds of problems tend to emerge: personalities clash or work schedules fail to coincide. Either problem can result in a dysfunctional group and work being shifted unfairly from one person to another. Avoiding a person you are supposed to work with, or missing meetings where work is done, add up to the same thing: a lack of productive interaction. Just as your personal feelings should not be a part of your professional writing, your personal reactions to co-workers should not be allowed to affect a work project.

Fixing scheduling problems is fairly easy: pull out calendars and coordinate meeting times. Set a time to meet that can fit into everyone's schedule on a regular basis. Exchanging two levels of contact information (work email and personal phone number, for example) will give you the option of checking in with a person who has missed a meeting or is home sick. Be proactive about schedules and communication, as regular contact is essential to productive collaboration.

Personality issues are more difficult to manage. The best response to someone who drives you crazy is to use your best manners: imagine the most gracious person you have ever met, and be that individual in all interactions. Good manners—saying "please" and "thank you" and other small niceties—make personal interactions easier.

Attending to assignment preferences can help the group avoid dysfunction. A writing group, like any other team, needs leaders and followers and people who can fill either role. You need people who can write, who can design, who can plan, and who can be available for last-minute editing. A person stuck with a task he or she does not like will not be eager to get it done, and may become a drag on the project.

To help define what kind of team player you are, and thus what role is best for you in a team project, try taking the little quiz below.

Defining Collaboration Roles *Quiz*

Are you happiest when . . .	✔
A. You know that you have final say about edits?	
B. You are working on page design and organizing the document?	
C. You are writing parts that other people will insert into the document?	
D. You are doing last-minute edits?	
Are you most confident when . . .	
A. You are outlining a plan for a project?	
B. You are planning ways to make a document easier to read?	
C. You are working on a task that has a clear purpose and endpoint?	
D. You are revising other people's work?	
Are you most frustrated when . . .	
A. Team members argue about how things should be done?	
B. The document looks unattractive, and no one seems to care?	
C. Others in your work team slack off, and you have to take on their work?	
D. People say they don't need your help to complete the document?	

If you checked "A" most often, you will do best as the leader or planner of the group. You should be the one to hold the schedule and remind people of meetings. If you checked "B" at least twice, you will be happy as a team member in charge of establishing a style sheet for the document and making sure that the document narrative unfolds in a logical and attractive way. If you checked "C" most frequently, you will be most valuable at writing special pieces or individual sections of the document. If you checked "D" at least twice, you will be the person who is best at working under pressure at the last moment and making sure the document is submitted or sent to the printer in time.

All these group members are essential to the success of the writing project; try to make sure that everyone is working in the way that he or she can best contribute. Some people can be quite versatile and can work in more than one way.

EXTERNAL AUDIENCE *Worksheet*

Male? Female?
Approximate age?
Where do they live?
What is their income?
What is their education/reading level?
Is the audience computer-savvy?
What is their marital status? (married, single, widowed, etc.)
What is their occupation, or occupations?
What is their ethnic background?
What are their attitudes about my topic?
What are their beliefs about my topic?
What are their needs?
What are their wants?
What is their lifestyle?
What are typical behaviors?
What are their interests and hobbies?
Is the audience fluent in standard English?
What is the audience's most comfortable language?

INTERNAL AUDIENCE *Worksheet*

Who is the primary audience?
Who is the secondary audience?
Hierarchy position in relation to you: Below Peer Superior
What is their job function?
What are their attitudes toward your topic?
What are their needs and wants?
Do they prefer written or oral communication? What type?
What is their educational/reading level?
Are they fluent in standard English?
How much knowledge do they already have about your topic?
What reaction might you expect from your document?
Does your audience use the computer at work?

WEB AUDIENCE *Worksheet*

Who is the primary audience?
Who is the secondary audience?
What is the purpose of the web site?
What is the subject matter of the web site?
What is the audience's job responsibility?
How old is the audience? Male? Female?
What might the audience like and dislike?
What ethnic values might the audience have?
What attitude might the audience have toward the website or content writer?
What attitude might the audience have about the web site's subject matter?
What does the audience expect to gain from visiting this site?
How might the audience want to navigate the web site?
What kind of information is important to this audience?
How computer-savvy is this audience?
What kind of computer might this audience have?
Does the audience have disabilities?
What is the audience's reading level, educational level?
Does the audience speak English as a second language?
Does the audience want to print out information?
How much time will the audience spend at this site per visit?

DISCUSSIONS

1. Find a letter or email you have received recently. This may be a junk mail letter inviting you to apply for insurance or credit; an actual letter from a business you have patronized; a note from a teacher, or even a communication from a friend. Make a copy, blocking out personal identification information, and share it with your class or post in your discussion group. What does the sender assume about you, the intended audience? Can you identify at least two purposes in the document? How would you describe the tone? Is the communication professional? ethical? effective? Why or why not? Explain, pointing out words or phrases in the document for support.

2. Read an opinion article about a controversial current event, such as a Supreme Court ruling, a government policy, or an election. (Your instructor may assign a particular news story for this exercise. Newspapers such as the *New York Times,* the *Washington Post*, and the *Chicago Tribune* all carry vigorous opinion columns, accessible on their websites.) Analyze the speaker's message to the audience. What is his or her stance toward the topic? What seems to be the writer's purpose? How do you know? For evidence to support your assertions about attitude, tone, and purpose, point to specific words and phrases in the article. How might this story be told differently? Try reporting the story in a new way to your discussion group, or writing it to produce a different stance on the issue and a different effect for your readers or listeners. What did you change? Why?

3. In your discussion forum, or in the classroom, brainstorm about things that can go wrong in the process of completing a project and suggest ways of using scheduling to help make these problems disappear. Try to come up with a general schedule that includes all important parts of the writing process. Does your schedule work for all possible documents? Why or why not?

4. Imagine that you are planning the construction of a park in a city-owned vacant lot and you are preparing to write letters about the project. In your discussion forum or in the classroom, brainstorm a list of groups who would be logical recipients of the letter, and which facts should be included. Which groups might logically receive identical letters?

5. Imagine that you are working for Monogram Industries, a company that employs skilled labor to sew highly individualized monograms on clothing. There is a problem on the work floor: the workers at Machine 5 can't seem to get the machine positioned correctly for a clear, clean monogram. You call the manufacturer and their service department tells you how you can fix the problem. The machine operators need to perform three simple steps to line up the fabric correctly. There is a slight chance of injury when performing these three steps. Use the "Choosing Format" flowchart to discuss what type of communication you might use to solve this problem.

EXERCISES

1. Imagine that you have been assigned to a small group (3-4 people) to complete a project together that involves researching several different products and coming up with a recommended product for a student consumer. The group will need to do research, construct tables or graphs, and write up the group's findings. **Write an email** to the rest of the group proposing a role for yourself in the group that will

    - ensure that you have some control over the quality of the product;
    - demonstrate that you are an equal contributor to the project;
    - and prevent you from having to do the whole thing yourself.

    (Objective: manage more than one purpose; write to a specific internal audience; choose tone successfully)

Use the following to get you started:

Subject: My Role in the Product Research Project

To: sgrouse@rgelectric.com, lfitty@rgelectric.com, twalker@rgelectric.com

October 2, 2:15 PM

Hello team members,

I'm very excited about working with you all on the upcoming project. I would like to propose that I be responsible for...

Thanks,

[your name]

2. For the project imagined for Exercise 1, **create a Gantt chart** that includes a plan for the review and revision process of the document cycle. (Objective: make a workable plan for a project involving more than one person)

3. Imagine that you are a marketing analyst and the Marketing Director, Georgia Allbright, has assigned you a task. You are to analyze the audience for the Senior Classic Recreational Vehicle (SCRV), an economy motor home that sleeps two. Your analysis will be turned over to the writer and artist who will create a brochure. The brochure will be handed out to weekday visitors as they look over the SCRV (Senior Classic Recreational Vehicle) at Motor Home Expos throughout the United States.

   Use the External Audience Worksheet on page 44 to cover all aspects of the audience, and then **write a two-page analysis to the Marketing Director in memo format, describing the target audience for the proposed brochure.** Who are the people who would be attending the event, and who will be most likely to be interested in the SCRV? What do these people need? What are their interests? What kind of information might be important to provide?

   Resist the urge to tell the writer and artist what to include in the brochure or how the brochure should look. Your job is to analyze the audience.

4. **Rewrite the letter on the next page** to correct for tone.

Sample 2-2 Letter for Exercise 4

5603 Lexington Drive
Gregory, GA 60590
555-555-5555

April 22, 2017

Customer Service
Farmstead Enterprises
Box 102
Marietta, GA 60500

Hi,

I'm a customer and I'm frankly VERY UPSET about the quality of the tomato plants you sent to me!!!! They are crushed and not fit for selling, or even planting. I can't tell you how ANGRY I am because this is tomato planting season and I'm going to lose a lot of customers due to your delivery of these crappy plants.

I expect you to immediately send me another complete shipment, or else! Don't bother calling unless you're going to tell me when the next delivery is going to be.

Todd Nelson

3 - Short Communications

Short communications are the everyday methods of conveying critical, time-sensitive information in the workplace. They are often better than personal conversations, especially when specific instructions are given or conditions explained. Written communication also has the advantage that it can be retrieved to aid memory and offer evidence of agreements.

Many workplace exchanges happen face-to-face, on the telephone, or in meetings, with the advantage that the participants can see and/or hear each other and understand tone and intent clearly. Those conversations aren't usually recorded; however, important details in face-to face or telephone conversations require a follow-up email that summarizes what was discussed and agreed to. Business meetings always have a note-taker who captures the minutes and records the attendees.

Short communications such as emails, memos, and letters usually have a very narrow scope and a central message. It's important to be clear, polite, and efficient with words in all communications, but especially in shorter ones.

Courtesy words such as "please" and "thank you" are essential, especially when you are making a request.

I-Centered vs. You-Centered Language

Strong communication establishes a positive connection between writer and reader; it can help promote understanding and cooperation. One way to build this connection is to write from a reader-centered point of view, implying that you value the reader's concerns and have taken the time to consider his or her needs. Simply starting with "you" rather than "I" can help you adjust your own perspective to communicate with your audience effectively.

Figure 3-1, on the next page, shows the differing directions of "I-" vs. "You-" centered communication. "You-centered" language helps direct the message toward the reader; "I-centered" language fails to make a connection.

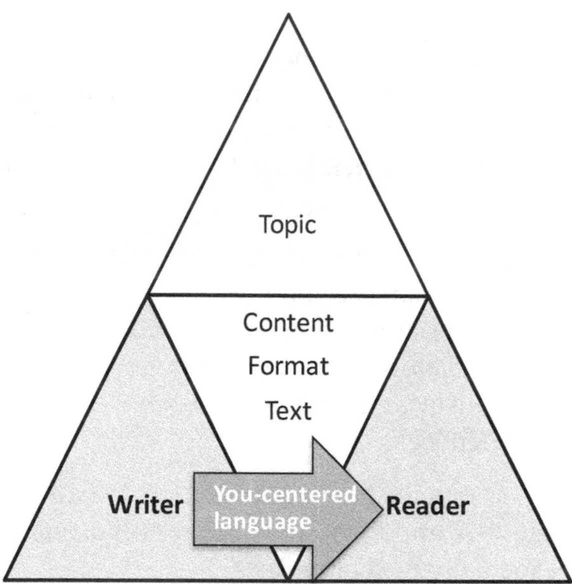

Figure 3-1 Communication Triangle for Reader-Centered Perspective

The chart below compares I-centered sentences on the left with more positive, you-centered statements on the right:

Table 3-1 Comparison of I-Centered and You-Centered Language

I-Centered	You-Centered
I want to invite you to our conference in Portland, where I am putting together a leadership council.	Your input at the conference will be invaluable in considering leadership for next year.
I was disappointed when I learned that you rejected the proposal.	Thank you for your helpful comments about the proposal.
I am unable to send you the fall catalog until October.	You will receive the fall catalog in October.

Bad News

Most messages are neutral: establishing meeting times, confirming understandings, or delivering information. Some messages carry good news (You have won the lottery for the reserved parking space! You have been promoted to manager!) and are easy to write effectively, as your audience finds that positive spark and forgets the rest.

Other messages are much harder to write effectively—the bad news kind. Messages correcting inappropriate behavior, denying admission or promotion, or refusing refunds, for example, are difficult to write gracefully. Your goal in this type of letter should be to make your reader feel recognized and valued, despite the bad news.

The person receiving a bad news letter, unlike the good news recipient, will remember every part, and may even go back to reread the letter, looking for anything positive. A writer reading a rejection notice from a publisher, for example, hopes to find a positive comment about at least some aspect of his or her work along with the "No" message.

A bad "bad news" letter is an obvious form letter that offers no recognition of the individual or his or her concerns. An even worse version is one that adds rudeness to the injury. Of course, you must treat your audience with courtesy and use a cordial tone, as with any correspondence.

People pay most attention to the first and last parts in any piece of writing, so begin and end with praise or positive statements. This way, the necessary negative parts become psychologically secondary, and you also have the chance to put the bad news in reasonable context.

The examples below show two versions of a bad news email—one abrupt and rude, and the other recognizing the individual and sandwiched with positive statements:

Example - Bad news delivered abruptly

Dear Ms. Lopez,

Your application for the manager position is denied. I have hired a better candidate.

Sincerely,

Axel Pincherton

Example - Bad news delivered effectively

Dear Ms. Lopez,

You have worked hard for the company for several years, and I appreciate your dedication. In interviewing several candidates for the manager position, the hiring committee found there were several very qualified candidates. Unfortunately, the committee has decided not to hire you for that position this time.

You are doing a good job as assistant manager in the Forms Department, and our staff is lucky to have you.

Sincerely,

Axel Pincherton

EMAILS

Emails have almost entirely replaced business letters in business communication. Advantages are that they are instantly delivered and can convey even very brief information effectively. A telephone conversation is a better choice when personal contact is needed. Unlike a telephone call, however, an emailed message provides an important record of contact and allows the reader to think about his or her response before replying.

Always use complete words and sentences when writing a work email. Taking the time to explain your meaning and make sure that words are spelled properly shows respect for your reader. Many people are in the habit of using casual, friendly, abbreviation-filled exchanges in personal emailing or texting and continue that practice in documents that should be professional. Casual acronyms such as LOL are not appropriate in business writing, for example. Since emails so common, they are a good place to start in separating the professional, work world from conversations with friends and family.

Paragraphs

Paragraphs in an email should be short and begin at the left margin, without an indent. Readers scroll through quickly and are likely to skip very long chunks of text. Parts that require special emphasis, such as appointment times or action times, need to have white space before and after, to focus the reader's attention.

An email is a unit of thought recognizable to your computer. If you need more than about four paragraphs to convey what you have to say, there is a good chance that you are covering more than one thought and that you should send separate emails for each subject to separate different projects or problems in the email thread.

Readers of email tend to check messages often and respond quickly. If you have a lot of complex information to convey, consider writing a report and sending it as an attachment to a brief email. That way, your reader can easily download the file and read it later.

On the next page is a sample work email that meets professional standards:

Professionalism & Ethics

Workplace correspondence is never private (as much as it may seem so) and can be potential evidence in lawsuits involving you and/or the company you work for. Avoid saying anything in a letter, memo, or email that is not demonstrably true, that reflects badly on colleagues (gossip), or that suggests a conflict of interest, establishes unnecessary liability or invites lawsuits.

In writing to a customer or other external correspondents, it is wise to have a supervisor, or even the company's legal advisor, review your message for appropriate tone and content if you are uncertain. Sometimes even well-meaning expressions of sympathy can be interpreted as admission of fault.

Sample 3 -1 Business Email

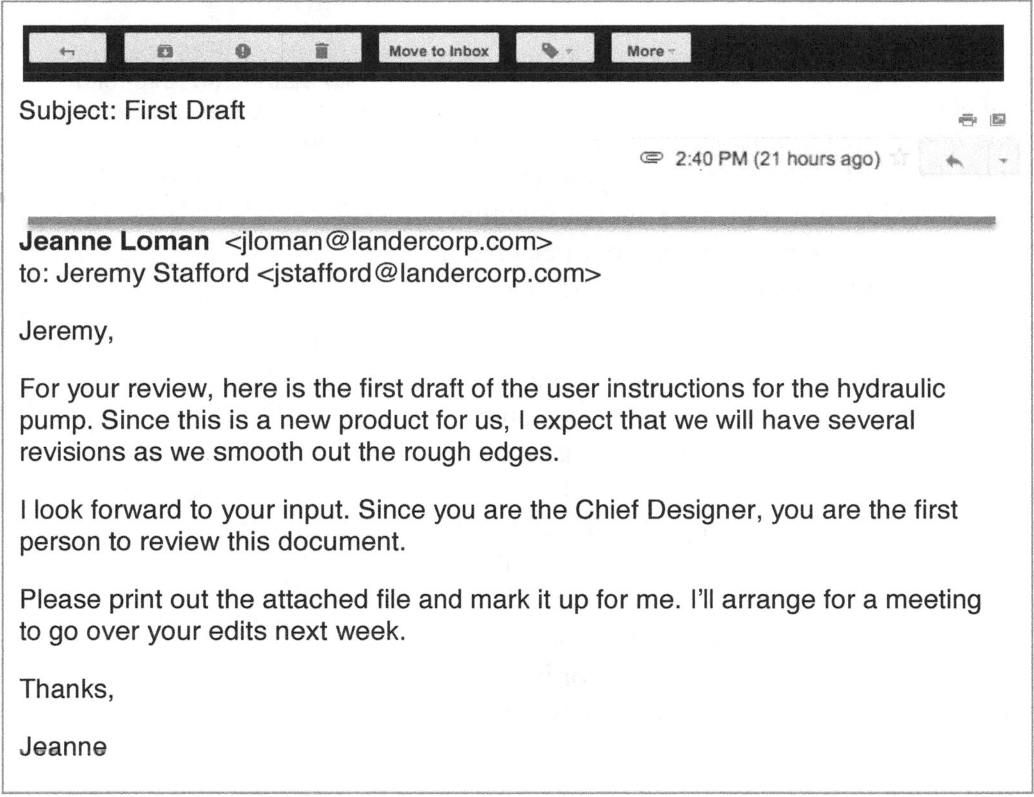
Move to Inbox
More
Subject: First Draft
2:40 PM (21 hours ago)

Jeanne Loman <jloman@landercorp.com>
to: Jeremy Stafford <jstafford@landercorp.com>

Jeremy,

For your review, here is the first draft of the user instructions for the hydraulic pump. Since this is a new product for us, I expect that we will have several revisions as we smooth out the rough edges.

I look forward to your input. Since you are the Chief Designer, you are the first person to review this document.

Please print out the attached file and mark it up for me. I'll arrange for a meeting to go over your edits next week.

Thanks,

Jeanne

One disadvantage of emails compared to letters is that problems in delivery are frequent. Best practice in professional correspondence requires a brief confirmation that you have received the message, even if you cannot respond in detail right away. Below is an example of a brief confirmation email:

Sample 3 -2 Confirmation Email

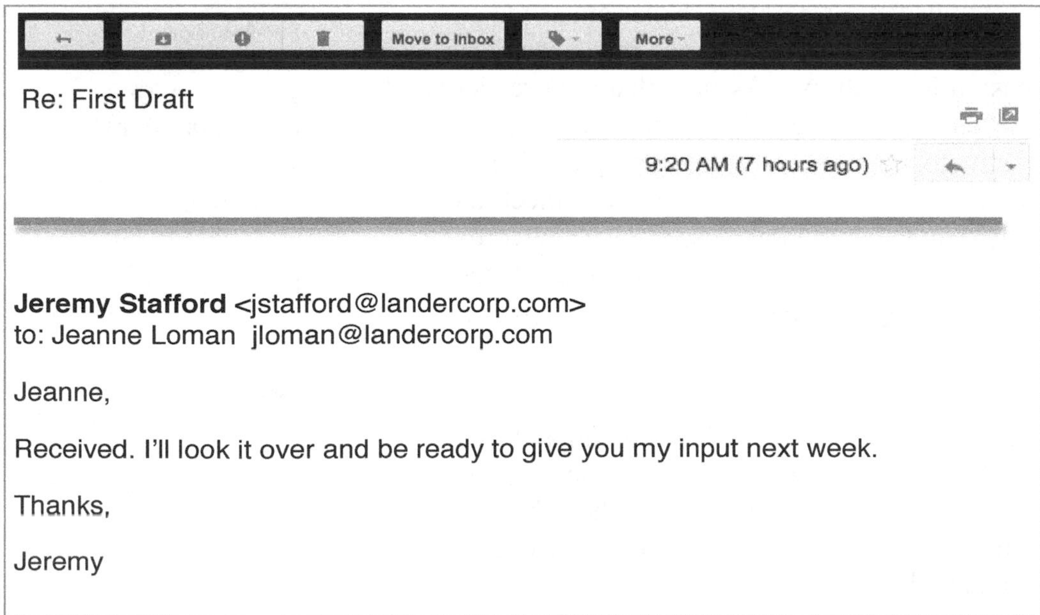
Move to Inbox
More
Re: First Draft
9:20 AM (7 hours ago)

Jeremy Stafford <jstafford@landercorp.com>
to: Jeanne Loman jloman@landercorp.com

Jeanne,

Received. I'll look it over and be ready to give you my input next week.

Thanks,

Jeremy

Professional Email Address

At work, many people have a standard work email address, such as *firstname.lastname@company.org.* That email address should be used for work only; discourage your friends and relatives from clogging your work inbox. Email in your work account is *not private*. Keep your personal life separate from your work life, including separating email accounts according to purpose.

Your email address is part of your work persona. Even if you do not yet have the job that you want, you can make sure that your email address matches the image that you want to portray. Funny or embarrassing email addresses may ensure that the person receiving your message does not open it, or if he/she does open the message, will never take you seriously. Keep your funny/casual email address for friends, and, if you do not have one already, create an email account that is specifically for business correspondence. Some recognizable version of your formal name is appropriate for this, such as *allen.brown* or *mjmckenzie*.

Subject Line

The subject line, for some reason, is easy to overlook when writing an email, but it is extremely important. It can determine whether or not your reader opens the message, where the message goes once it has been read, and how easy it is to retrieve. Assume that your reader is busy and needs a way to identify the specific topic quickly. Instructors appreciate it, for example, when students include their course number in the subject line, because they may teach several classes. Use keywords to reflect the topic of the message, and adjust the subject line when an ongoing conversation shifts to a new focus.

Many people click "reply" on an old email as a convenient way to locate the recipient's email address, especially when writing to a person who is not in their contact list. If you do that, be sure to edit the subject line to make it reflect the new subject matter. Otherwise, your email may be sorted in the wrong thread and lost.

Professionalism & Ethics

Courtesy titles are a way to maintain a respectful distance between writer and recipient. The title "Dr." or "Professor," for example, signals polite respect for a professional's education and authority.

"Mr." and "Ms." are the standard courtesy titles used in correspondence and personal address. The titles "Miss" or "Mrs." are no longer used professionally (unless by personal request), as they label women according to marital status.

Because not everyone identifies as simply male or female, there is a need for gender-neutral titles. Although no gender-neutral has been universally accepted for professional correspondence at this time, a few options exist, in order of preference:

1. **Professional titles**, abbreviated or spelled out (Dr., Prof., Mgr., Barista)
2. **M.** (gender neutral in English, but masculine in French)
3. **Mx.** (has been adopted widely in the UK)
4. **Ind.** (stands for "individual")

Salutation

Emails are a lot like letters, especially when they are written to contact people whom you might not know very well, or when they initiate a new workplace discussion. It is professional practice to include a brief first-name opening for friends, family, and close co-workers, such as "Janine," or "Hi Dave," and a more formal opening such as "Dear Ms. Truhana," for a person you do not know well. If you do not know the recipient's name, it is acceptable to address your reader by title, such as "Dear Human Resources Specialist." When writing to a group, you may use the group name, such as "Hello Iowa City Recyclers." If you are truly stumped about what to call someone, "Greetings" is better than nothing. A comma after the salutation is correct.

Do not use time-of-day salutations such as “Good morning, Tim” because you don’t know when the reader will open and read your email. The reader may be slightly put off that you assume your email will be read first thing in the morning. Many professionals block off a specific time in their day for the purpose of reading and responding to emails.

When you are replying to an ongoing discussion with a brief answer, it is acceptable to skip a formal salutation and get right to the reply. If your answer will be more than a line or two, however, a "Hi [Name]," salutation is the best practice.

Threaded Email

An email "thread" is a sequence of emails (often replies to each other) that share the same subject line. You can use your email settings to organize conversations by “thread,” so you can easily see what people have written on the subject. Readers can also use the subject line to sort emails on a particular subject to locate the complete thread.

When you click "reply," email programs often open a message box showing the email you are replying to —and all the other messages in the thread. This can be a very long list of messages, with signature lines from various people over and over. Massive threads, with copied messages from many individuals, can get unwieldy. It is best to drop messages that are no longer current from your reply, if the entire conversation is saved under the subject line.

When writing your reply, **write at the top of the message box.** If you type your contribution below another person's message, it may not be read. Readers will be looking for the new responses to appear at the top and may not search for what you have written.

Although it is a good idea to eliminate extra baggage from your email, you should not send your message bare of context. Keep at least the last email or two within your reply, as they are very useful to jog the busy reader's memory. Especially if the subject line is at all unclear, your reader will be grateful for a little review of what is happening and will then be able to be more helpful and knowledgeable in their reply.

Closing

Email format is not quite as standardized as that of the memo or the letter, but the best professional emails have a closing and signature line.

In an informal email, you can usually close with "Thanks" and your first name, as shown on page 61. In a more formal message, use a closing such as *Best regards* or *Sincerely.* Do consider the meaning of that ending line, to avoid misunderstandings. For example, *Cheers* might not be the best one to use (at least not all the time), as it suggests raising an alcoholic beverage in a toast. Closing lines help convey a cordial tone and establish a final, formal connection with the reader.

One good reason to include a signature is that a person's email address does not necessarily reflect a complete name. If the recipient does not know you, he or she may be flummoxed by *pmartin*, for example (is it Patricia? Paul? Padma?).

Many professionals use a standard signature block that includes their full name, job title, contact information, and even a small company logo. This is a good way of making sure that your reader always knows your name, your position, and your organization or company affiliation. If you do include a job title and contact information in your signature, make sure to update it when you change positions or switch phones or change your email address.

For many emails, a personal touch is required. It is a kindness to your reader to sign the email in the way you would like to be addressed: for example, if your signature line reads Theodore R. Signer but everyone calls you Rick, your reader needs to know.

Since no one has any expectation that you will actually sign your emails with a pen, it is not necessary to mimic a signature, unless required by a particular form or company rule.

Professionalism & Ethics

In business communication, writers often set up group lists or distribution lists and need only to click on the name of the group (e.g. Focus Team) in order to send emails to everyone on the list. This shortcut is convenient, but can also can be dangerous when writers do it habitually, without considering who is on the list: you probably don't want Fred T. (a member of the Performance Review Committee) to see you discussing *his* job performance before *his* annual review, for example. Think about who is receiving the email and scrutinize your cc list.

CC and BCC Lists

The letters "cc' in the pre-photocopy days stood for "carbon copy," and "bcc" stood for "blind carbon copy." In those days, a typist inserted several sheets of paper into the typewriter, separated by carbon paper, to create faint copies that were sent to interested parties. The cc list was limited to very few people, since only the strongest typist could hit the keys hard enough to create more than one or two readable copies. The indication "cc:" with the name of the person receiving the copy is included at the bottom of every copy of a formal letter. A person receiving a "blind carbon copy" (bcc) is indicated only on the file copy—the addressee is "blind" to the fact that another person is seeing the correspondence.

In emails, "cc" indicates people who will be receiving a copy of the email; those addresses are listed publicly in a line under the "To" line. Those listed in the "bcc" will receive a copy of the email but they will be “blind” to other email addresses in the list.

Use the bcc function when writing mass emails, such as newsletters or marketing material, to maintain privacy of individuals and to avoid having an enormous address section in recipients' email messages.

Proofread!

Before you hit that "send" button, check the recipient's email address (no typos? still the same as it used to be?). If sending to a work email address, is the recipient still employed there?

Most email programs have a built-in spell check. Because email is quick and easy, a lot of writers don't remember to use this resource. Take the extra minute to proofread and run spell check in the body of your message.

MEMOS

A memo, or *memorandum*, is usually used to convey a simple but important message to a group of people. Memos are often workplace announcements. Sometimes they posted on a bulletin board in the break room, or dropped in a physical “IN” box. More often, they are sent in emails to “distribution lists,” a pre-set group of addressees.

Use the memo format selectively and wisely to gain support and respect of coworkers and superiors. Use it unnecessarily and your memos will reflect badly upon you and your workgroup. Your memos may even be ignored.

Hard copy (printed) memos and email memos have slightly different formatting rules. As you can see in the chart below, the format expectations for emailed memos are more flexible than for hard copy memos:

Table 3-2 Hard Copy (Printed) Memo vs. Emailed Memo Format:

Format Feature	Hard Copy Memo	Emailed Memo
Salutation	NO	YES
Closing	NO	YES
Handwritten signature	NO	NO
Includes Memo or Memorandum as title	YES	NO
All important words capitalized in subject line	YES	YES
Includes job titles in From and To lines	YES	NO

Sample 3-3 Memo in Hard Copy Format

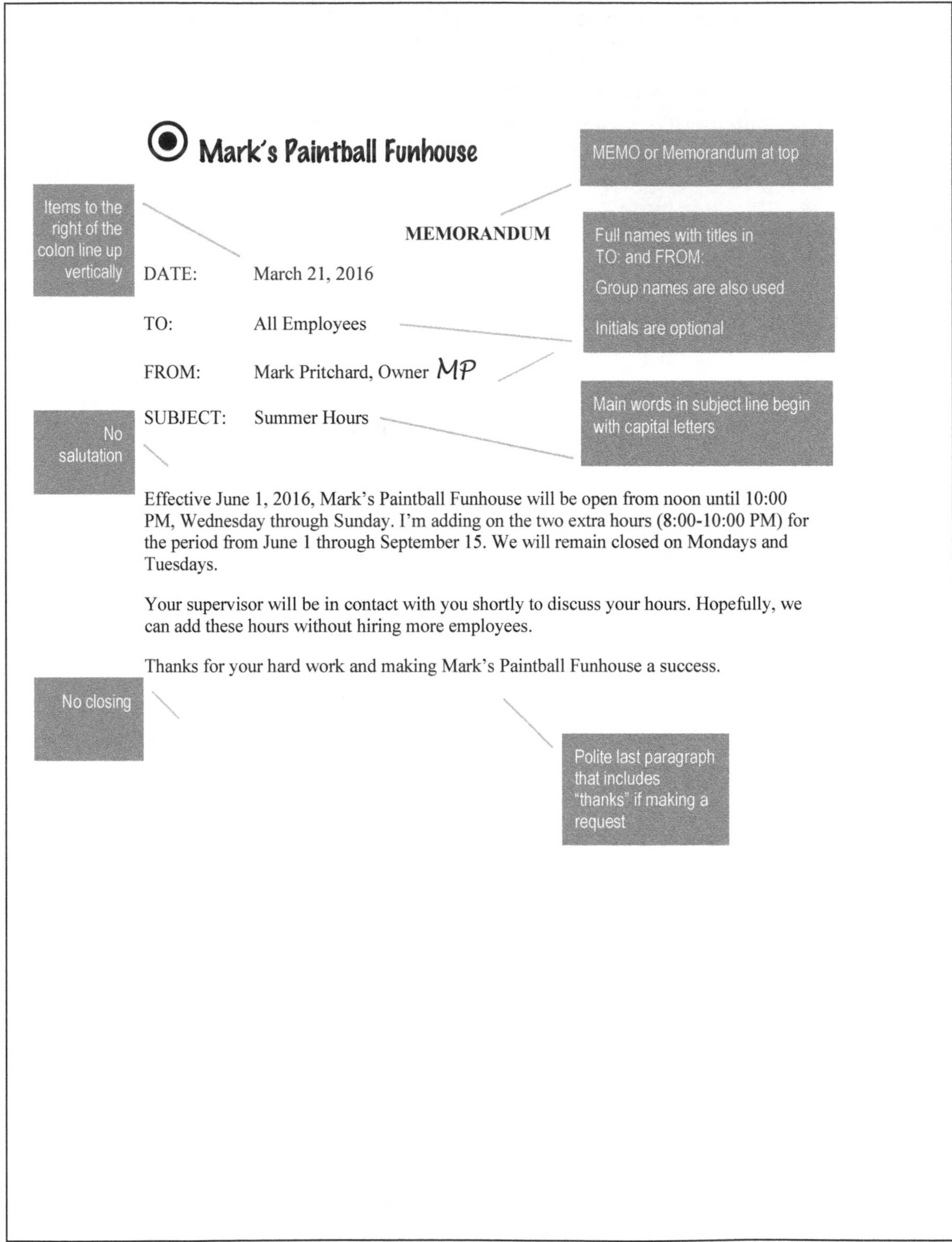
Mark's Paintball Funhouse

MEMORANDUM

DATE: March 21, 2016

TO: All Employees

FROM: Mark Pritchard, Owner MP

SUBJECT: Summer Hours

Effective June 1, 2016, Mark's Paintball Funhouse will be open from noon until 10:00 PM, Wednesday through Sunday. I'm adding on the two extra hours (8:00-10:00 PM) for the period from June 1 through September 15. We will remain closed on Mondays and Tuesdays.

Your supervisor will be in contact with you shortly to discuss your hours. Hopefully, we can add these hours without hiring more employees.

Thanks for your hard work and making Mark's Paintball Funhouse a success.

MEMO or Memorandum at top
Items to the right of the colon line up vertically
Full names with titles in TO: and FROM:
Group names are also used
Initials are optional
Main words in subject line begin with capital letters
No salutation
No closing
Polite last paragraph that includes "thanks" if making a request

Sample 3-4 Memo in Email Format

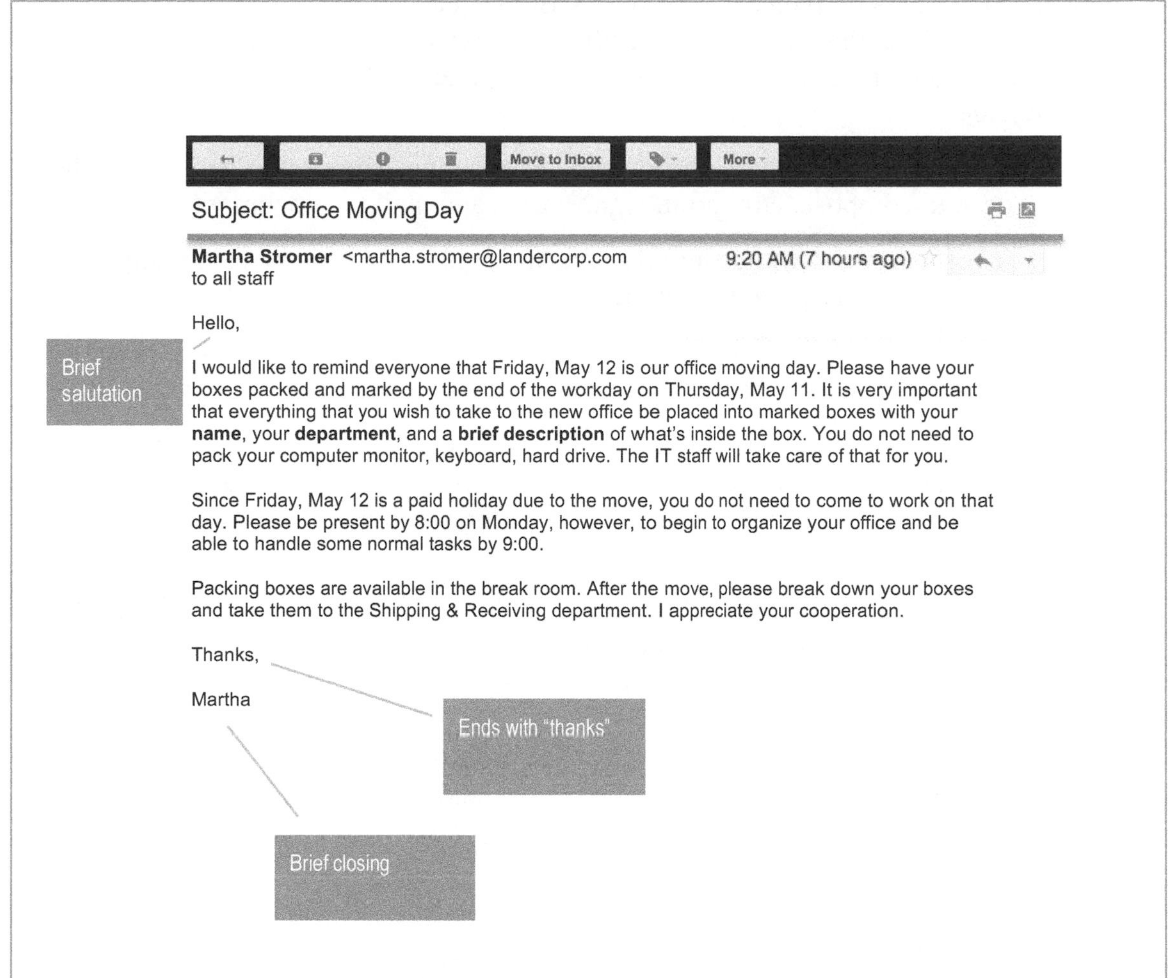
Move to Inbox

More

Subject: Office Moving Day

Martha Stromer <martha.stromer@landercorp.com 9:20 AM (7 hours ago)
to all staff

Hello,

I would like to remind everyone that Friday, May 12 is our office moving day. Please have your boxes packed and marked by the end of the workday on Thursday, May 11. It is very important that everything that you wish to take to the new office be placed into marked boxes with your **name**, your **department**, and a **brief description** of what's inside the box. You do not need to pack your computer monitor, keyboard, hard drive. The IT staff will take care of that for you.

Since Friday, May 12 is a paid holiday due to the move, you do not need to come to work on that day. Please be present by 8:00 on Monday, however, to begin to organize your office and be able to handle some normal tasks by 9:00.

Packing boxes are available in the break room. After the move, please break down your boxes and take them to the Shipping & Receiving department. I appreciate your cooperation.

Thanks,

Martha

Memo Reports

Some memos are expanded to include a report. A memo report is an internal document that follows the memo format, but can include headings and expanded content. An example of a simple memo report to an individual is given in Chapter 6, **Short Reports**, Sample 6-5, page 130.

LETTERS

You may think that the printed business letter has gone the way of the typewriter—an archaic way to communicate. But there is not a more powerful way to reach an external audience (an audience outside your company or organization). It's very easy to pick up the phone, or "shoot off" an email. (The expression "shoot off an email" is especially appropriate because you can "shoot yourself in the foot," especially if you write while angry.)

A hard copy document is assigned more importance because it exists in a concrete format. It arrives, gets delivered, sits in the IN BOX, gets handled by human beings, is physically opened (tactile and auditory reinforcements), and is easily read (hard copy is still easier to read than online). When you send an actual printed letter, you put yourself at an advantage:

- You show that you are serious enough about your request to have taken the time to compose, edit, print, sign, stamp, and mail the document.
- Your handwritten signature reminds the reader that you are personally attesting to the content of the letter.
- Your recognition of the relative weight that a letter carries, versus an email or phone call, shows that you are a savvy business person.
- You give yourself the opportunity to state your purpose clearly and confidently without the interferences that can sometimes accompany phone calls or emails, such as noise and connection troubles.

For memo and letter format, use **Full Block Style** (See Sample 3-5 on page 63). Full block is very easy to read because each line begins at the left edge of the margin, where English speakers look for the beginning of text. It also makes letters look more organized and helps eliminate formatting problems. For example, you don't have to worry about how much to indent paragraph one versus paragraph two. However, you do need to have extra white space between paragraphs to distinguish paragraph breaks.

For simplicity and consistency, use the following table to find the official two-letter code for states to use in your address lines:

Table 3-3 State Two-letter Codes

Alabama – AL	Kentucky – KY	North Dakota – ND
Alaska – AK	Louisiana – LA	Ohio – OH
Arizona – AZ	Maine – ME	Oklahoma – OK
Arkansas – AR	Maryland – MD	Oregon – OR
California – CA	Massachusetts – MA	Pennsylvania – PA
Colorado – CO	Michigan – MI	Rhode Island – RI
Connecticut – CT	Minnesota – MN	South Carolina – SC
Delaware – DE	Mississippi – MS	South Dakota – SD
District of Columbia – DC	Missouri – MO	Tennessee – TN
Florida – FL	Montana – MT	Texas – TX
Georgia – GA	Nebraska – NE	Utah – UT
Hawaii – HI	Nevada – NV	Vermont – VT
Idaho – ID	New Hampshire – NH	Virginia – VA
Illinois – IL	New Jersey – NJ	Washington – WA
Indiana – IN	New Mexico – NM	West Virginia – WV
Iowa – IA	New York – NY	Wisconsin – WI
Kansas – KS	North Carolina – NC	Wyoming – WY

Sample 3-5 Letter in Full Block Style

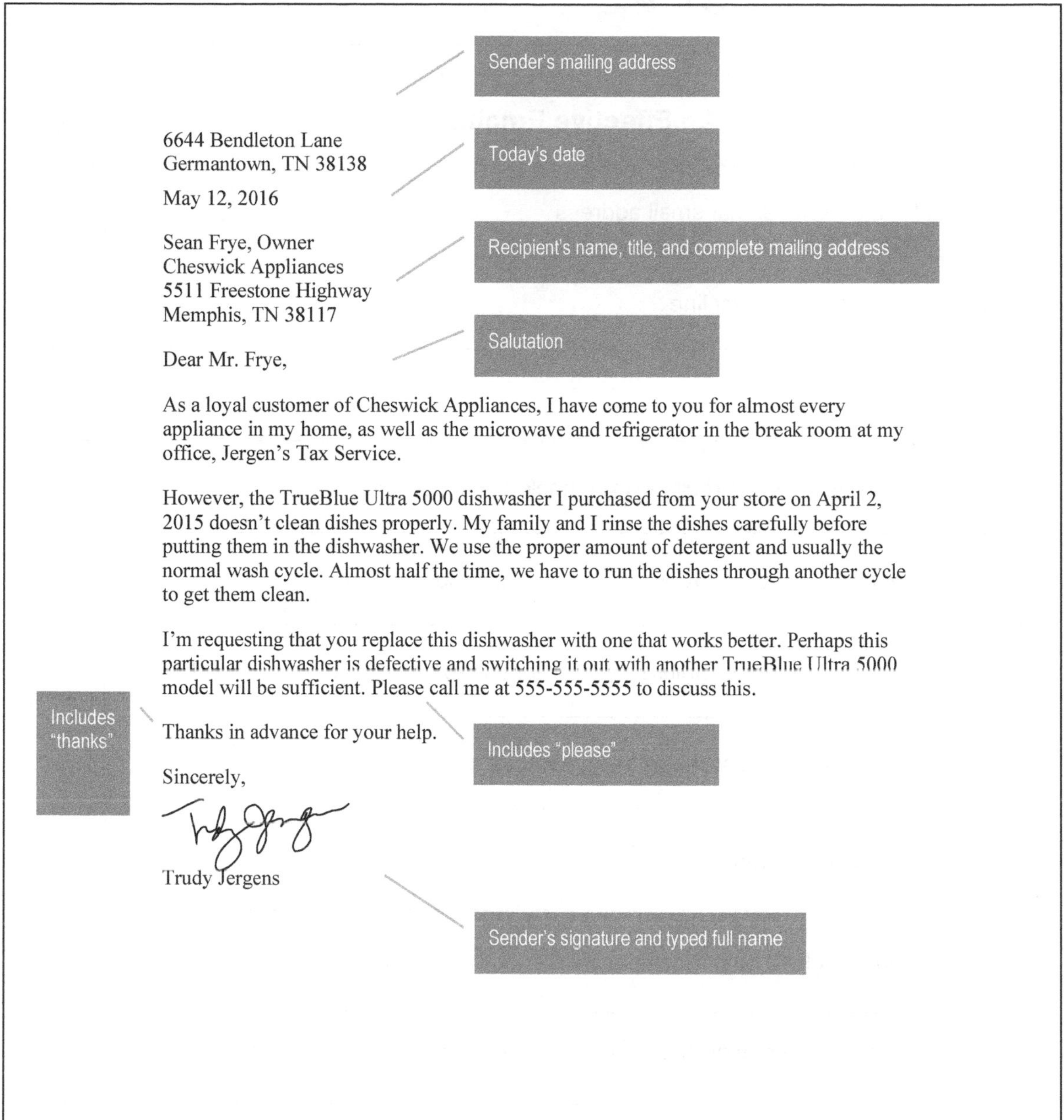

6644 Bendleton Lane
Germantown, TN 38138

May 12, 2016

Sean Frye, Owner
Cheswick Appliances
5511 Freestone Highway
Memphis, TN 38117

Dear Mr. Frye,

As a loyal customer of Cheswick Appliances, I have come to you for almost every appliance in my home, as well as the microwave and refrigerator in the break room at my office, Jergen's Tax Service.

However, the TrueBlue Ultra 5000 dishwasher I purchased from your store on April 2, 2015 doesn't clean dishes properly. My family and I rinse the dishes carefully before putting them in the dishwasher. We use the proper amount of detergent and usually the normal wash cycle. Almost half the time, we have to run the dishes through another cycle to get them clean.

I'm requesting that you replace this dishwasher with one that works better. Perhaps this particular dishwasher is defective and switching it out with another TrueBlue Ultra 5000 model will be sufficient. Please call me at 555-555-5555 to discuss this.

Thanks in advance for your help.

Sincerely,

Trudy Jergens

Letter Reports

Letter reports are simply letters written to an external audience with expanded content. They may contain headings and even sub-headings. See Sample 6-6 on pages 132-133 in Chapter 6, Short Reports for an example of a letter report.

EMAIL *Checklist* ✔

An Effective Email...	✔
Is sent from a professional email address	
Uses a descriptive subject line	
Is limited to one subject	
Is sent to the appropriate recipient(s) (check to, cc, bcc lists)	
Uses a salutation (e.g., Hi George, Dear Ms. Johnson)	
Uses paragraph breaks or bullets to call attention to action items or appointments	
Uses cordial closing line with preferred name of sender	
Is written in a professional tone	
Uses natural English, language appropriate for the audience	
Uses please and thanks or thank you if requesting information or action	
Uses correct grammar, spelling, and punctuation	

MEMO *Checklist* ✔

An Effective Memo...	✔
Uses standard memo format for hard copy or email, including full block style	
Uses a descriptive subject line with initial capitalization	
Correctly spells the name(s) of the recipients, and gives their title(s)	
Is limited to one subject	
Uses an appropriate tone for the purpose and audience	
Uses natural English, language appropriate for the audience	
Uses paragraph breaks or bullets to call attention to action items or appointments	
Uses please and thanks or thank you if requesting information or action	
Uses correct grammar, spelling, and punctuation	

LETTER *Checklist* ✔

An Effective Letter...	✔
Uses standard letter format (full block style), with sender's contact information, date, recipient's name and contact information, salutation, body, and closing	
States the purpose clearly in the first paragraph	
Organizes content into paragraphs that cover one topic each	
Ends politely in the final paragraph	
Uses a professional tone	
Uses natural English, language appropriate for the audience	
Uses paragraph breaks or bullets to call attention to action items or appointments	
Uses please and thanks or thank you if requesting information or action	
Uses correct grammar, spelling, and punctuation	

DISCUSSIONS

1. Reflect on an instance in your life in which your email completely missed its mark. Perhaps you wrote the email while angry and immediately regretted the action. Perhaps you unknowingly cc-ed everyone in the company on a private or delicate subject. Discuss one of your email mishaps with the class and reveal what you learned from the experience.
2. For a week, save and copy all the junk mail letters and spam emails you receive. Share two or three with the class (or with a small group, assigned by your instructor), and analyze them according to the checklists provided in this chapter. Which are the worst or best, and why?
3. Respond to the following quotations by relating them to the material in Chapters 1-3:
    - "The language of truth is simple."
      Euripides
    - "Not the fastest horse can catch a word spoken in anger."
      Chinese Proverb
    - ". . . the most valuable of all talents [is] that of never using two words when one will do."
      Thomas Jefferson
    - "The letter I have written today is longer than usual because I lacked the time to make it shorter."
      Blaise Pascal

EXERCISES

1. You are the owner of a small business, and you have noticed that lately you have had several people calling in sick on Fridays. You do not want to have people working while they are ill, but you suspect that this "Friday sickness" is, in reality, a way for workers to add a day to the weekend. Fridays are typically busy days, so you have often been left short-handed, resulting in frustrated customers. **Write a memo to your staff to resolve this problem.**
2. You work for a boutique that sells high quality, expensive women's clothing. A customer has recently returned a blouse that, when worn, left dye on her skin and bra. **Write a letter to the dissatisfied customer.**
3. You have been assigned to a product evaluation project along with several co-workers. The project involves testing various competitors' athletic shoes by wearing them during daily runs and other exercise activities. Each person in the group has agreed to investigate one company's product in terms of design, manufacturing, and pricing; all participants are testing the shoes. One colleague's

input is always late, and you have had to do some of his work yourself to avoid missing deadlines. It is unclear whether he has actually been wear-testing the shoes. The other people in the group have missed meetings now and then but are generally keeping up with the work. You are frustrated but you will need to work with this person in the future, so you need to be courteous. **Write an email to your work group in an attempt to begin to resolve these matters**.

4 - Page Design

Deciding which elements to include on a page, and then formatting these elements, requires an understanding of the subject matter, how the document will be used, and who will read it. For example, the page design for a set of instructions for the installation of a baby car seat would look very different from the page design for a yearly stockholders' report. They have vastly different subjects, audiences, and purposes. Page design is at the center of the communication triangle:

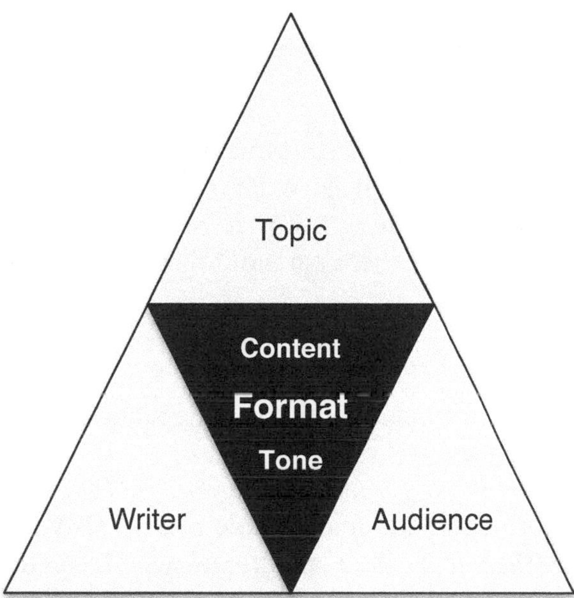

Figure 4-1 Communication Triangle for Page Design

No matter how different two documents may be, they should still follow some basic principles of good page design:

- **Application of cognitive theory**. How do human beings read? How do human beings learn new information? The field of cognitive psychology has given writers valuable information about how best to design documents.

- **Readability**. Use an appropriate font and type size for ease of reading for the audience. Factors such as alignment, justification, and spacing between lines also affect readability.

- **Use of white space**. Unused space on the page is not wasted. The interaction between the white space and the text or graphics helps the reader interpret the content. Also, adequate white space is visually pleasing to the reader and gives the eyes a break.

- **Organization**. Think of your document as a map. The reader is guided along a path using guideposts (headings, subheadings, paragraphs, bullets, numbered lists, page numbers).

- **Use of graphics**. Integrate graphics into the page design in a way that optimizes the understanding and impact of the page content. The effective use of graphics is covered in Chapter 7 of this textbook.

HOW READERS READ

Cognitive psychologists have researched how humans take in, process, and remember new information. As writers, we can use this knowledge not only to write effectively, but also to format the page.

Western readers (in Europe and the Americas) start tracking a page from the left side. We look for quick clues to answer questions such as: What is important on this page? What is this page about? Does this look like something I want to read? Have I been prepared to receive the information on this page? Are there parts of this page I can skip?

Use this knowledge about reading patterns to invite the reader into the page. Put important text on the left side, or at least have it begin on the left side. Notice the headings and sub-headings in this textbook. They are formatted with the understanding that you look to the left side to guide yourself through the page.

The concept of "chunking" information into manageable bites is also a revelation brought to us by research (Miller). Rather than using long paragraphs, which can intimidate some readers, try to "chunk" or group information into shorter paragraphs that the reader can access and process easily.

For more information on using paragraphs, see "Paragraphing" on page 289 in the "Resources – Grammar" section at the back of this textbook.

Compare the relative ease of reading the following two examples. Which would you rather read, and why?

Example 1 - Without paragraph breaks

When authors write they have an idea in mind that they are trying to get across. This is especially true as authors compose paragraphs. An author organizes each paragraph's main idea and supporting details in support of the topic or central theme, and each paragraph supports the paragraph preceding it. A writer will state his/her main idea explicitly somewhere in the paragraph. That main idea may be stated at the beginning of the paragraph, in the middle, or at the end. The sentence in which the main idea is stated is the *topic sentence* of that paragraph. The topic sentence announces the general theme (or portion of the theme) to be dealt with in the paragraph. Although the topic sentence may appear anywhere in the paragraph, it is usually first - and for a very good reason. This sentence provides the focus for the writer while writing and for the reader while reading. When you find the topic sentence, be sure to underline it so that it will stand out not only now, but also later when you review.

[Note: Paragraph breaks were taken out of original material for the purposes of this example.]

Example 2 - With paragraph breaks

When authors write they have an idea in mind that they are trying to get across. This is especially true as authors compose paragraphs. An author organizes each paragraph's main idea and supporting details in support of the topic or central theme, and each paragraph supports the paragraph preceding it.

A writer will state his/her main idea explicitly somewhere in the paragraph. That main idea may be stated at the beginning of the paragraph, in the middle, or at the end. The sentence in which the main idea is stated is the *topic sentence* of that paragraph.

The topic sentence announces the general theme (or portion of the theme) to be dealt with in the paragraph. Although the topic sentence may appear anywhere in the paragraph, it is usually first - and for a very good reason. This sentence provides the focus for the writer while writing and for the reader while reading. When you find the topic sentence, be sure to underline it so that it will stand out not only now, but also later when you review.

Source: Taranaki Literacy NLC. http://taranakisecondaryliteracynlc.wikispaces.com/Identify+and+understand+main+ideas?showComments=1

READABILITY

Some pages are easier to read than others. That's because the person who designed the readable page made conscious decisions about how to present the text to a particular audience.

Fonts and Style

One of the important decisions is the typeface or font. Writing software (e.g., MS Word) offers many choices for font. However, for readability purposes, a handful of fonts suffice for all our purposes.

Fonts are divided into two major types: serif and sans serif. "Serifs" are the small details added to simple letter shapes. For example, the "d" in Times New Roman has a small horizontal line at the top of the vertical line. In contrast, the Arial font, which is a sans serif (without serif), has only the basic letter shape:

d Times New Roman (a serif font)

d Arial (a sans serif font)

Font families are comprised of the basic font with variations that can be used in different ways. For example, the Arial font family contains the following variations:

Arial
Arial Black
Arial Narrow

The font can be further specified to be **bold**, *italic*, ALL CAPS, or underlined. The size of the type can be adjusted almost infinitely, either by choosing a size on the drop-down size menu or entering a size in the size field.

A word about underlining: Since underlining has become the standard method for formatting URLs and hyperlinks, they are no longer used for adding emphasis. If you underline text, the reader will expect it to be a link.

In general, the safest choice for readability is a serif font, such as Times New Roman, which should be used for the text of a document. Sans serif text can effectively be used for headings. Using both a serif and sans serif gives the page some graphic interest, and clearly separates the headings from the text. Note that the heading below is a sans serif and the text is serif.

This Heading is Arial Rounded MT Bold, 14 pt.

This text font is Palatino, type size 12. As it is smaller and different from the heading, it is clearly the paragraph that goes under the heading.

Typography, or the study of the use of typeface, is a very complex subject that is beyond the scope of this textbook. Graphic artists study typography to produce the right impression for a graphic layout.

For writers who do not need that level of knowledge about type, the following general guidelines are helpful:

Guidelines for Typeface Choices

- Use a serif font for the text, and sans serif for headings.
- High-level headings should be larger than lower level headings. Use the type size to show hierarchy. Headings should be larger than the rest of the text.
- **Arial** and **Times New Roman** are the most commonly used typefaces and will suffice for most documents.
- Use 11 or 12 point type for the main text of any document. Smaller text can be used for notes or in tables, but take extreme care that the text remains legible.
- Adjust the type size for the audience. Small children and older adults prefer larger type size.
- Use black type on white for the easiest readability. In all cases, use a high contrast between the type color and the background color.
- Do not exceed more than two or three font families on the same page. Using too many fonts and styles will give the document a "ransom-note" appearance.
- Use color carefully. Use red only for warnings or cautions. Use other colors only when the color is used to add meaning to the text, not to "prettify" it.

Alignment

Alignment is another critical decision for readability. Since Western readers start at the left margin, it's a good idea for you to start there. There are exceptions to this general rule, such as for a heading that you would like to center. Rarely, you may choose right-aligned text to hug up against an item, such as a description for a graphic. For example, the description in Figure 4-2 is right-aligned to "attach" it to the graphic.

Trails such as the North Sylamore Creek trail offer family enjoyment.

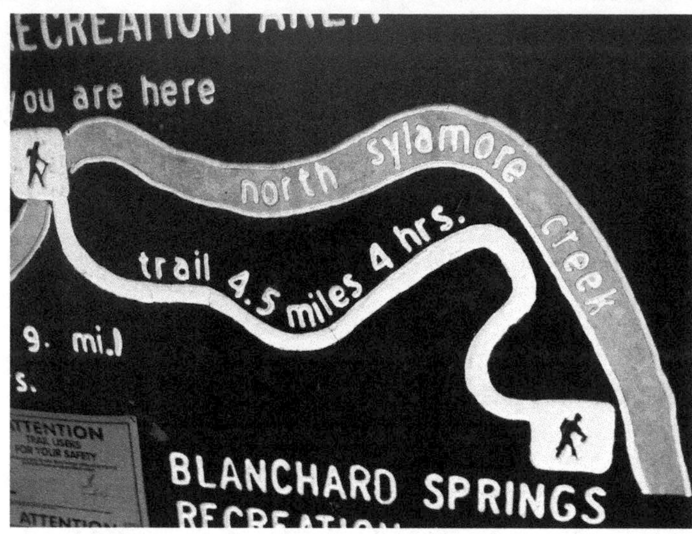

Figure 4-2 North Sylamore Creek Trail Sign. Photo by Nell Johnson

With left-aligned text, use "ragged right" margin for maximum legibility. "Ragged right" means that the text at the right margin doesn't line up. The right margin has a ragged appearance because each line of text ends where it naturally needs to, and wraps to the next line. The spacing between words is consistent. A ragged right line helps our eyes to move from left to right and then left again to the next line, keeping our place in the page. It also helps legibility by keeping the spacing between words consistent.

Justified vs. Ragged Right

Avoid the urge to use justified margins, which means that the words are spaced so that the text lines up along both the left and right margins. While this may look neat and organized, it doesn't usually help the reader. The examples below show a justified margin and a ragged right margin. Notice the white space swimming between the words in the justified example.

Example 1 - Justified paragraph

> Avoid the urge to use justified margins. While this may look neat and organized, it doesn't usually help the reader. Notice that the right margin is straight, but white space is swimming between the words in this paragraph.

Example 2 - Ragged right paragraph

> Avoid the urge to use justified margins. While this may look neat and organized, it doesn't usually help the reader. A ragged right margin allows for even spacing between words.

Justified margins can be used effectively in newspaper and magazine columns. They give the text a neat appearance, usually at the loss of some readability. However, in newspaper and magazine columns, as well as some web pages, the justified right margin serves an important purpose: the text is seen as a block of material. The block appearance helps the reader identify and separate articles. The blocks of text also allow for an easier integration of graphics.

However, for the purposes of workplace communications, it's best to avoid the justified right margin.

Sentence and Line Spacing

Use only one space between sentences. The era of using two spaces after a period ended when typewriting lost popularity to word processing. Adding two spaces between sentences and using justified text can create a situation with extreme spacing between sentences:

Example - Justified paragraph with two spaces between sentences

> Use only one space between sentences. The era of using two spaces after a period ended when typewriting lost popularity to word processing. Adding two spaces between sentences and using justified text can create a situation with extreme spacing between sentences.

In a paragraph, line spacing should allow enough room to see each line of text clearly, yet still show a connection to the other lines of text in the paragraph. Put more space between the paragraphs than between the lines within the paragraph. This strategy reinforces the organization of your document by easily revealing paragraphs. For example, the paragraphs in this textbook use single spacing within the paragraph and double-spacing between paragraphs.

WHITE SPACE

The effective use of white space is probably one of the most difficult concepts for writers to grasp. Unfortunately, we've been trained to fill a page and not waste space. Using a generous amount of white space strategically can help communicate content effectively. The space allows the reader to move through the page rather than getting stuck on dense blocks of text.

Use generous margins, ensuring that the lines of text are not so long that the reader has trouble tracking back to the next line of text. In general, 1-inch margins all around are adequate.

The following example from a professional resume shows how using white space, chunking, and two font families can use about the same amount of space, but with greater comprehension:

Example 1 - Before

Positions Held: Chief Dietician, Ft. Smith Hospital, Ft. Smith, AR
Staff Dietician, Portland Community College, Portland, OR, Head Chef, Providence Hospital, Portland, OR, Line Cook, Providence Hospital, Portland, OR, Service Staff, Chipotle Restaurant, Portland, OR
Education: 2003, MS Dietetics, University of Alabama, Tuscaloosa, AL
2001, BS Biology, University of Alabama, Tuscaloosa, AL

Example 2 - After

Positions Held

- Chief Dietician, Ft. Smith Hospital, Ft. Smith, AR
- Staff Dietician, Portland Community College, Portland, OR
- Head Chef, Providence Hospital, Portland, OR
- Line Cook, Providence Hospital, Portland, OR
- Service Staff, Chipotle Restaurant, Portland, OR

Education

- 2003, MS Dietetics, University of Alabama, Tuscaloosa, AL
- 2001, BS Biology, University of Alabama, Tuscaloosa, AL

Notice how the serif font is used for the text and the sans serif is used for the headings in Example 2. The text has ample white space, clearly separating the items in the bulleted lists. Note that the type size is actually smaller in the "after" example, yet it is more legible because of the bullets and white space.

BULLETS AND NUMBERING

Bulleted and numbered lists are very practical ways to show a listing of items. It's much easier to see the items in a list when they are not side-by-side in a paragraph. For example, the items in a typical desk drawer can be written in two ways:

Example 1 - List without bullets

The contents of many desk drawers include pencils, pens, CDs, paper clips, note pad, business cards, chewing gum, stapler, and staple remover.

Example 2 - List with bullets

The contents of many desk drawers include:

- Pencils
- Pens
- CDs
- Paper clips
- Note pad
- Business cards
- Chewing gum
- Stapler
- Staple remover

Bulleted Lists

Use bullets for lists that are longer than two or three items, or when you want to especially highlight the particular items, as in showing your skills in a resume. Remember that bulleted lists do not show order or hierarchy. You can read the items in any order and the meaning is the same.

Bullets should also be parallel. That means that they should use the same parts of speech and the same grammatical pattern or verb form. Notice how the items in Example 1 below are parallel (all with an understood "you") and the items in Example 2 are not.

Example 1 - Parallel list items

- Buy groceries
- Feed the dog
- Finish homework

Example 2 - Non-parallel list items

- Buy groceries
- Dog gets fed
- Homework

Lines of text in bullets (and numbered lists) line up with each other. You should be able to draw a ruler line vertically down the left side of the text in the bullets as shown below:

Example 3 - Text indentation for bullets and numbering

- Lake Tahoe – a large, fresh water lake that is a popular tourist attraction.
- Yosemite – a national park featuring beautiful rock formations and waterfalls.

Numbered Lists

Use numbered lists (ordered lists) for items that occur in order or have an order of importance. Steps in a set of instructions are the perfect use for numbered lists. For example, the following steps for buying a soft drink from a vending machine must occur in sequence:

Example - Numbered steps

1. Slide a dollar bill into the slot with a picture of the face of a dollar bill. Make sure the dollar bill is oriented in the same way as the picture.
2. Choose a selection from the soft drinks by pressing the button beside the picture of the soft drink you prefer.
3. Collect your soft drink in the tray at the bottom.

HEADINGS AND SUBHEADINGS

Use headings and subheadings liberally to let your readers know what they can expect. As the name implies, headings are phrases that briefly describe the general material that follows. Subheadings further divide the general material into smaller topics.

Unless you are instructed otherwise by corporate guidelines, follow these generally accepted guidelines:

- Capitalize the first major word in each title, heading, and subheading.
- Use parallel structure. (For more on parallel structure, see "Parallel Structure" on page 290 in "Resources – Grammar" at the end of this textbook.)
- Make your headings larger than your subheadings.
- Do not use sentences as headings or subheadings.
- Do not use periods at the ends of the headings or subheadings.
- Omit "the," "a," "an" or other unnecessary modifiers from the beginning of the heading or subheading.

ORGANIZATION

Organization of your material can be clearly demonstrated using visual techniques. For example, even though there is no meaningful text in the "Lorem Ipsum" examples below, you can discern the heading, the paragraphs, the unordered list, and the ordered list.

You can see that the headings give the topic of the material that follows in Examples 1 and 2. You can assume that the paragraph is a cohesive treatment of one topic, which is presented in the first, or topic, sentence. In Example 1, the bullets are an unordered list of items that pertains to the paragraph above it. In Example 2, a numbered list follows some explanation. The numbered list could be instructions or a description of a process that must be followed in a particular order.

All of these expectations are generated by the organization of the text. In this way, the design of the page helps us to understand what we are reading.

Example 1 - Organization with heading, paragraph, and unordered list.
Source: www.loremipsum.org

Lorem Ipsum

Lorem ipsum dolor sit amet, consectetur adipisicing elit, sed do eiusmod tempor incididunt ut labore et dolore magna aliqua. Ut enim ad minim veniam, quis nostrud exercitation ullamco laboris nisi ut aliquip ex ea commodo consequat. Ut enim ad minim veniam, quis nostrud exercitation ullamco laboris.

- Ut enim ad minim veniam, quis nostrud exercitation ullamco laboris.
- Ut enim ad minim.

Example 2 - Organization with heading, paragraph, and ordered list.
Source: www.loremipsum.org

Lorem Ipsum

Lorem ipsum dolor sit amet, consectetur adipisicing elit, sed do eiusmod tempor incididunt ut labore et dolore magna aliqua. Ut enim ad minim veniam, quis nostrud exercitation ullamco laboris nisi ut aliquip ex ea commodo consequat.

1. Lorem ipsum dolor sit amet, consectetur adipisicing elit, sed do eiusmod tempor incididunt ut labore et dolore magna aliqua.

2. Ut enim ad minim veniam, quis nostrud exercitation ullamco laboris nisi ut aliquip ex ea commodo consequat.

STYLE SHEETS

A style sheet is the collection of all the elements used in a document, from terminology to major headings and graphic captions.

For example, the style for the paragraphs in this textbook contains the following choices:

> Paragraph Style: Font: Times New Roman 12 point; Space after: 12 points; Keep lines together

This information means that the Paragraph style uses the *font* Times New Roman, 12 point. The amount of *spacing after* each paragraph is 12 points, meaning that each paragraph is separated from the next paragraph by a single line (12 points) of white space. *Keep lines together* means that the paragraph is not allowed to break across pages. If the paragraph doesn't fit at the bottom of the page, the whole paragraph will move to the following page. This avoids "widows" and "orphans," small amounts of text that gets separated from their paragraphs or other components by bad line, column, or page breaks.

Style sheets, or style guides, are collections of word usage and formatting choices applied to elements of the page (paragraphs, headings) that contribute to the consistency of language and page design. Style includes indentation, font choice, type size, type style, spacing within the element and around it.

Fortunately, MS Word and other programs already have default styles that you can use. It is not necessary to set up a style sheet for simple office documents unless the corporate style requires it. In many cases, a company may have established templates that include predesigned style sheets. The templates and style sheets help to create a consistent corporate image.

The following sample style sheet (Sample 4-1) contains terminology to be used in an owner's manual and also formatting for Caution and Warning headings and text. The complete style guide for an owner's manual would be several pages longer than this example. In fact, style guides grow during the creation of a large project as the writers must decide answers to such questions as "How shall we refer to the "ink-jet printer"? Hyphen or no hyphen? Spacing? I've seen it both ways in our drafts." Usually, writers reach a consensus and then add the item to the style guide.

A style guide of this type helps writers working together to follow the same formatting and usage as they create a collaborative project. It ensures that Writers A, B, and C will use "arrow keys" to refer to the keyboard keys with arrows on them. Even if Writer B believes that "cursor keys" is a more descriptive term for the same keys, he or she follows the style guide.

Sample 4-1 Owner's Manual Style Sheet

Owner's Manual Style Sheet

Correct	NOT Correct	Comments/Examples
AC outlet	AC power supply	
adapter	adaptor	Plug in the adapter.
arrow keys	cursor keys	Press the arrow key.
back paper tray	back paper slot	Place the clean paper in the back paper tray.
brightness control	video	
Caution and Warning headings		***Helvetica, 12 pt., bold, italics, red***
Caution and Warning text		**Helvetica, 10 pt., bold**
clicks	pops	The latch at the bottom of the monitor clicks shut.
cut off	truncated	
dialog box, window	screen, display	
email	e-mail, E-mail	
heading		**Arial, 18 pt., black**
heading 2 (subheading)		**Arial, 14 pt.**
inkjet	ink-jet	
main menu	MAIN MENU	Go to the main menu.
monitor	CRT	Plug in the monitor.
paragraph text		Times New Roman, 12 pt.

DISCUSSIONS

1. Imagine a scenario in which you must produce a one-page job aid (short written procedure) for an assembly line worker. What choices in page design might you make? Why?

2. Analyze the following section of text from a magazine article on dog health for adherence to page design principles. Work in groups to re-format the text. Present your revised text to the class and explain why you changed the formatting.

Dogs need exercise. That's what every veterinarian will tell you. Why? Because dogs are active, curious, playful, intelligent animals. What are the benefits of exercising your dog? Stronger muscles, leaner body, happier disposition, better social skills, closer bonding to owner, increased intelligence, less boredom. **Exercise can also be an opportunity to teach your dog important skills like coming to you when you call him or her, learning to sit and stay, learning to fetch a ball.**

It can even save your dog's life should he or she run toward a busy street while playing in an off-leash area. What excuses can we come up with to avoid exercising our dog? Many! It's too wet outside, too muddy, too cold, I'm too tired, I'll make up for it tomorrow, I'll get my kids to do it, Buffy doesn't seem to mind anyway, she gets plenty of exercise walking to her food bowl. Procrastinating dog owners are missing out on an opportunity to have a best friend, a friend who looks forward to their coming home, patting their head, and providing some excitement. Take an adventure with your dog and you'll both be happier and healthier. Ruff, ruff!

EXERCISES

1. **Create a style sheet** using the three-column layout shown in Figure 4-3. Then follow the style sheet to write a short description of your desk at home, or the top of your kitchen counter. Make sure that your description follows the guidelines in your style sheet. Your style sheet should include:

    - Formatting style for one major heading (title of description)
    - Formatting style for paragraphs
    - Formatting style for bulleted items
    - Usage style for at least one term

2. **Pick out the items** that are not parallel in the following list:

To Do List for Next Thursday

- Feed dog
- Newspaper
- Get to work on time
- Bill paid
- Go out to lunch with boss
- Sunny day!
- Hanging around with friends

3. **Rewrite the list in Exercise 2** to make all the items parallel, or **create an unordered list** of your own with at least six parallel items. Use hierarchy of importance to **change the unordered list to a numbered list**.

4. Analyze the page design of the document on the next page. **Write a well-designed memo report** to your instructor with some advice about how to reformat the page. Explain the benefit of the changes. **Show a complete example of the reformatted text** in your memo.

Testing the Document

To set up a testing phase, add some time into your schedule after the second or third draft. You don't want to use a draft that is too primitive because the user will not have confidence that the information is correct.

To perform a basic user test:

If possible, choose a tester who is a member of your targeted audience.

Give the tester a copy of the instructions that looks professional and complete.

Set the tester in the surroundings, with equipment or products, where he or she would be using the instructions.

Tell the tester that you will watch and take notes (on your own, separate set of instructions), but you won't answer questions. The user should rely only on the instructions.

Ask the tester to "think out loud" as they ponder the meaning or intent of each part of the document. This is valuable information for you, and you must capture it in your notes, and use it for your next revision. If the tester comes to a dead end and is truly stuck, make your notes exactly where the user stalled, and then give the tester minimal information to get them unstuck. Emphasize that the problem is not them; it's a failure of the instructions. You don't want your tester to feel that he or she is being tested.

Thank the tester and then get busy making improvements to your document.

5 - Summaries

One of the most important writing functions—but least honored—is summarizing. Whether you are an unpaid intern, a research analyst, or an editorial assistant, you may be asked to read and summarize long documents or even books—so that other people don't have to read them. You may find yourself interpreting and summarizing data for reports, or synthesizing research findings for a presentation. One reason summarizing is not glorified is that people generally imagine that it is simplification: "just give me the highlights," someone might say, or "what's the gist of it?"

In fact, simplification is often a very difficult task. It requires a complete understanding of the text and a confident analysis of your audience's concerns. When you summarize, you act as a filter for your reader, deciding what is most important to know and to remember about the source. The summarizer influences not only *what* is understood about the original piece of writing, but also *how* it is understood. The ability to write an accurate summary of your reading is an important skill. The triangle below shows the mirroring/filtering effect of the summary:

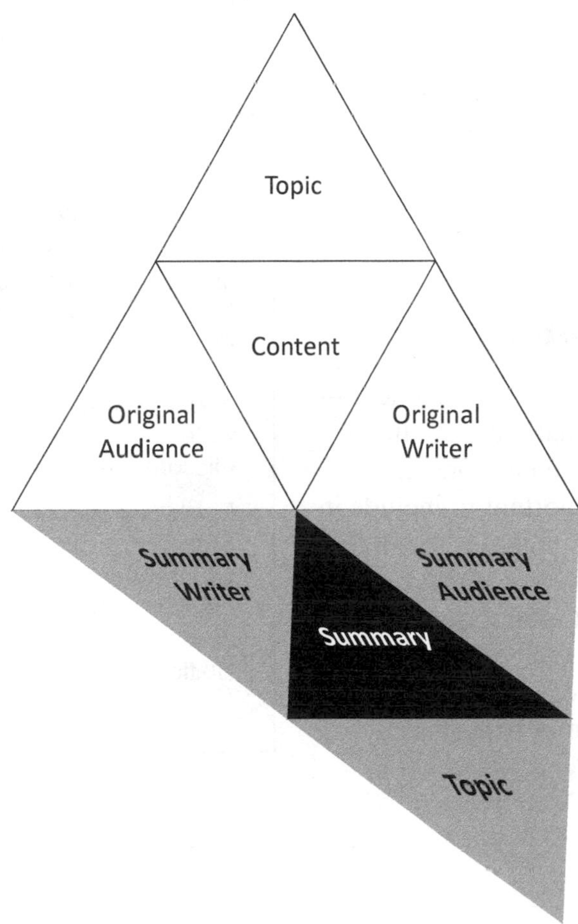

Figure 5-1 Communication Triangle: Mirroring Effect of Summary

THE SUMMARY WRITING PROCESS

When summarizing, a large part of the technical writer's job is to read and understand the original piece of writing completely. The summary must present complicated information more simply and briefly than the original. Simplifying can be dangerous, however, as important facts can be overlooked, resulting in misunderstandings. Before summarizing, read carefully to make sure that you understand both the factual information and the original author's approach to that information.

Summaries are necessary so that your audience does not have to read the entire piece of writing. The length of any type of summary should not exceed 25% of the original, and some types are much shorter. They save readers time and enable them to make decisions based on facts in the article, or based on the summarizer's judgment about facts in the article. Some summaries simply describe content; others help the reader see how the content applies to information already known. The type of summary depends upon the intended readers and their needs.

Reading for Content

Content means what is "in" the document—what it says. There is usually a LOT in the document, so you will need to consider which parts are most important to include in a summary. If the article includes numbers or statistics, for example, which of these might make the "highlights"? Learn to recognize the ways that articles in your field are organized: being aware of common patterns will help you judge what is important.

Professionalism & Ethics

Plagiarism—using another writer's words, ideas, art, or research without acknowledgment—is theft. Any time you use the same words or even echo the same sentence structures as the original writer, you are plagiarizing. When you are summarizing, it is sometimes particularly difficult to come up with original phrasing, so the danger of plagiarism is significant.

To guard against plagiarism, first, read carefully so that you understand the source material thoroughly. Then, close the tab or turn over the page, and DO NOT look at the original again until you have finished writing.

If you want to use some of the original writer's words intentionally, for emphasis or example, be sure to put those words in quotation marks.

In every type of summary except the "abstract" (which is usually directly connected to the original work), you should make sure to refer to the author or title of the original article to emphasize that you are not the writer of the original document. In the course of revision and re-use of your summary, the original writer's work can be forgotten or misconstrued if not directly referenced.

Finally, always provide a complete citation for work summarized to direct your reader to the original work and to credit the original writer. Use MLA or APA citation format, or the specific type of citation style used in your field.

Look for Key Parts in First/Last Positions

If you have trouble understanding the article you are reading, try looking especially at sentences and paragraphs at the beginnings and ends of paragraphs, of sections, and of the entire article.

Parts in first and last positions provide a frame for the document. Topic sentences and concluding sentences, for example, introduce and review content; introductions and conclusions develop and review key concepts.

Middle parts illustrate, explain, and support; they are essential to a full understanding of the subject presented, but only after you understand the main idea or the author's approach to the concept.

Look for Key Headings

Even long, technical documents usually have some parts that are clearer and simpler than others and that can give you a wedge to get into the more technical and tedious parts. Look for headings like "Abstract," "Summary," "Overview," "Discussion," and "Conclusions," and give these sections reading priority. For example, reading the "Conclusions" section first, rather than last, can give you perspective on the rest of the document. Plowing straight through from beginning to end can be a way to get bogged down or lost.

> **Professionalism & Ethics**
>
> As a summarizer, you have a responsibility to the original writer to be true to his or her intent and purpose. You have the power to influence how your audience understands what authors have written. Do not ignore important qualifiers or quote statements or figures out of context.
>
> You have a responsibility to your reader to include important or useful facts from the original. For example, if the original article relies on a key number or reveals a startling statistic, you would be remiss to omit that from your summary.

Study Illustrations

Visuals tend to present information more clearly and effectively than the written explanation, so they provide another entry into dense texts. If an author has used a graphic to illustrate or explain text, study it carefully so that you know what it says, and why it is there. Graphics are difficult to produce and insert, so they are included only if important. Fortunately, they are usually not as difficult to read as they are to create; understanding their meaning and noting key terms used within them will help you get the sense of the rest of the reading.

ABSTRACTS

An abstract is a small but important part of a research article, often written by writers of the original document to give a clear overview and emphasize its main point. Librarians or bibliographers write abstracts to provide brief summaries of books or articles to guide readers. Sometimes abstracts are included as the first section at the top of an article, and sometimes they appear alone in a catalog, with a link to the full text.

The abstract allows interested readers—the public, students, or researchers—to see the scope of an article and make a decision about whether to read it. Abstracts are also used in cataloging literature for search engines and libraries, so key words relevant to the subject are important to include.

Abstracts are usually only one paragraph and are usually written from the point of view of the author. Sample 5-1, on the next page, shows the abstract that is included as the first section of an article in *Accident Analysis and Prevention.* The full article is six pages long and about 6000 words. Notice that although the abstract is comparatively short—only 280 words—the writers cover the general question, the types of experiments performed, and the overall findings.

The second example, only 36 words (Sample 5-2), is an excerpt from another article about the increasingly technological and dynamic role of public art. Like many non-scientific articles, this one does not include a formal abstract, but this excerpt could serve well as an overview for cataloging purposes, with the addition of at least one more key phrase ("kinetic art"). The full article is 1860 words and includes examinations of specific art installations.

Key Word Search Terms

Since abstracts are often used for cataloging, search terms become very important to include.

In Samples 5-1 and 5-2, potential search terms are shown in bold type and shaded. This emphasis is simply to show you where search terms can be found. Do not shade or bold search terms in your own abstracts.

Sample 5-1 Published Abstract of Online Scientific Journal Article

ABSTRACT: **Driver drowsiness** has been implicated as a major causal factor in road accidents. Tools that allow remote monitoring and management of driver fatigue are used in the mining and road transport industries. Increasing drivers' own awareness of their drowsiness levels using such tools may also reduce risk of accidents. The study examined the effects of real-time blink-velocity-derived **drowsiness feedback** on driver performance and levels of **alertness in a military setting**. A sample of 15 Army Reserve personnel (1 female) aged 21–59 (M = 41.3, SD = 11.1) volunteered to being monitored by an **infra-red oculography**-based **Optalert Alertness Monitoring System (OAMS)** while they performed their regular driving tasks, including on-duty tasks and commuting to and from duty, for a continuous period of 4–8 weeks. For approximately half that period, blink-velocity-derived Johns Drowsiness Scale (JDS) scores were fed back to the driver in a counterbalanced repeated-measures design, resulting in a total of 419 driving periods under "feedback" and 385 periods under "no-feedback" condition. Overall, the provision of real-time feedback resulted in reduced drowsiness (lower JDS scores) and improved alertness and **driving performance ratings**. The effect was small and varied across the 24-h **circadian cycle** but it remained robust after controlling for time of day and driving task duration. Both the number of JDS peaks counted for each trip and their duration declined in the presence of **drowsiness feedback**, indicating a dynamic pattern that is consistent with a genuine, entropy-reducing feedback mechanism (as distinct from random re-alerting) behind the observed effect. Its mechanisms and practical utility have yet to be fully explored. Direct examination of the alternative, random re-alerting explanation of this feedback effect is an important step for future research. (8)

Other relevant key words for this article: driver fatigue; drowsiness monitoring, military personnel alertness

Aidman, E., Chadunow, C., Johnson, K., & Reece, J.. (2015). Real-time driver drowsiness feedback improves driver alertness and self-reported driving performance. *Accident Analysis and Prevention*, *81* (2015) 8-13. Retrieved from http://dx.doi.org/10.1016/j.aap.2015.03.041. Used under Creative Commons License 4.0 International <http://creativecommons.org/licenses/by/4.0/legalcode>

Note: Shading and bold type are NOT normally part of any summary or abstract. This example highlights elements for study only.

Sample 5-2 Abstract of Online Arts Journal Article (Excerpt)

Sculptural public art is changing; it is moving away from the long-held static, form-focused style to the dynamically developing **intersection of technology, art and communication**, where the art changes, interacts, and even communicates with the viewers. (100)

Other relevant key phrases for this article: kinetic art, interactive art

Gschwend, R. (2015). The development of public art and its future passive, active and interactive past, present and future. *Arts*, *4*(3), 93–100. MDPI AG. Retrieved from http://dx.doi.org/10.3390/arts4030093. Used under Creative Commons License 4.0 International <http://creativecommons.org/licenses/by/4.0/legalcode>

Note: Shading and bold type are NOT normally part of any summary or abstract. This example highlights elements for study only.

DESCRIPTIVE SUMMARIES

Like an abstract, a descriptive summary presents an overview of the article, mentioning important facts or observations made by the authors. Unlike an abstract, a descriptive summary takes an outside, third-person point of view.

Signal Phrases

Summarizers use signal phrases to give credit to the original writer and to establish an outside point of view. A signal phrase alerts the reader of a difference between voices in the text. Common signal phrases are shown in the list below:

- **According to** [author's name],
- **In** [author's name]**'s words,**
- **From** [author's name]'s **point of view, . . .**
- [Author's name] **writes . . .**
- [Author's name] **explains . . .**
- [Author's name] **describes . . .**
- [Author's name] **questions . . .**
- [Author's name] **shows . . .**
- [Author's name] **demonstrates . . .**
- In an article published in **[publication title]**, **[author's name]** writes,

Signal phrases often refer to the author or title of the article, as in "Frieda Odwaller writes that pure joy is an unusual emotion," or "the article 'A Good Woman—Redefined' questions cultural paradigms."

General Content

A well-written descriptive summary includes enough information about content to present a responsible and honest condensation of the article, but does not usually cover minor details. Even though some details are inevitably excluded, the summary maintains the general proportions and emphasis of the original document. Because descriptive summaries are neutral in tone and contain key content, they can be useful to help survey current thought or research on a topic. Sometimes writers include several brief descriptive summaries in a survey of current research to show objectively what is being studied or in progress.

These types of summaries can save reporters time and can help students learn concepts.

No Judgments or Extra Information

In a descriptive summary, try to present the writer's ideas and information as neutrally as possible. Resist the temptation to disagree or praise. Do not try to debate the original writer or bring up parts he or she has forgotten to mention to support his or her point.

You may comment on the original writer's point of view only briefly, in the most objective way, preferably in a signal phrase. For example, "Republican Roy James maintains . . ." or "Challenger Maria Mitchell argues against . . ." both inform your reader of the original writer's point of view without inserting your own bias.

Maintains Proportion and Emphasis of the Original

Because any summary condenses information and thus must exclude some details, it is important to be aware of the possibility of distortion and try to avoid it. No matter how interesting specific detail might be to you, your judgment of whether to include it in your descriptive summary should be based on how important it seems to be to the writer of the text. A descriptive summary's function is simply to report reliably what is said in the original.

Below are examples of descriptive summaries for the two articles already profiled in the abstracts. Note that these summaries make direct reference to the authors and the sources.

In the examples on the next two pages, signal phrases are shaded to show you how they are used in the summary. Do not shade signal phrases in summaries that you write.

Sample 5-3 Descriptive Summary of Online Scientific Journal Article

Because driver fatigue is a factor in many accidents, it is important to find a way to identify and reduce drowsiness. A recent article in *Accident Analysis and Prevention* reported an experiment by an Australian research team that sought to measure whether a particular alerting device, the Optalert Monitoring System (OAMS) was helpful in reducing sleepiness while driving. Volunteers from the Australian Army Reserve agreed to wear anti-drowsiness glasses that measured their eyelid movements; greater "blink velocity" indicated drowsiness. Along with the measurements collected by the device, participants evaluated their own sleepiness and driving performance. The experiment collected data from 14 drivers for 804 driving trips. Researchers correlated results for the time of day (circadian phase) and the length of the drive, as well as whether the feedback from the device was in the "on" or "off" position. The team concluded that the device's effect on drowsiness and driving performance was "robust and significant"(13). They recommended further testing of the device with workers in different industries that involve driving, to see if results can be replicated.

Aidman, E., Chadunow, C., Johnson, K., & Reece, J.. (2015). Real-time driver drowsiness feedback improves driver alertness and self-reported driving performance. *Accident Analysis and Prevention*, *81* (2015) 8-13. Retrieved from http://dx.doi.org/10.1016/j.aap.2015.03.041. Used under Creative Commons License 4.0 International <http://creativecommons.org/licenses/by/4.0/legalcode>

Note: Shading and bold type are NOT normally part of any summary or abstract. This example highlights elements for study only.

Sample 5-4 Descriptive Summary of Online Arts Journal Article

Ralfonso Gschwend, a co-founder and president of the Kinetic Arts Organization, writes in the July 2015 issue of *Arts* that incorporating interaction with the audience is an important component of public art today. He offers examples of seven different kinetic public art installations, from Chicago to Beijing. According to Gschwend, China is the leader in this kind of interactive art. In many countries around the world today, sculptures move and interact with the viewer, reflecting not only weather, light and movement, but also technology such as SMS messaging and Internet connection. He says that young people, in particular, enjoy art that offers a quickly-changing display and interactive communication. He sees a new connection between art and science; advancing technology has enabled art not only to change over time, but also communicate with its audience. And, because the potential audience for these public displays can extend to those who view and communicate with it via webcam, Gschwend declares that such art has the potential to transcend culture.

Gschwend, R. (2015). The development of public art and its future passive, active and interactive past, present and future. *Arts*, *4*(3), 93–100. MDPI AG. Retrieved from http://dx.doi.org/10.3390/arts4030093. Used under Creative Commons License 4.0 International <http://creativecommons.org/licenses/by/4.0/legalcode>

Note: Shading and bold type are NOT normally part of any summary or abstract. This example highlights elements for study only.

EVALUATIVE SUMMARIES

This type of summary includes all the aspects of a descriptive summary (content in broad strokes, signal phrases) but adds the aspect of judgment and support for an opinion. The writer of an evaluative summary writes not just to inform his or her audience of content, but also to share his or her perspective on that content.

Source Credibility

Some evaluative summaries focus on the reliability or accuracy of the original article. Below are some red flags that should arouse suspicions about credibility:

- Uses emotional tone
- Uses loaded words that prevent neutrality
- Ignores opposing perspectives
- Shows clear bias (religious, political, other loyalty)
- Attempts to sell reader something
- Presents either/or choice
- Exaggerates facts
- Fails to give sources, citations, or links to related information
- Echoes other texts without citing sources (potential plagiarism)
- Violates logic (See the list of fallacies in Chapter 1, pages 1-2 for a list of faulty logic and biased statements.)
- Found on a wiki (open editing) site, such as Wikipedia

Audience Needs and Perspective

The point of view of your audience will determine your focus in an evaluative summary. What aspects of the original are important from the audience's point of view? In this kind of summary, you need to give not only a faithful account of the original text, but also approach it in a way that will be useful to your readers.

For example, if you work for a movie studio, you might summarize the plot of a novel accurately, but executives who read your summary are probably interested in whether that novel will make a good screenplay; making that judgment requires looking at that novel with specific questions in mind: are there parts of the novel that do not lend themselves to staging or visualization?

Informed Judgment

An evaluative summary includes a judgment based on an analysis of the original text. Often, that analysis springs from the summary writer's deep understanding of the topic. For example, you might write, "Molina's discussion of the banking industry's history leaves out the factors leading up to the recent crisis."

Sometimes an evaluative summary involves a professional estimation of the significance of a document. For example, a food industry executive might want to know whether an article about the safety of food coloring seems to be well-founded.

If asked to write an evaluative summary about a topic you are unfamiliar with, you may need to research context so that you know what may be useful to your audience. For example, if you work for a waste treatment facility and are asked to report on an article about recycling disposable diapers, you would need to be familiar with other methods of diaper disposal, as well as the company's current procedures, if any.

Judgment Supported with Evidence

Be aware of claims that you make in an evaluative summary, and make sure that each is supported with specific examples from the original article, or from your background reading. Giving examples from your personal experience is not appropriate in professional writing; you must cite published work. An exception can be made for examples from an ongoing work project that is as yet unpublished.

Outside Sources Cited, If Used

If you bring in specific examples from your background reading, you must cite sources for that information. Citing sources shows that you handle information carefully and responsibly and can provide factual support for claims you make in your evaluation.

In the two examples that follow, the evaluative parts to to differentiate evaluation from description. This shading is for demonstration purposes only. Do not shade any part of your own summary.

Sample 5-5 Evaluative Summary of Online Scientific Journal Article

AUDIENCE: Lay readers interested in ways to help drivers recognize when they are too sleepy to drive.

Because driver fatigue is a factor in many accidents, it is important to find a way to identify and reduce drowsiness. A new device, the Optalert Monitoring System (OAMS), shows promise in helping drivers recognize sleepiness and adjust driving behavior. A recent article in *Accident Analysis and Prevention* reported an experiment by an Australian research team in which volunteers from the Australian Army Reserve wore the OAMS glasses that measured their eyelid movements; greater "blink velocity" indicated drowsiness. Along with the measurements collected by the device, participants evaluated their own sleepiness and driving performance. The experiment collected data from 14 drivers for 804 driving trips. Researchers correlated results for the time of day (circadian phase) and the length of the drive, as well as whether the feedback from the device was in the "on" or "off" position. The team concluded that the device's effect on drowsiness and driving performance was "robust and significant"(13). They recommended further testing of the device with workers in different industries that involve driving, to see if results can be replicated.

Although any technology that can reduce road accidents is welcome, there are several reasons that this study's results are unreliable. The experiment used only 14 drivers, and the drives taken did not give significant data for the time between 10 pm and 4 am, presumably the sleepiest driving times. The drivers also measured their own driving performance, which may not have been entirely objective. There was no standard drive length or drive route; drive length varied considerably from person to person, and was not clearly correlated with the effect of the device. It appears that most drivers drove when they were not particularly drowsy. Although researchers did alternate portions of the drives with the device "off," they did not include a separate control group to address the question of whether merely wearing the device (as opposed to depending on its alerting functions) increased alertness.

Aidman, E., Chadunow, C., Johnson, K., & Reece, J.. (2015). Real-time driver drowsiness feedback improves driver alertness and self-reported driving performance. *Accident Analysis and Prevention*, *81* (2015) 8-13. Retrieved from http://dx.doi.org/10.1016/j.aap.2015.03.041. Used under Creative Commons License 4.0 International <http://creativecommons.org/licenses/by/4.0/legalcode>

Note: Shading and bold type are NOT normally part of any summary or abstract. This example highlights elements for study only.

Sample 5-6 Evaluative Summary of Online Arts Journal Article

AUDIENCE: Lay readers interested in the interplay between art and technology

In a wide-ranging article that attempts to show how the revolution in information technology has affected public art, Ralfonso Gschwend of the Kinetic Arts Organization writes that an important development in public art today is the inclusion of movement and communication through technology. He offers examples of seven different kinetic public art installations, from Chicago to Beijing. These sculptures move and interact with the viewer, reflecting not only weather, light and movement, but also even SMS messaging and Internet connection. Gschwend predicts a new and evolving connection between art and science; advancing technology has enabled art not only to change over time, but also to expand its audience. Because the potential audience for these public displays can extend to those who view and communicate with it via webcam, Gschwend declares that such art has the potential to transcend culture. He compares ancient and immense public art such as the Sphinx with its undeniable relation to culture and place, to 21st century sculptures such as his own EX STRATA, with fixtures in Beijing and the Netherlands. His view of how kinetic art is related to older forms is somewhat difficult to understand: the main idea seems to be that the newest art takes new advantage of the element of time in showing movement and response.

Gschwend is a well known international sculptor of kinetic art, so he is a very knowledgeable reviewer and theorist of the genre. However, he may not be an objective critic of the sculptures' historical or cultural importance, since he is not only an insider to that particular artistic community, but also profits from creating this type of art.

Gschwend, R. (2015). The development of public art and its future passive, active and interactive past, present and future. *Arts, 4*(3), 93–100. MDPI AG. Retrieved from http://dx.doi.org/10.3390/arts4030093. Used under Creative Commons License 4.0 International <http://creativecommons.org/licenses/by/4.0/legalcode>

Ralfonso Gschwend (n.d.) in Sculptor Directory. *International Sculpture Center.* Retrieved from http://www.sculpture.org/portfolio/sculptorPage.php?sculptor_id=1000748

Note: Shading and bold type are NOT normally part of any summary or abstract. This example highlights elements for study only.

EXECUTIVE SUMMARIES

An executive summary is geared to readers who have specific needs and interests and are generally written about texts that are very long, to save the reader time. An executive summary might be requested if your supervisor needs to have a working knowledge of the material in the document but does not have time to read the whole thing from beginning to end. A reasonable executive summary should include not only an overview of the document, but also an easily-read presentation of relevant facts and figures and even some quotations from significant parts, particularly if there are memorable phrases that may come up in conversation.

A wise summarizer will include strategically-selected information based on the parts that are likely to be controversial or will be key to decision-making on relevant topics. A Cliff Notes or Spark Notes summary is an executive summary, designed to give the reader a working knowledge of the text with a minimal time investment. If you are writing an executive summary, write as if your reader needs to discuss the issues related to the text with reasonable competence.

Overview of Document

Like other types of summaries, executive summaries offer an overview of the original document. Unlike other types, this overview may be divided into sections that mirror or rearrange those in the original, especially if the original text is long.

Executive summaries are often longer than other type of summaries. Since the reader may need to go from the summary to the original, to read a piece in more depth, the page numbers for the original section are sometimes included as a reference.

Headings and Page Design

Use principles of page design to guide your reader through the summary. For example, headings are important in executive summaries, as the reader needs to be able to skip to the appropriate area quickly. A manager involved in a telephone conference may need to find a section on the spur of the moment. Bulleted lists or sidebars can be very helpful to set up content in a graphic way for quick access to facts or figures. Creating an accessible design might involve rearranging the order of the information, or gathering disparate parts together. See Chapter 4, Page Design, for instructions about how to create a convenient, consistent, and readable layout for your document.

Key Graphics from the Original

An effective graphic can convey a concept, process, or relationship more easily than a paragraph or a page of explanation. You do not need to reproduce every graphic from the original text in an executive summary, but you should give your reader the benefit of the most striking or important ones. These graphics may come up in discussions about the topic.

Numbers in Easily-Accessible Format

Numeric figures are particularly important to reproduce in the executive summary, and the expert summarizer presents these in a clear and easy-to-find format, such as a list or table, so that the reader does not need to search through pages of text to find them. If numbers or statistics are sprinkled throughout the text, consider gathering them into a space where they will be easier to locate.

Points for Research, Discussion or Controversy

Like the evaluative summarizer, the executive summarizer shares his or her expertise by offering some perspective on the topic. In an executive summary, however, the original text is usually not being evaluated, but rather used as a way to talk about an important subject. An executive summary should highlight, either at the beginning or end of the summary, some relevant questions or recommendations for areas that need investigation, based on an understanding of the content of the original text.

The executive summaries below are geared to the perspective of their stated audiences. The executive summary of the research study about driver alertness (Sample 5-7) presents the information about the type of device used, as well as a general survey of the observed results and a brief breakdown of the problems with the study. The reader of this particular summary is not specifically concerned about the physiology of sleep or alertness, but rather with the potential use of the device by company drivers. An executive summary of the same article for a sleep researcher might look very different.

The executive summary of the article about public art breaks down the article into distinct parts to make the points easier to understand at a glance, and shows one of the examples from the article, with a link to its website where the user can both view and control the installation to experience the effect of public kinetic art.

Notice that the second executive summary puts information about the author near the top of the page; for this audience, the credibility of the author is important to consider before spending the time to read his views.

Sample 5-7 Executive Summary of Online Scientific Journal Article, Page 1

AUDIENCE: ABC Trucking Company executive interested in an anti-drowsiness device for use by truck drivers

Article: Aidman, E., Chadunow, C., Johnson, K., & Reece, J.. (2015). Real-Time Driver Drowsiness Feedback Improves Driver Alertness and Self-Reported Driving Performance. *Accident Analysis and Prevention,* 81 (2015) 8-13. Retrieved from http://dx.doi.org/10.1016/j.aap.2015.03.041. Used under Creative Commons License 4.0 International <http://creativecommons.org/licenses/by/4.0/legalcode>

Overview:

An Australian research team, using a small group of volunteer military reservists, found that the OAMS (Optalert Monitoring System) increased drivers' perceived alertness and driving performance. More study is needed.

Use of the OAMS:

- Driver wore glasses that measured blink velocity (rise in blink speed = rise in drowsiness)
- Electronic display was shown in the vehicle
- Display beeped when blink velocity reached medium risk level
- When driver was in low risk for 5 minutes, display blanked out
- Display reactivated by touch

Results of the Study:

Time of day was the most important variable in determining the effectiveness of the device. In times considered most alert generally, such as between 6 and 7 a.m., the OAMS effect was negligible. The greatest effect was observed in the 10 p.m. to 4 a.m. period, when sleepiness is known to be highest. The study also revealed an unexpected period of drowsiness in the evening from about 5 to 8 p.m. In Figure 1 below, from the research article, the X axis shows the drive times and the Y axis indicates the JDS (Johns Drowsiness Scale) score:

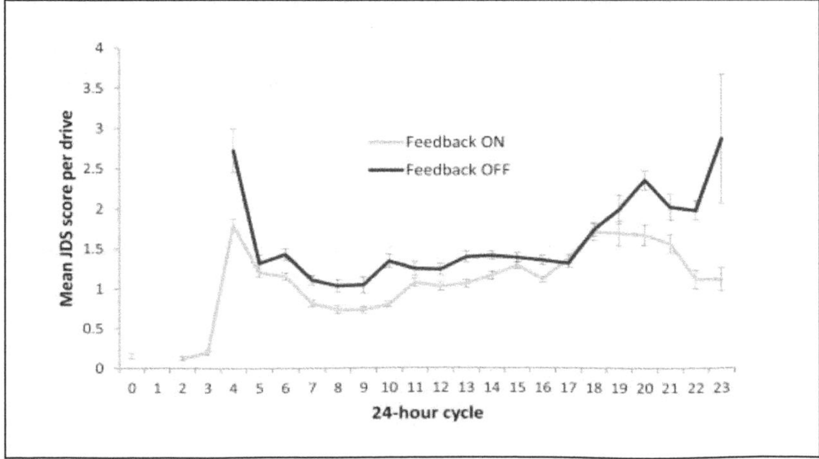

Figure 1. The Effect of Feedback on Drowsiness Levels

Sample 5-7 Executive Summary of Online Scientific Journal Article, Page 2

Considerations:

Although the OAMS device showed promise in reducing drowsiness, some factors in the design of this study give concern:

- Subject group was limited (only 14 participants)
- Drives ranged dramatically in route and duration
- Drive performance was evaluated by the drivers themselves
- Most dangerous drive time had the fewest drives

The time when the device seemed to be most effective (late night) was coincidentally the same time period when the participants had the fewest drives, so the most promising conclusion of the study—that using OAMS could have a beneficial effect in the late night hours—unfortunately has the least reliability.

Conclusion:

Although this study suggests that the OAMS may improve safety by alerting sleepy drivers, more investigation is needed. Although a drowsiness-warning system could be very valuable for the company, this particular study does not show conclusively that the OAMS is effective.

References For Further Reading:

Adell, E., Várhelyi, A., Fontana, M.d., 2011. The effects of a driver assistance system for safe speed and safe distance – a real-life field study. Transp. Res. C: Emerging Technol. 19, 145–155.

Breuer, J., 2008. Attention assist: don't fall asleep. Daimler Tech. Report.

CaterpillarGlobalMining, 2008. Operator Fatigue Detection Technology Review. Caterpillar, Peoria, IL.

Corbett, M., 2009. A drowsiness detection system for pilots: Optalert. Aviat. Space Environ. Med. 80, 149.

Haraldsson, P., Akerstedt, T., 2001. Drowsiness-greater traffic hazard than alcohol. Causes, risks and treatment. Lakartidningen 98, 3018–3023.

Horne, J., Reyner, L., 1995b. Driver sleepiness. J. Sleep Res. 4, 23–29.

Kircher, A., Uddman, M., Sandin, J., 2002. Vehicle Control and Drowsiness. Swedish National Road and Transport Research Institute, Stockholm.

May, J.F., Baldwin, C.L., 2009. Driver fatigue: the importance of identifying causal factors of fatigue when considering detection and countermeasure technologies. Transp. Res. F: Traffic Psychol. Behav. 12, 218–224.

Thiffault, P., Bergeron, J., 2003. Monotony of road environment and driver fatigue: a simulator study. Accid. Anal. Prev. 35, 381–391.

Sample 5-8 Executive Summary of Online Arts Journal Article, Page 1

AUDIENCE: City Council considering a new public art installation

Article: Gschwend, R. (2015). The Development of Public Art and its Future Passive, Active and Interactive Past, Present and Future. *Arts*, *4*(3), 93–100. MDPI AG. Retrieved from http://dx.doi.org/10.3390/arts4030093. Used under Creative Commons License 4.0 International <http://creativecommons.org/licenses/by/4.0/legalcode>

Overview:

Art and science intersect in new "kinetic" public art sculpture, where the art has the capability to change and shift with time, weather, and user interaction. According to sculptor Ralfonso Gschwend, 21st century viewers especially appreciate this addition of another dimension to their experience of art.

About the Author:

Ralfonso Gschwend (professional name: *Ralfonso*) is an artist who specializes in public art kinetic and light sculptures. He works from studios in West Palm Beach, Florida and Geneva, Switzerland.

Author's Website: http://www.ralfonso.com

Notable Quote:

I feel very strongly that, in our modern world, public art will be more interesting and engaging if it continuously changes, or, **even better—if the art has a two way communication and interaction with the environment (wind, water) and/or the viewer. (98)**

Central idea:

Art is no longer passive or static. New sculptures are being designed, with the assistance of modern technology, to change and react to the viewer.

Examples:

- Cloud Gate by Anish Kapoor, Chicago Millennium Park (2006)
- Crown Fountain by Jaume Plensa, Chicago Millenium Park (2004)
- Shiny Ball Mirror by Daniel Rozin (2003)
- EX STRATA SMS and Internet Light Sculpture by Ralfonso Gschwend, Tsinghua University, Beijing (2011)
- Ned Kahn kinetic wind sculpture, Brisbane Airport, Australia
- Light and Kinetic Wind Sculpture by K. Dimopoulos, Australia

Figure 5-8 Executive Summary of Arts Article, Page 2

Figure 1 shows a light and kinetic sculpture designed by Ralfonso.

A similar sculpture , EX STRATA #3, is installed in the Netherlands, and global viewers can communicate directly with it at http://exstrata.nl/

Figure 1. Ralfonso's EX STRATA SMS and Internet Light Sculpture, Tsinghua University, Beijing.

Main Points:

1. Public art can be analyzed by considering four main criteria. Each of these reflects the evolving expectations for this type of art, within cultures. It is natural for public art to incorporate and respond to the needs and technologies available. Arrows indicate Ralfonso's sense of the way public art is evolving.

- Form: representative → abstract → interactive
- Function: personal expression → monument → cultural focus point
- Technology: wood→ceramic→bronze→metal→informational
- Time: significance evolves with context and culture, and in recent times has become a dimension of the art itself.

2. Young people today are interested in art that changes quickly and interacts with them, as they have come to expect in other areas of their lives.

3. Kinetic art is a global phenomenon that transcends region and culture through the Internet and associated communication possibilities.

CHOOSING SUMMARY TYPES

Summary Type	Summary Features						
	Covers the general content of original work	Written from point of view of the original work	Separates summary's view from that of original writer	May include judgment about original article	Considers audience's needs, interests	Refers directly to the author or title	Maintains proportion & emphasis of the original
Abstract	✔	✔					✔
Descriptive Summary	✔		✔			✔	✔
Evaluative Summary	✔		✔	✔	✔	✔	
Executive Summary	✔		✔	✔	✔	✔	

SUMMARY *Checklist* ✔

An Effective Summary . . .	✔
Accurately and fairly represents the point of view of the original	
Contains the main points of the original	
Is faithful to the context of the original	
Contains features of the desired summary type (see table above)	
Considers the interests and needs of the summary's audience	
Cites the original source properly	
Is no more than 25% of the length of the original	
Uses correct grammar, spelling, and punctuation	

DISCUSSIONS

1. Compare the four types of summaries for one of the articles in this chapter. What seem to be the key differences?
2. Read a news article distributed by your instructor or find one on your own. Write a one-sentence summary. Share your sentence with those written by other students in the class. Discuss differences in your summaries, and reasons for those differences. Which one is the best?
3. What steps might you go through as you summarize to make sure you don't use the same wording as the original or otherwise plagiarize?
4. Read an article provided by your instructor and, with a small group of students, come up with a list of key words you might try to include in an abstract, to help people find the information in a database. Share your list with the class, and discuss your reasons.

EXERCISES

1. Find a professional article in your field and read it carefully. Then, **write two of the following summaries:**
   a. Write a **descriptive summary** of the article for another student who is also interested in the same field of study but who doesn't have time to read the article.
   b. Write an **executive summary** for an instructor who is going to use the article in his or her research and needs to understand the most important points.
   c. Write an **evaluative summary** for a student who is considering using the article in a research report.

2. Find an article that interests you in any field and **write an abstract that could be included in a library database**. The abstract should not be more than 100 words long. List potential search terms relevant to the topic, underneath your abstract.

6 - Short Reports

Short reports are very common in the workplace. They serve many functions:

- To describe an incident (Incident Report)
- To report meeting proceedings (Meeting Minutes)
- To record events, such as training trips or software loads (Trip Report, Software Load Report)
- To show progress on a project or program (Progress Report)
- To make an evaluation or recommendation (Evaluation/Recommendation Report)
- To report financial information (Budget Report)

The audiences for short reports are almost always internal. They are usually written for management, and should be considered permanent records. They are formalized, structured vehicles for passing important information. They may take many hours to create and go through many revisions. They may involve research, sometimes contain graphics, and always use a professional tonc.

When you are asked to write a workplace report, accept the responsibility with the knowledge that you have been given an opportunity to demonstrate your thinking and writing skills. You have been given an opportunity to stand out. The rest of this chapter will help you write reports that will reflect positively on your credibility and professionalism.

General Formats

Short reports can be written in an email, hard copy memo or letter format. For longer reports, a "free-standing" booklet format is appropriate, with an accompanying cover letter or memo.

- **Email Report Format:** Some emails report an occurrence, progress, or other information. Sample 6-1 on page 111 shows an email report. An email report should be relatively short and addressed to only one person. If you have more than one recipient, choose memo report format. You can, however, email an attachment memo report to the recipients.
- **Memo Report Format:** Some memos are expanded to include a report. A memo report is an internal document that follows the hard copy memo format, but can include headings and expanded content. Sample 6-5 on pages 130-131 is an example of a hard copy memo report.

- **Letter Report Format:** Letter reports are simply letters to external audiences with expanded content. They may contain headings and even sub-headings. Sample 6-6 on pages 132-133 shows an example of a letter report.
- **Booklet Report Format**: A report in booklet form has its own title page and organizational structure. This type of report is usually chosen for documents longer than two or three pages. It can be copied for insertion in a binder or for presentation at a formal meeting. When these reports are sent by email or postal mail, they are sent as attachments or enclosures, with a cover letter or memo. See Sample 6-3 on pages 115-126 for an example of booklet report format.

INCIDENT REPORT

Incident reports are short reports describing a recent, unexpected occurrence. They are critical for capturing details of a particular event very soon after the event occurred. Capturing details in a business setting can help to avoid a lawsuit, defend against a lawsuit, or launch a lawsuit. Examples of an incident that would require this type of report might be:

- An accident that occurred on company property
- An accident that occurred using a company vehicle
- Receipt of inferior products that were passed on to customers

Some incident reports help to analyze a problem or to provide evidence of a situation that may require change. Examples of this type of incident are:

- Unacceptable employee behavior
- System outage
- Criminal activity (break-in, theft, graffiti)

Incident reports use first-hand knowledge only. No assumptions, opinions, or judgments are made. Like good journalism, the incident report gives the who, what, when, why, and how of an unexpected event. The following incident report written in **email report format** gives details of an apparent break-in (Sample 6-1):

Sample 6-1 Incident Report in Email Format

RE: Break-in Last Night 10:30 AM (1 hour ago)

Todd Small tsmall@musicom.com

to me ▽

Jane,

The following is a description of what occurred today when I arrived to work and discovered that we had experienced a break-in.

When I came to work this morning at 8:50 AM, I noticed that the front door was closed but not locked.

I walked in, and noticed that the door key we keep by the cash register was not there. I called Todd Leyburn, and he stated that he distinctly remembered locking the door the evening before and that Shane Barberry had witnessed his locking it. He did not recall whether the key by the cash register was still there.

I opened the cash register and didn't see anything unusual. Since we don't keep money overnight in the cash register, there was no money missing. However, the shelves where we keep automotive stereo products were nearly empty. I called police at 9:10 AM, and then checked our inventory online. Here is a list of what is missing:

- Six (6) Sony XAV-63 Receivers
- Twelve (12) Pioneer DEH-150MP Receivers
- Four (4) JVC KD-X150BT Receivers

I unlocked the storage room (it uses another key besides the front door key), and everything seemed normal, with apparently nothing missing. I checked for anything unusual in the rest of the store, including the bathroom. Nothing seemed disturbed.

The police arrived at 9:20 AM. Officers Warnoff and Fleury took a police report and told me that there were two other reported break-ins in the North Precinct last night. The police took the names of the customers who had come in the store yesterday, the names of the other employees, and permission to look at our security camera recording.

After checking with Reggie Foss, I gave the security camera disk to the officers. I gave them your phone number as well as mine so they could get back with us. Officer Fleury said that their investigator, Katrina Hibbins, would call within a week.

The officers left at 9:45, as the first customers began to enter the store. If you have any questions, I'd be glad to provide more information.

Todd

MEETING MINUTES REPORT

At meetings, information is brought forward, opinions are voiced, and decisions are made. To avoid discrepancies in interpretation of what actually happened at a meeting, someone is usually appointed to "take the minutes." Having a record of the meeting not only preserves the events, but helps to hold attendees responsible for what they report or promise. See Sample 6-2 on the next page for an example of a minutes report.

If you are called upon to take the minutes in a meeting, keep the following guidelines in mind:

- Pass around a sheet of paper for each participant (attendee) to write his or her name and email address. You will send this group an email with the meeting minutes attached.
- Write down an overview of what happens at the meeting. You can use a pad of paper or you can use your laptop.
- Use the agenda as a handy "cheat sheet" for an overview of the topics. Each article in your minutes should cover the topic mentioned on the agenda. If one of the items isn't covered, give the reason. For example, "Budget item was not covered because Sandy Kline was absent."
- Record all action items, who they are assigned to, and the deadline for completion. An Action Item is a task that one of the meeting attendees must complete. Action items can be the result of a discussion about one of the agenda items. For an agenda item named "Construction: Next Step," an action item may be assigned to Joe Smith to make sure that the lot is cleared and ready for construction by May 1.
- Record "New Business" during the last section of the meeting. In this part of the meeting, participants can bring up items that are not already on the agenda. The meeting leader, sometimes called the facilitator, or the chair, can decide if an item should be handled at the meeting or is best added to the agenda for the next meeting.
- When possible, give the name of the speaker and a summary of what he or she said. Ask for clarification if you do not understand something or if you think something is missing. If you need an extended explanation, wait until the meeting is over, so as not to hold up the meeting.
- State decisions clearly and include any time constraints. For example, "Phase 1 is scheduled to complete by June 1."
- If you have an important role to play in the meeting, besides taking notes, you may ask another person to take minutes when your segment comes up.
- Promptly write your meeting report and send it to the meeting participants as an email attachment. Attendees will have a chance to read the report and either accept it as written at the next meeting or make corrections to be approved at the next meeting.

Sample 6-1 Meeting Minutes Report

TREEHAVEN COMMUNITY ASSOCIATION

Minutes of 4/17/2016 Executive Council Meeting, held at Treehaven Community Room.

Prepared by Sean Mogley, Secretary

Attendees: Marcy Scott, President; Merle Falstaff, Vice President; Charles D'Angelo, Treasurer; Sean Mogley, Secretary; Trish Bingham, Outreach Committee Chair; Fletcher Moss, Treasurer.

The meeting was called to order at 7:00 PM by President Marcy Scott. The minutes from last month's meeting were accepted.

Agenda Items:

- **Item 1: Swimming Pool Opening Date.** The first item on the agenda was determining when to open the community swimming pool each year. Trish brought up the point that most students aren't out of school until the end of June, and the pool water temperature is too cold to swim in before July. Charles added that some adult swimmers like to use the pool swim lanes in June, even when the water is cool. Fletcher stated that the cost for opening the pool (cleaning, adding water, cleaning dressing rooms) is $500, but that cost is the same no matter when the pool opens. The cost of maintaining the pool (daily water testing, adding water, daily cleaning) is $200/week. Charles made a motion that the pool be opened each year on Father's Day weekend in mid-June. The motion was seconded and passed.

- **Item 2: Budget Report.** The second item on the agenda was the budget report. Charles stated that the association has $4000 currently, and expects more as the mid-year dues are received. The annual budget for maintaining the pool, grounds, and Holiday Party is $6000.

- **Item 3: Dues Increase.** The third item on the agenda was a request by Charles to possibly increase dues. He pointed out that similar neighborhoods around the city charge around $50 more per year. After much discussion, an action item was created. Merle made a motion that Charles write a report in which the feasibility of raising dues is researched. The executive committee wishes to see the "pro's and con's" of raising dues. Merle asked that Charles write the report and bring copies to the next meeting. The agenda item will be added for next month.

New Business:

The Outreach Committee Chair, Trish Bingham, announced that she and her family are moving to Tulsa, OK, and she will not be able to continue his role as Outreach Committee Chair beyond July 1. Sean made a motion that that Trish pass along this information to the newsletter editor and ask him to place a note asking for a volunteer replacement from the community. The motion was seconded and passed. All wished Trish well, and were sorry to hear of her leaving.

Meeting was adjourned at 8:30.

Next meeting: 5/18/2016, 7:00 PM, Treehaven Community Room

EVENT REPORT

An event report, such as a travel report or project report, is similar to an incident report, but the event is a planned event with specific expectations for the outcome. For example, if you are sent to China to find out about the feasibility of relocating your company's manufacturing facility there, the expectations for your report will be fairly high. You must provide concrete details and new knowledge. If you are called upon to write a report describing the last software load your company implemented, you'll also need a very high level of detail along with a comprehensive overview of the event.

An event report is usually created in a **booklet report** because it includes several parts. The parts of a booklet report include:

- Cover Letter or Memo
- Cover or Title Page
- Table of Contents
- Glossary (Optional)
- Introduction
- Body of Report
- Conclusion
- Directory of Contacts (optional)
- Sign-offs or Document Version Information (optional)

Booklet reports will vary in content and format according to the audience and the expectations of your organization. Headings and sub-headings are used to organize the material; graphics can be useful to explain concepts. Reports are usually printed double-sided and either bound or stapled at the left margin.

Sample 6-3 beginning on the next page is an example of a software load report for a complex development effort involving 12 teams in two locations.

Sample 6-2 Event Report in Booklet Format, Cover Memo

MEMORANDUM

DATE: 6/2/2014

TO: All Managers

FROM: Gina Gilliam, Software Certification Manager *GG*

SUBJECT: Post Release Report for April/May 2014 Load
Release 4

Attached, please find the Post Release Report for Release 4. It covers the following areas:

- Scope
- Lessons Learned (new topic)
- Outstanding Issues from Previous Releases
- Metrics and Measurements

I am pleased with the quality of the reporting and I hope you will find this report valuable as you make important decisions for Release 5.

If you have any questions, please contact me, Gina Gilliam (ggilliam@gbc.com).

Sample 6-3 Event Report in Booklet Format, Title Page

Post Release Report

April/May 2014 load
Release 4

Prepared by GRS Software Certification Group
Gina Gilliam, Manager

Page 1 of 11

ISO 9000 Controlled Document
Owner: GBC Software Certification Group
All paper copies are for reference only.
Master copy: GBC\postrelease\reports\AprilMay2014

Sample 6-3 Event Report in Booklet Format, Table of Contents

Table of Contents

Page 2 of 11

ISO 9000 Controlled Document
Owner: GBC Software Certification Group
All paper copies are for reference only.
Master copy: GBC\postrelease\reports\AprilMay2014

Sample 6-3 Event Report in Booklet Format, Introduction

Introduction

This GBC Post Release Report summarizes the issues and successes of each GBC revenue software development release. This document is distributed after each quarterly load to the managers, team leads, and participants of the groups directly involved with GBC development and testing:

- Program Management
- Business Architecture
- Application Architecture
- Data Architecture
- Operations Architecture
- Application Development
- Computer Operations
- Product Test
- Training and Communications
- Software Process Improvement
- Software Certification

The purpose of this document is to ensure continuous improvement in the GBC development program through a retrospective analysis. Comments and suggestions should be made to Gina Gilliam, gina.gilliam@gbc.com.

Page 3 of 11

ISO 9000 Controlled Document
Owner: GBC Software Certification Group
All paper copies are for reference only.
Master copy: GBC\postrelease\reports\AprilMay2014

Sample 6-3 Event Report in Booklet Format, Body, Page 1

Release Summary

During development, Release 4 became a split load with capabilities implemented on two days, April 21, 2014 and April 28, 2014.

April 21, 2014 Capabilities Implemented:

- EDI Billing using the new invoice format
- Continued data migration from ERGA to Customer Accounts
- Accounts receivable for TLSD
- Additional revenue cycle controls
- Additional Verify Credit reports

April 28, 2014 Capability Implemented:

- Automated Business Bonus rebate to Customer Invoicing

On May 5, 2014, the Post Release Review meeting was held in Seattle. On May 12, 2014, a second Post Release Review meeting was conducted in Sacramento. Both meetings were facilitated by the GBC Software Certification Group. A representative from each area associated with Release 4 was invited to attend. Application Development, Computer Operations, Operations Architecture, and Technical Architecture did not provide representation for the Release 4 Port Release Review. The list of names below were identified as contacts/participants for the Post Release Review meeting by Program Management and their respective teams:

TEAM/AREA	REPRESENTATIVE
Application Architecture	Maddie Olson
Application Development	Jim Slidfelt, Terry Reagan
Business Architecture	Regina Lee, Tim Slicer
Computer Operations/Technical Architecture	Ray Fisher, Judy Goldberg
Data Architecture	Rhonda Matsoff, Lyla Spencer
Product Test	Amy Regent, Bill Loberman
Program Management	Felicia Simpson
Software Process Improvement	Reggie Grayson, Tim Newberry
Training and Communications	Marilyn Freeland, Shawna Miller

Page 4 of 11

ISO 9000 Controlled Document
Owner: GBC Software Certification Group
All paper copies are for reference only.
Master copy: GBC\postrelease\reports\AprilMay2014

Sample 6-3 Event Report in Booklet Format, Body, Page 2

Release 4.0 Scope

The following features, arranged by phases of service, were included in Release 4. This information was imported from GBC\Users\PubData\Release4\Scope.doc.

Initiate Service

Verify Credit

- Create a monthly report of accounts with a credit limit override date greater than zero for the Credit & Collections department
- Access new accounts receivable during credit verification process

Accounts Receivable

- Support new accounts receivable processes throughout system

Provide Service

- Nothing for Release 4

Request Settlement

- Calculate for US Payors

Process and Acknowledge Settlement

- Nothing for Release 4

Revenue Controls

- Provide prediction functionality
- Support legal entity and multiple currency
- Implement research data infrastructure

Page 5 of 11

ISO 9000 Controlled Document
Owner: GBC Software Certification Group
All paper copies are for reference only.
Master copy: GBC\postrelease\reports\AprilMay2014

Sample 6-3 Event Report in Booklet Format, Body, Page 3

Lessons Learned

Lessons Learned is a cumulative list grows with each release. A lesson learned is defined as a "good work practice" or "innovative approach" that is captured and shared to promote repeat application. A lesson learned may also be an adverse work practice or experience that is captured and shared to avoid recurrence. The purpose for capturing this information in the Post Release Report is to publicize what works well and to share the benefits of experience. All teams associated with Release 4 were asked to provide lessons learned.

LESSON LEARNED	RELEASE	TEAM
Adequate and thorough assembly testing resulted in an efficient and successful product test.	2	Accounts Receivable
Adhering to process standards insured a quality software release. The processes also controlled the workload and kept it manageable throughout.	3	Application Development
Operation Architecture, Data Architecture will have separate environment files.	4	Application Development
Conduct a walkthrough with SMEs prior to instructions design walkthrough	4	Training and Communications

Page 6 of 11

ISO 9000 Controlled Document
Owner: GBC Software Certification Group
All paper copies are for reference only.
Master copy: GBC\postrelease\reports\AprilMay2014

Sample 6-3 Event Report in Booklet Format, Body, Page 4

Outstanding Issues from Previous Releases

The following issues were documented in the Release 3 Post Release Report. Of all the issues listed in the previous report, these are the issues left unresolved. Since the issues have not been closed, the closed column has been changed to a status column. The status is reported directly from the Issues management database. This information was extracted on 5/30/2014. All information in this chart, except for status, is the original information listed in the previous report. Any modifications to the original information are noted in the status section.

ISSUE NUMBER	ISSUE	RELEASE	ACTION	ASSIGNED TO	DUE DATE	STATUS
1689	What are the responsibilities and deliverables for Business Architecture and Application Development in regard to corporate initiatives?	3	This issue was written as a result of concerns raised by Terence Rogan. He will update the issue with more information and a concrete example.	Program Management – George Riley	3/3/2014	In Process
1655	Values (IP, port #s) need to be verified that they are accurate.	2,3	Identifying actual system names, IPs, ports, etc. for both test and production systems.	Business Architecture – Mary Walker	3/3/2014	Rejected – Insufficient detail to assign to a specific team.

Page 7 of 11

ISO 9000 Controlled Document
Owner: GBC Software Certification Group
All paper copies are for reference only.
Master copy: GBC\postrelease\reports\AprilMay2014

Sample 6-3 Event Report in Booklet Format, Body, Page 5

Metrics and Measurements

The measurements in this section correspond to Release 4.0 only. Any questions should be directed to Molly Bronchowski at molly.bronchowski@gbc.com.

The results were recorded after the load on April 28, 2014. Note that several production fixes have been implemented since this date and may slightly affect these numbers.

In future reports, we plan to expand these measurements by development team.

Source Code Files Statistics

	NUMBER IN APPLICATION DEVELOPMENT			NUMBER IN TECHNICAL ARCHITECTURE			TOTALS		
Release	*2.0*	*3.0*	*4.0*	*2.0*	*3.0*	*4.0*	*2.0*	*3.0*	*4.0*
C++ code	251	527	647	111	125	166	362	652	813
Java code	150	245	354	10	12	143	160	257	497
UNIX scripts	52	153	256	33	40	45	85	193	301
Total Files	453	925	1257	154	177	354	617	1102	1611

Database Statistics

	RELEASE TOTALS		
Release	*2.0*	*3.0*	*4.0*
Tables	191	235	379
Stored Procs	492	642	835

Page 8 of 11

ISO 9000 Controlled Document
Owner: GBC Software Certification Group
All paper copies are for reference only.
Master copy: GBC\postrelease\reports\AprilMay2014

Sample 6-3 Event Report in Booklet Format, Body, Page 6

Measurement of Team Problems

The V-model has been a contributor to the software engineering efforts of GBC since its inception. Much of the current and future Deliverable flow stems from the theory of the V-model. Until recently, the particular stages of the V-model had not been directly mapped to the deliverable flow. Therefore, determining the entry point of a change request has too often been subjective, and determining the source stage of a problem has been guess-work at best. Therefore, the Software Certification and Metrics group has undertaken the task to eliminate these gray areas.

The first three columns in the table below show the types of problems that occurred and were found by each team during release 4.0. A *problem* is a type of change request that is an error, a defect, a fault, or a change to scope. Problems exclude *work requests* (WR). An *error* is a problem generated and found in the same stage, such as when a code review uncovers a coding typo. A *defect* is a problem generated in a previous stage of software development, such as when Application Development discovers an error in a programming work unit during Assembly Test. A *change to scope* modifies, lessens, or enhances deliverable content that has already gone through Verification Sign-off, such as when detailed requirements are changed during high level design. Hence, all change to scope types have been included in the defect type. A *fault* is a problem that was found in production. *Requirement* and *enhancement* are former options which will be categorized with *defect* and *work request* (WR) respectively.

The totals for each team are included in this table. Every stage and category are included in the summations.

	ERROR	DEFECT	FAULT	WR
Business Architecture	0	2	1	1
Application Architecture	0	3	0	2
Data Architecture	11	104	10	10
Operations Architecture	3	33	47	35
Product Test	30	436	10	22
Application Development	0	2	0	1
Computer Operations	1	11	0	13
Training & Communications	0	0	0	1
Software Process Improvement	0	1	1	0
Software Certification	0	0	0	1
Unassigned	0	0	0	2
Totals	45	592	69	88

Page 9 of 11

ISO 9000 Controlled Document
Owner: GBC Software Certification Group
All paper copies are for reference only.
Master copy: GBC\postrelease\reports\AprilMay2014

Sample 6-3 Event Report in Booklet Format, Conclusion

Conclusion

Release 4 was a successful load. However, limited participation from the contacts impacted the effectiveness of leaning from our experiences. The GBC Software Certification Group will work with all departments to increase the level of support and involvement for Release 5 and beyond.

Continuous improvements for the Release 5 report will include:

- The Software Certification Group will formulate and distribute a survey to gather improvements, suggestions, and feedback from report recipients.
- The Software Certification Group and the Software Process Improvement group will create and keep the Lessons Learned repository. This will reduce the work for participants and it will give all GBC members the opportunity to record lessons learned.
- The Measurement of Team Problems section will be expanded.

This report is located in GBC\postrelease\reports\AprilMay2014 and on the GBC intranet web page.

Page 10 of 11

ISO 9000 Controlled Document
Owner: GBC Software Certification Group
All paper copies are for reference only.
Master copy: GBC\postrelease\reports\AprilMay2014

Sample 6-3 Event Report in Booklet Format, Directory of Contacts

Directory of Contacts

These team members are considered contacts because they participated in the Release 4 Post Load Review meeting on April 21, 2014 or April 28, 2014, or both dates. All data in the report are provided by these participants.

Group	Name	Phone	E-mail
Application Architecture	Mary Stevenson	555-555-5555	mary.stevenson@gbc.com
Accounts Receivable	Lyla Tompkins	555-555-5555	lyla.tompkins@gbc.com
Business Architecture	Nigel Ford	555-555-5555	Nigel.ford@gbc.com
Data Architecture	Robin Lawrence	555-555-5555	Robin.lawrence@gbc.com
Product Test	Jim Bookman	555-555-5555	Jim.bookman@gbc.com
Program Management	Kareem Soji	555-555-5555	Kareem.soji@gbc.com
Software Certification	Winston Cleary	555-555-5555	Winston.cleary@gbc.com
Software Process Improvement	Frederick Shantell	555-555-5555	Frederick.shantell@gbc.com
Training and Communications	Charles Franklin	555-555-5555	Charles.franklin@gbc.com

Page 11 of 11

ISO 9000 Controlled Document
Owner: GBC Software Certification Group
All paper copies are for reference only.
Master copy: GBC\postrelease\reports\AprilMay2014

PROGRESS REPORT

A progress report is invaluable for keeping a project on schedule. Knowing that a project team must report what it has accomplished, and how much is left to do adds motivation to keep going. A progress report can also show management where actual or potential problems are showing up so that management can correct the problem.

Progress reports typically have the following sections:

- Title and author info (department, manager, etc.)
- Introduction
- Project Scope (What is the project about? What does it cover? What are its major parts? Has there been a change?)
- Work Completed
- Work Remaining
- Issues/Risks (use a table with numbered rows)
- Conclusion

Progress reports usually use a graphic to show the parts of a project, when they should begin and end, and how long they last. Usually Gantt charts are used to show an overview of the project and indicate when tasks are scheduled. There is an example of a simple Gantt chart in the progress report on the next page (Sample 6-4), and in Figure 2-10 on page 40, in Chapter 2. They can be created in Microsoft Excel or Word relatively easily.

Below is a progress report for a thesis writing project. The writer is using an email report format.

Sample 6-4 Progress Report in Email Format, Page 1

To: rpschiffler@nyu.edu <Richard Schiffler>

From: mthornton@nyu.edu <Freda Thornton>

Date: 10/1/2012

Subject: Thesis Progress Report

Dr. Schiffler,

As you requested, here is a report of my progress toward completing my thesis, "The Rhetoric of Forestry: The Wetland as a Case Study." If you have any questions, please let me know.

Project Scope:

The scope of my thesis remains the same. I am including the following sections:

- History of Forestry Rhetoric
- Shifting Paradigm
- Shifting Terminology: Swamp to Wetland
- New Rhetoric of Forestry

Work Completed:

I have completed three drafts, which you have reviewed. The following chart shows my overall progress. The dark blocks are completed work. The diagonally-shaded blocks represent work yet to be finished.

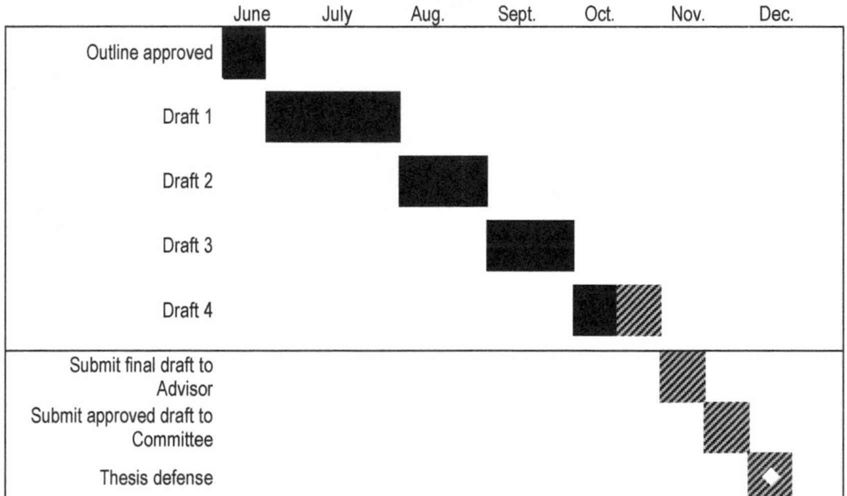

Sample 6-4 Progress Report in Email Format, Page 2

Work Remaining:

I am currently revising my third draft and expect to submit my fourth and final draft for your review by November 1. Incorporating your input, I would like to complete my final draft by November 15. If I can complete—and the committee approves—my final draft by December 1, I will seek to schedule my thesis defense for December 15.

Issues/Risks:

One of my major professors, Dr. Tarnhouse, will be extremely busy during the time my thesis will be reviewed by the committee. As you know, she will be on a hectic book touring schedule. She has expressed a wish to remain on my committee, nonetheless.

Conclusion:

I am confident that my final draft will be ready for you to read by November 1. If so, the timeline for approval will take place before graduation, and I'll have earned my MA in Rhetoric.

Thanks for all your help!

Freda

EVALUATION/RECOMMENDATION REPORT

An evaluation or recommendation report usually involves a considered evaluation of two or more alternatives. This kind of report can be very simple or quite complex, depending upon the topic. You may be asked to write a straightforward comparison of a few different refrigerators for possible purchase for the employee break room, for example. Or, you might be asked to compare three complex manufacturing systems and project how they will contribute to profitability.

Whether small or large, the evaluation/recommendation report generally includes the following sections:

- Introduction
- Statement of Problem or Need (criteria can be included here)
- Solutions (evaluation of solutions or alternatives using criteria)
- Recommendations
- Conclusion

The following (Sample 6-5) is an example of an evaluation/recommendation report in memo format.

Sample 6-5 Evaluation/Recommendation Report in Memo Format, Page 1

FERGUSON & RILEY REALTORS
KIM BRADLEY, REALTOR
1220 RIVER ROAD | CHARLESTON, SC 29401 | 803-555-5555 | FERGUSONRILEY.COM

MEMORANDUM

DATE: March 20, 2015
TO: Cheryl Goldberg, Office Manager
FROM: Kim Bradley, Realtor
SUBJECT: Recommendation for Welcome Packet

Introduction

As you know, I've been working at Ferguson & Riley for over five years. During this time, I've dealt with over a hundred clients who are moving to this region from other parts of the US and even from other countries. I would like to propose an idea that will help them acclimate to our region.

Statement of Need

Many of our new leads and potential customers relocate to the Charleston, SC vicinity from all over the US and the world. Because of the naval base, especially, we have an influx of a diverse population. Adding to the stress of moving and getting used to a different house, these new residents are also faced with the stress of adapting to new jobs, schools, businesses, roads, weather, etc. These new residents need a way to learn about the city and the region, making their adaptation easier.

Solutions

You and I have discussed some solutions to this problem, including asking the Chamber of Commerce to begin a Welcome Wagon program. However, as we learned, the Chamber of Commerce doesn't have the funds to dedicate to this program.

Criteria for Solution

Nonetheless, the new residents need a way to:

- quickly adapt
- gain knowledge of the area
- adopt a positive impression of Charleston

Sample 6-5 Evaluation/Recommendation Report in Memo Format, Page 2

Page 2

Recommendation

I recommend that Ferguson & Riley begin compiling our own packets for newcomers. We could include only free or very low cost items, such as road maps, brochures of local attractions, copies of local newspapers, a copy of the state magazine, free samples and coupons from local businesses. We could even include a monetary incentive in the form of a voucher for customers who bring us another home-buying customer.

I estimate that you and I could put together this packet in our slack time, which is coming up next month. On a budget of $50, we could assemble 50 packets and test them in the Spring. I can follow up with my clients and see if they enjoyed receiving the packets and if they have used them.

Conclusion

I'm looking forward to discussing this with you. I think that our "Ferguson & Riley Welcome Packet" will be a memorable way to help our clients adjust to and appreciate all our region has to offer.

In the next sample document, the same writer sends a recommendation report in letter format to her clients, giving them information about neighborhoods and making suggestions.

She is trying to make her clients lives easier by narrowing down the number of homes they will consider when they come to town for a home-buying trip. Notice that although there are no formal section headings, the sections are included.

Sample 6-6 Evaluation/Recommendation Report in Letter Format, Page 1

FERGUSON & RILEY REALTORS

KIM BRADLEY, REALTOR

1220 RIVER ROAD | CHARLESTON, SC 29401 | 803-555-5555 | FERGUSONRILEY.COM

March 20, 2017

Introduction

Roger and Mindy Clayborne
1605 NE Treble Lane
Ft. Lauderdale, FL 33301

Dear Roger and Mindy,

Need

Criteria for Solution

I'm looking forward to your visit in early April. It will be very exciting to find just the right home for you and your young family. I've been doing some research to get ready for your visit, hoping to steer you in the right direction. This letter will give you a good idea of neighborhoods that might be suitable, and my recommendations for you based on your criteria: affordable (less than $300,000), at least three bedrooms and two baths, fenced in back yard, good public schools, small town atmosphere, low traffic streets, nearby recreation (swimming, golf).

You stated that you want to find your home as soon as possible so that you can sell your home in Ft. Lauderdale and start planning your move. I hope to make this transition as easy for you as I can.

From what you've told me, I've narrowed down the neighborhoods to the following three choices:

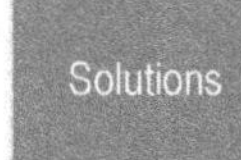

- Summerville Crest Lake
- Frasier Forest
- Golden Beach Acres

Summerville Crest Lake is a subdivision in the town of Summerville, right outside of Charleston. Home prices are affordable now, but they are rising quickly due to the outstanding test scores for the public schools. You can find a home with the amenities you're looking for in the upper $290,000 range. Summerville Crest Lake is within the city limits of Summerville, which has a public golf course and municipal swimming pool for all residents. The lot sizes are large, and virtually all have cedar privacy fencing. The streets have sidewalks and low traffic. Summerville Crest Lake does have a small lake that can be used for boating or fishing.

Sample 6-6 Evaluation/Recommendation Report in Letter Format, Page 2

Client: Roger and Mindy Clayborne, 3/20/2017 - Page 2

Frasier Forest is a very new subdivision being built in a heavily forested area. The home prices average $250,000, and you would be able to choose carpeting and paint colors for any home that is now under construction. Frasier Forest has a very good elementary school. The middle and high school students go to North Charleston High currently, but there is a good possibility that a new middle and high school will be built in the Frasier area within the next 5 years. Frasier Forest subdivision has its own swimming pool. The nearest golf course is in North Charleston, only about a 20-minute drive.

Golden Beach Acres is on Traymore Island, accessible from Charleston by the Green River Bridge. You can find older homes in your price range, and even below $250,000, but I must caution you that the flood insurance can be quite steep due to hurricane flooding. There is an established school system with excellent state standings. The lot sizes are a bit smaller than Frasier Forest or Summerville Crest Lake, but there are sidewalks, speed bumps, and it is considered a very walkable neighborhood. Most homes have 2-3 bedrooms and 1-1/2 to 2 baths. To swim, you can always go to Golden Beach. For golf, you would need to join the Regents Golf Club if you wanted to play nearby. Otherwise, you can play on a municipal course in North Charleston.

Recommendation

I would like for you to first look at Summerville Crest Lake because I believe it has more of what you are looking for, and in your price range. I believe it's an excellent choice for a growing family. I look forward to showing you a mint condition 3 bedroom, 2 bath home on the lake, that probably won't stay on the market long. It's move-in ready, and I think it may have your names on it.

Go to our website, and enter code 4043 to see a video of the home: 595 Lancelot Lane. Let me know what you think. It's a pleasure to work with you.

Conclusion

Sincerely,

Kim Bradley

Kim Bradley

BUDGET REPORT

Budget reports are written to provide regular updates to managers about expenses and income. They are not to be confused with accounting spreadsheets or the process of budgeting itself.

In small, nonprofit organizations such as a neighborhood club or co-operative daycare, a budget report can be very simple, as the expenses are few and the income is almost nonexistent. In larger organizations, materials, overhead and labor are important considerations, and managers are concerned with profit and loss.

Remember that the report needs to be simple enough that your audience can comprehend the information quickly and easily. Just providing a spreadsheet is not enough (even though you should be prepared to provide that if asked). Use your writing skills to interpret and emphasize the parts your readers will be most interested in knowing.

In a summary at the beginning of the report, present the facts that seem important to know or understand, so a manager with little time can feel informed by reading just that section. For example, a summary of the profit and loss for the time period will be important; if energy or labor costs have gone up, that is worth mentioning. If there has been an unexpected expenditure, that is crucial to note.

After summarizing, itemizing expenditures and income is important. An attentive manager will want to be informed about which products are selling, what supplies are most costly, and how much the company is paying for labor. If there are separate production or research groups within the organization with their own budgets, those should be presented separately.

Budget reports typically have the following sections:

- Summary or Overview
- Presentation of Expenditures and Income (usually in table or spreadsheet format)
- Itemized breakdown of expenditures: materials, overhead, and labor
- Itemized breakdown of income: sales, donations, grants, refunds
- Conclusion

If you are reporting on budget transactions over an extended period, or if you are requested to compare time periods, groups, or categories, your report may include a bar chart or a line graph of trends as an illustration. Sample 6-7 shows an example of budget report with a chart comparing budgeted and actual expenses.

Professionalism & Ethics

Budget reports are essential to the effective running of a business. When you create one, you are being trusted with information that can affect important decisions—sometimes including whether to keep the business open at all. Be careful to proofread all numbers carefully after each edit; Remember that when a change is made in one number, it may affect others. Check that decimal points are in the right place.

Sample 6-7 Budget Report in Memo Format

Memorandum

Date: May 5, 2014

To: Management Staff

From: Lucinda Jeffers, Bookkeeper *LJ*

Subject: April Budget Report

Summary:

Income rose by $12,000 last month, as we have enrolled three new families, adding five children to full time care. Note: the increase means that we now have the maximum child-to-teacher ratio allowed under State licensing in the toddler room.

Expenses rose by $2,422 last month. Most of that increase was a response to the sudden influx of new children: we scheduled more part-time staffers at hourly rates. The move to all-biodegradable diapers has meant that our materials cost has risen significantly. Last month we replaced the play kitchen area, so our expenses rose by over $300; that is an investment in the quality of our large play equipment.

Expenses			Income		
Materials	**Budgeted**	**Actual**	**Tuition**	**Budgeted**	**Actual**
Art supplies	$200	$212	Infants (full time)	$3,000	$3,000
Diapers	$625	$702	Toddlers (full time)	$4,000	$5,000
Cleaning supplies	$75	$50	Preschool (morning)	$10,000	$15,000
Books and Toys	$100	$95	Preschool (afternoon)	$12,000	$14,000
Play kitchen		$329	Kinders (morning)	$8,000	$9,000
Food/drinks	$850	$923	Kinders (afternoon)	$9,000	$10,000
Overhead					
Rent	$2,250	$2,250			
Gas	$200	$141			
Electricity	$150	$170			
Mowing	$100	$100			
Phones	$92	$92			
Labor					
Salaried staff	$22,000	$22,000			
Hourly rate staff	$4,000	$6,000			
Health benefits	$10,000	$10,000			
Total Expenses:	$40,642	**$43,064**	Total Income:	$46,000	**$56,000**

Conclusion:

Our expenses rose last month, and will continue to increase as we stock sufficient supplies to accommodate the new children. But, our income rose even more. We should consider hiring more full time staff to help with the new children.

SHORT REPORT *Checklist* ✔

An Effective Short Report...	✔
Is created in the appropriate format for the type of communication: memo, letter, or booklet format	
Follows all guidelines for the type of report. Booklet reports are more complex than memo or letter reports	
Begins with a brief introduction or summary	
Is well-organized, using headings and sub-headings whenever necessary; paragraphs divide the text into logical units	
Is written in a professional tone	
Is written clearly, covering the subject fully	
Contains graphics whenever necessary to clarify concepts or information	
Uses natural English, language appropriate for the audience	
Ends with a brief conclusion	
Uses correct grammar, spelling, and punctuation	

DISCUSSIONS

1. Brainstorm some instances in your current job in which a report might be useful. Is there information that is not being recorded that should be? How can a report help your work team do a better job?
2. Look at some reports about education in the nation or in your community. The National Center for Education Statistics (NCES) is a good source for reports on the national level. You can check your local school district website or State department of education for reports about education relevant to you. Print one out or share links with your classmates. What is the purpose of the report, and how could it be reorganized to be more useful for you?
3. Share a story about a particular report that you have written, for school or work. Why did you write it? Did it accomplish your purpose?
4. In a small group discussion, come up with at least one more criterion to add to the checklist on the previous page about a specific type of report, or about reports in general. Why do you feel strongly about adding this criterion?

EXERCISES

1. Consider this scenario: You are a writer in a group of eight technical writers, working for GBC, a large software company. You spend most of every day in your cubicle, on your computer. You have noticed some lower back pain which you and others in your group attribute to the 20-year-old office chairs that you are using. Several of your coworkers have complained about the chairs fixed height and the inability to adjust seat height. Your boss, Joseph Sitwell, Manager of Technical Communications, has listened to your complaints, and has heard complaints from others in your group. He has asked you to write a recommendation report for the purchase of eight new chairs. He has also asked you to keep prices as low as possible (under $200 each), while still gaining the comfort and adjustability you need. Therefore, your criteria are:

    - Price (under $200 each)
    - Comfort
    - Adjustability

    Do some Internet research and find several suitable chairs to compare. Include a graphic of each one, and give the source in the caption. **Write a recommendation report in hard copy memo format, evaluating several chairs, and naming the chair you believe will be the best for the group based on your stated criteria.** Use section headings as shown in Sample 6-5.

2. **Write a progress report to your writing instructor in hard copy memo format** in which you report your progress in this writing class. For Project Scope, list all the major topics the course covers. (The course syllabus may help you with this.) In Work Completed, give your grades as well as the assignments for each topic covered. In Work Remaining, describe what is yet to be done to complete the course. For Issues/Risks, discuss any problems you've had with the course, or any risks to your completing the course to your satisfaction. If you have any issues or risks, discuss how you plan to deal with them. End with a brief Conclusion.
3. **Write an incident report to your instructor in hard copy memo format** about an accident or unusual occurrence you recently witnessed or were involved in. Remember to include answers to who, what, when, where, why, and how.
4. **Volunteer to keep notes and write minutes for a group meeting in class.** Transcribe your notes in memo format and hand them in to your instructor at the next class meeting.
5. **Write an event report in booklet format about a recent vacation.** Include photographs of the location, as well as information about who, what, when, where, why, and how. Was the trip successful? Which parts were the most enjoyable, and which parts would you do differently in the future? How much did you spend, and on what? What did you learn, and what contact information (for hotels, travel agents, etc.) may be important to keep?
6. **Write a budget report** detailing one month's income and expenses for a job or project you are working on, such as a small home improvement project or a home-based business. (Some projects may be all expense and no income; jobs usually have both.)

7 - Graphics

Knowing when and how to use graphics (also known as "visuals") can make the difference between an uninteresting, hard-to-understand document, presentation, or web page and an outstandingly useful and professional one. Even if a document is well-written, the absence of needed illustration may cause it to fail. Of course, graphics are not needed in every document. The vast majority of emails, memos, and letters may not contain graphics. However, when a concept, action, or process can be clarified by illustration, effective writers find or create an appropriate visual, or commission a graphic artist to create one.

A graphic is an appeal to the part of our brains that processes forms, shapes, color, and movement. For some people (or possibly even most people), visual input is the primary way that they learn new information. We call these people "visual learners" because their preferred style of learning is "show me."

THE POWER OF SHOWING

As effective writers, we can tap into this powerful learning potential and use "show" or "show and tell" as alternatives to just "tell." For example, consider the three examples below, and how well they convey the same information.

Telling Only

Figure 7-1 tells us what to do in words. Is the step effective?

Step 1. Insert the shoe string into the first two holes.

Figure 7-1 Instructional Step that Tells

Showing Only

Figure 7-2 below shows us what to do without words. Is it adequate?

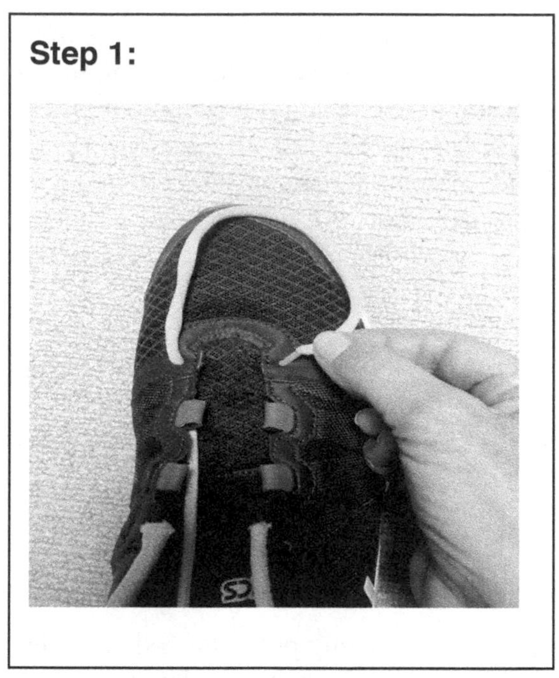

Figure 7-2 Instructional Step that Shows

Both of the examples so far lack clarity. Figure 7-1 is well-written, but the reader really doesn't know which two holes the writer is referring to. Figure 7-2 employs the user's perspective and is fairly clear, but it only shows one end of the shoe string.

Telling and Showing

Figure 7-3 is the best because it tells and shows. The meaning is very clear:

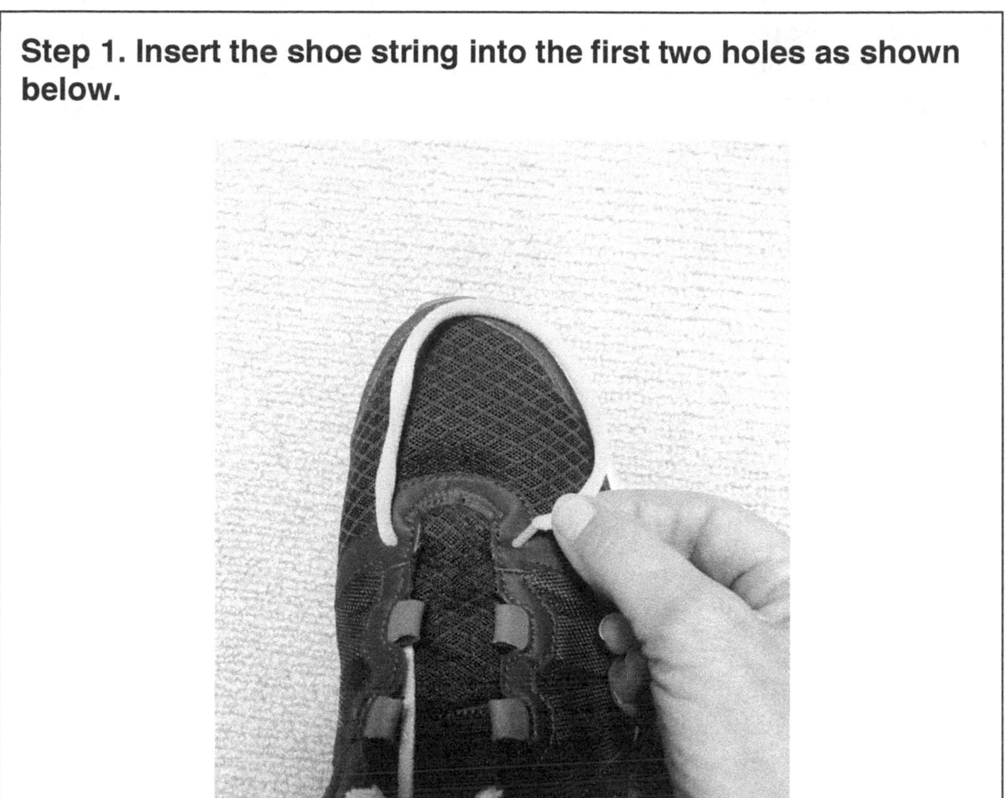

Step 1. Insert the shoe string into the first two holes as shown below.

Figure 7-3 Instructional Step that Tells and Shows

The focus for Figure 7-3 is precise and simple. The photograph clarifies the step to a degree in which misunderstanding is almost impossible. The combination of text + graphic is the most successful method for describing or instructing.

TYPES OF GRAPHICS

Choosing the type of graphic can be a difficult challenge. For example, the photograph in Figure 7-3 above could have easily been a black line drawing, with probably the same effectiveness. However, the photo is probably the cheapest and easiest type of graphic to create unless professional models and photographers are involved. Consider the many graphic choices that would have made the step more difficult for the reader: a cartoon, a tiny photo of only a shoelace, or a photo with little contrast between the shoe and the shoelace.

Adding graphics should be a very careful choice. Determine what the reader needs to know and what is the best way to show it. The list below shows the most common types of graphics.

- **Photograph** – used to show precisely what something or someone looks like. Photographs are especially useful in incident reports, damage reports, and identification. Very simple photographs in which extraneous details have been removed from the camera frame (as in Figure 7-3 above) can be used in almost the same way as a line drawing.

- **Drawing** – used to show a simplified depiction of a place, object, or person. Line drawings are often used to make a complicated subject matter appear to be much simpler. For example, a line drawing of the front of a black or chrome microwave can show the controls, knobs, or handles probably better than a photo. Drawings can be exploded, in which the pieces of a mechanism appear to be flying away from each other, or cutaway, in which the mechanism appears to be cut in half. Line drawings maintain the same scale as the original.

- **Diagram** – used in a similar way as the line drawing, but can be abstract. Usually diagrams show spatial relationships of parts. Diagrams do not necessarily maintain the same scale or physical appearance of the subject matter.

- **Graph** – used to show trends and volume in data relationships. Graphs are very handy for showing numbers in relationship to each other. Bar graphs are particularly good at showing volume relationships, and line graphs are perfect for showing changes over time.

- **Chart** – used to show relationships, progress, process, and organization. The pieces of a chart will only have meaning when shown with the other relevant pieces. For example, an organizational chart showing only a box with the word "Vice President" in it doesn't show who reports to the Vice President or who he or she reports to. A piece of a pie chart is only meaningful if we know what the entire pie consists of, and how each piece contributes to the whole.

- **Table** – used to present raw data, usually for comparison. Tables are less visual than other types of graphics because they consist of numbers, letters, and occasionally symbols. However, because tables handle raw data so elegantly (by use of the column/row matrix), they are very handy whenever quantities of data are important.

- **Logo** – used to deliver a single association quickly, usually for commercial purposes. For example, the logo for Portland Community College is used on all PCC documents and web pages so that the user recognizes where the information originates. Logos can be stylized letters (the IBM logo), an abstract shape (the Nike swoosh), or a stylized shape (the Apple, Inc. apple).

- **Symbol or Icon** – used to deliver a single message quickly, usually for general audience messages such as danger, directions, or prohibited activity. Common icons include the international symbols for danger, bathroom, radioactivity, merge, etc.

- **Clip Art** – used as a very quick and easy-to-understand depiction of a concept used in the text. Clip art is readily available on the Internet and for this reason, it has been often overused.

PHOTOGRAPHS

Digital photographs have become extremely common in all forms of communication. From smart phone snapshots to extremely high resolution studio shots, they are usually cheap and can be very effective. The downside to the photograph is it can be created without a discerning eye for controlling color, elements, and scale.

For example, compare the following two photographs, both depicting car maintenance procedures. Figure 7-4 is a little confusing because it's hard to discern what is below the model's hands. There is a tool in the model's right hand that doesn't appear to have a use in this photograph. In fact, the right hand doesn't really look like it belongs to the same person as the left hand. The area that catches our attention is the forearm of the model. There is a jack in the background but it's not obvious whether the car has been lifted or not. It is also unclear whether the dark, grimy rectangular object below the arms is an oil drip pan or a toolbox.

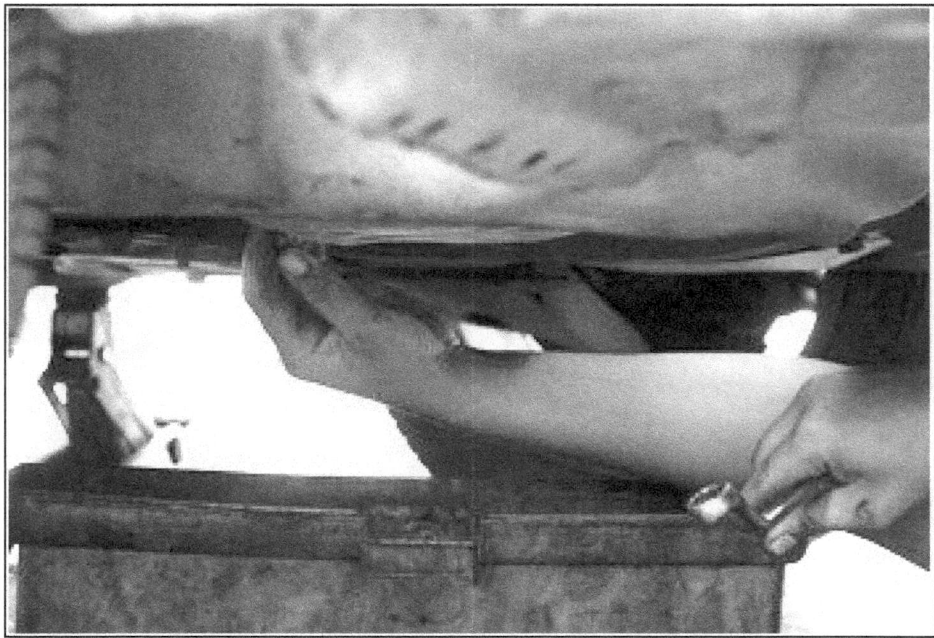

Figure 7-4 Draining the Oil. Source: Courtesy of WikiPhoto.

In contrast, Figure 7-5 is less complex, with the focus on the oil pan, and where the oil comes out.

Figure 7-5 Draining the Oil.
Source: Myke Waddy (2005). *Wikimedia Commons.* Public Domain

Guidelines for Using Photographs

The following list can give you a good idea of when and how to use photographs to clarify your documents:

- Use a photograph when precision and realism are required. Some examples include home-for-sale descriptions, evidence reports, and instances where a simplified photograph can be as effective as a line drawing.

- Size the photograph carefully, both in dimensions and file size. Use a resolution that is high enough to be effective, but not so high as to make your document file size unmanageable. The resolution (or DPI) should usually run from 300-400 DPI for most applications, with 300 being the standard.

- Make the photo as uncluttered as possible, with the main focus clearly visible and obvious.

- Get the permission of any model(s) appearing in your photo.

- Place a caption below the photograph.

DRAWINGS

Before the age of digital photography, drawings were the standard method used to show or illustrate. Drawings are still a very valuable tool, and the digital revolution allows for drawings to be created relatively easily by an experienced graphic artist. Using software such as Adobe Illustrator, line drawings (the most simple type of drawing, usually using black lines on a white background) can clarify an object or simple procedure.

Line drawings can be very simple black lines on a white background, or use carefully controlled color or shading, as in the figure below, demonstrating where to find the drain plug for opening a VW oil pan.

Figure 7-6 Finding the Drain Plug. Source: *WikiHow.* (2014). Used Courtesy of WikiHow.

Cutaway View

Other often-used drawings are the **cutaway** and **exploded** view. The cutaway is very good for showing the complexity of inner parts that can't be seen or accessed. Cutaway drawings remove parts of the subject so that the layers or internal components can be seen. Cutaway drawings are a type of "X-Ray vision," revealing what's hidden.

Figure 7-7 below shows an excellent cutaway drawing of the internal structure of a human heart. This level of detail and color definition is impossible to achieve in reality, even with an actual cadaver heart. Note that the parts are well labeled. The cutaway serves a valuable role in understanding a complex subject.

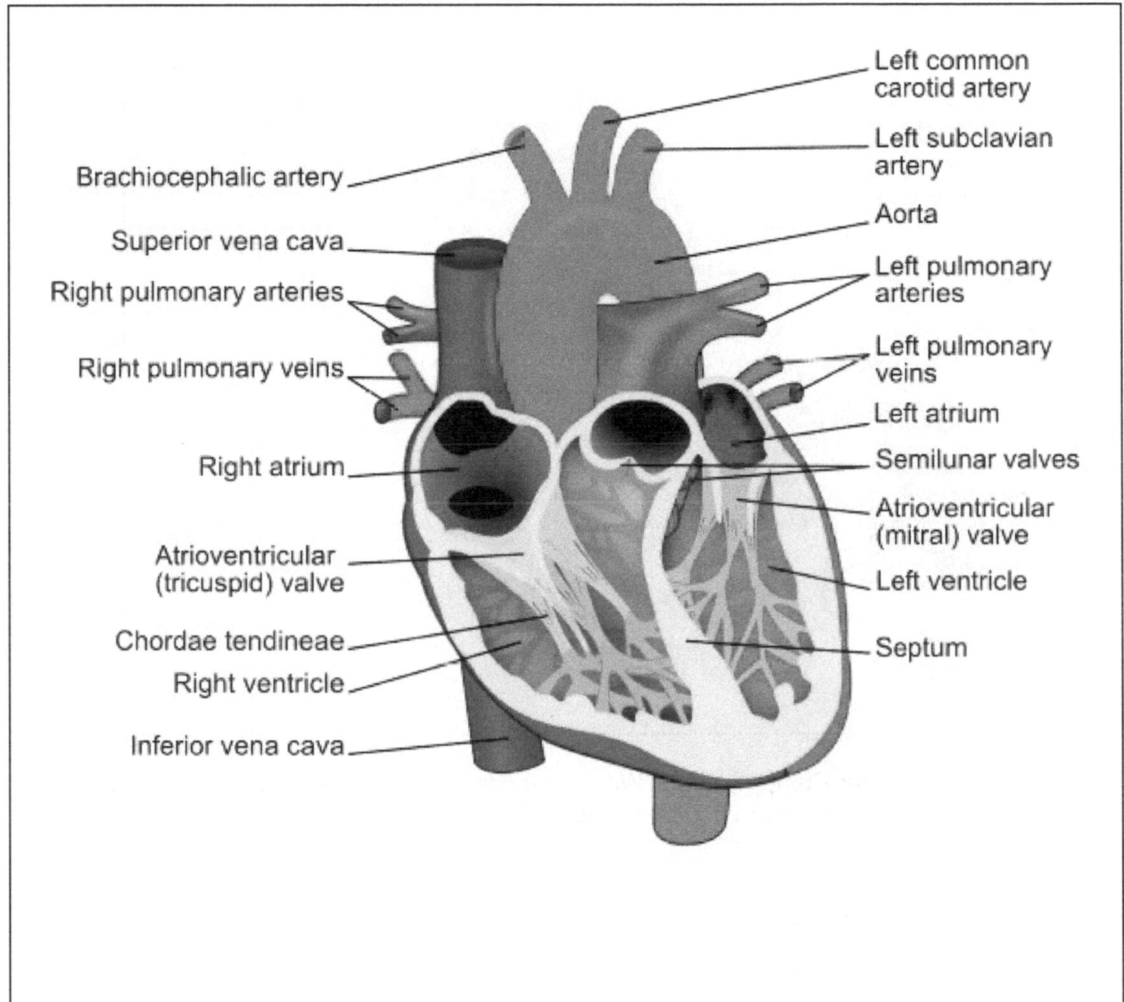

Figure 7-7 Cutaway View of Heart. Source: ZooFari (2010). *Wikimedia Commons*. Licensed under CC BY-SA 3.0 (http://creativecommons.org/licenses/by-sa/3.0)

Exploded View

The exploded view appears to be precisely that: the subject matter seems to be flying away in all directions. This view is helpful for assembling and disassembling mechanisms. Parts catalogs usually contain exploded views for the technician to use to assemble the parts in the correct order.

For example, Figure 7-8 below shows an exploded view of a gear pump. By referring to this diagram, technicians can see all the pieces involved in the part without disassembling it. Notice that the parts are labeled for easy reference.

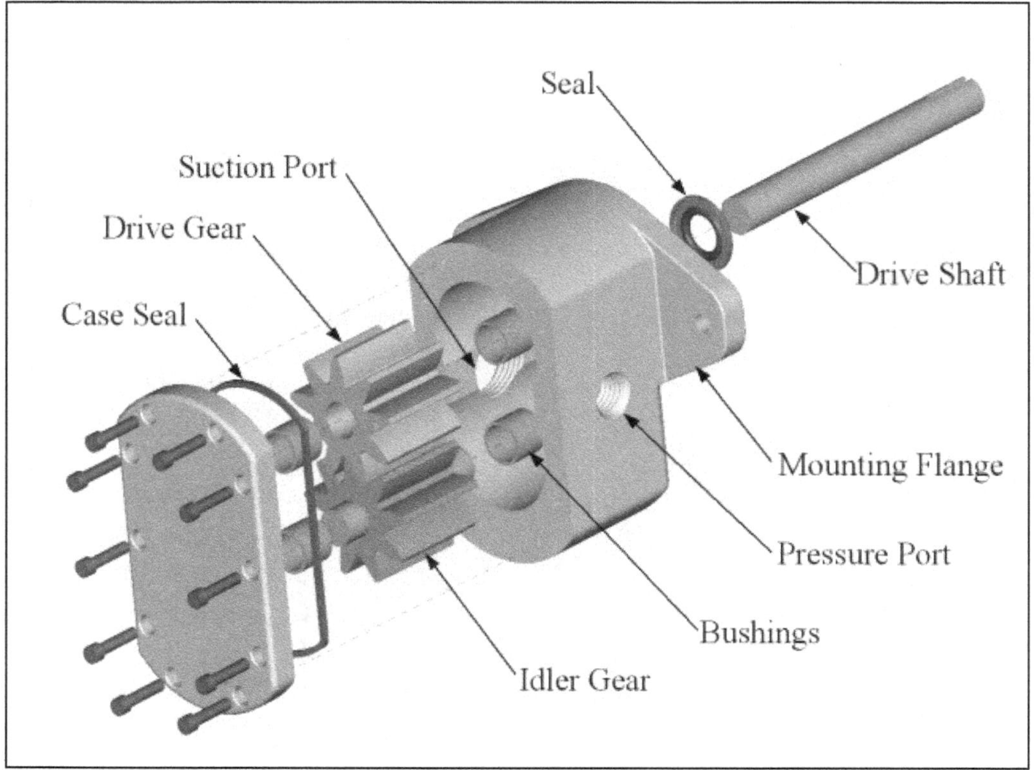

Figure 7-8 Exploded Gear Pump. Source: *Wikimedia Commons.* (2007). Licensed under CC BY-SA 3.0 (http://creativecommons.org/licenses/by-sa/3.0)

Guidelines for Using Drawings

With enough practice, some writers can use graphics software to create the line drawings that accompany their text. When this is not feasible, graphic artists are employed. The following suggestions should be kept in mind when creating line drawings.

- Maintain the same scale as the original subject. A line drawing should be somewhat realistic, but very simplified.
- Use arrows or callouts to point out important features.
- If you use more than one line drawing in a document, maintain the same color scheme and style. For example, don't switch from light blue and gray shadings to black on white. The graphics will not appear to relate to each other.
- Place a caption below the drawing.

Diagrams

Diagrams can be one of the most dynamic of all graphics because the artist has license to change the scale of the original—parts of the diagram may be much larger or smaller in relation to other parts than in reality. The artist also has license to simplify the subject matter considerably so that the primary parts and their relationship can be clearly seen. Diagrams depict a static state of the original, and not a change over time.

A very common use of the diagram is the wiring diagram. Figure 7-9 below shows a labeled drawing of the parts of a doorbell wiring configuration. Notice that the distances between the various connections are not to scale.

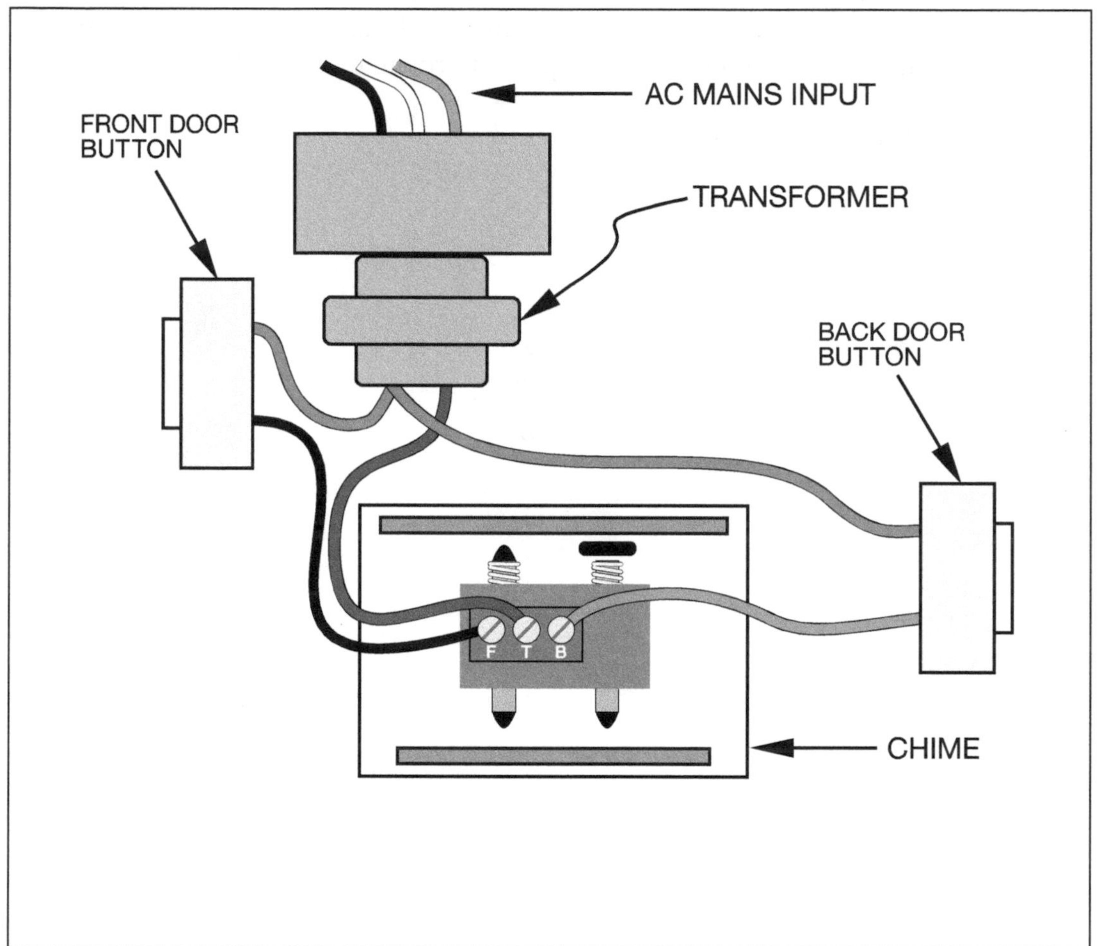

Figure 7-9 Diagram of Doorbell Wiring. Source: Hydrargyrum. (2013). *Wikimedia Commons.* Licensed under CC BY-SA 3.0 (http://creativecommons.org/licenses/by-sa/3.0)

Figure 7-10 below shows the same concept, in a less detailed and more symbolic way. This diagram could be used when only the basic idea needs to be conveyed. The intended user for the diagram below would probably be an electrician or construction professional because of the use of specialized shapes and symbols.

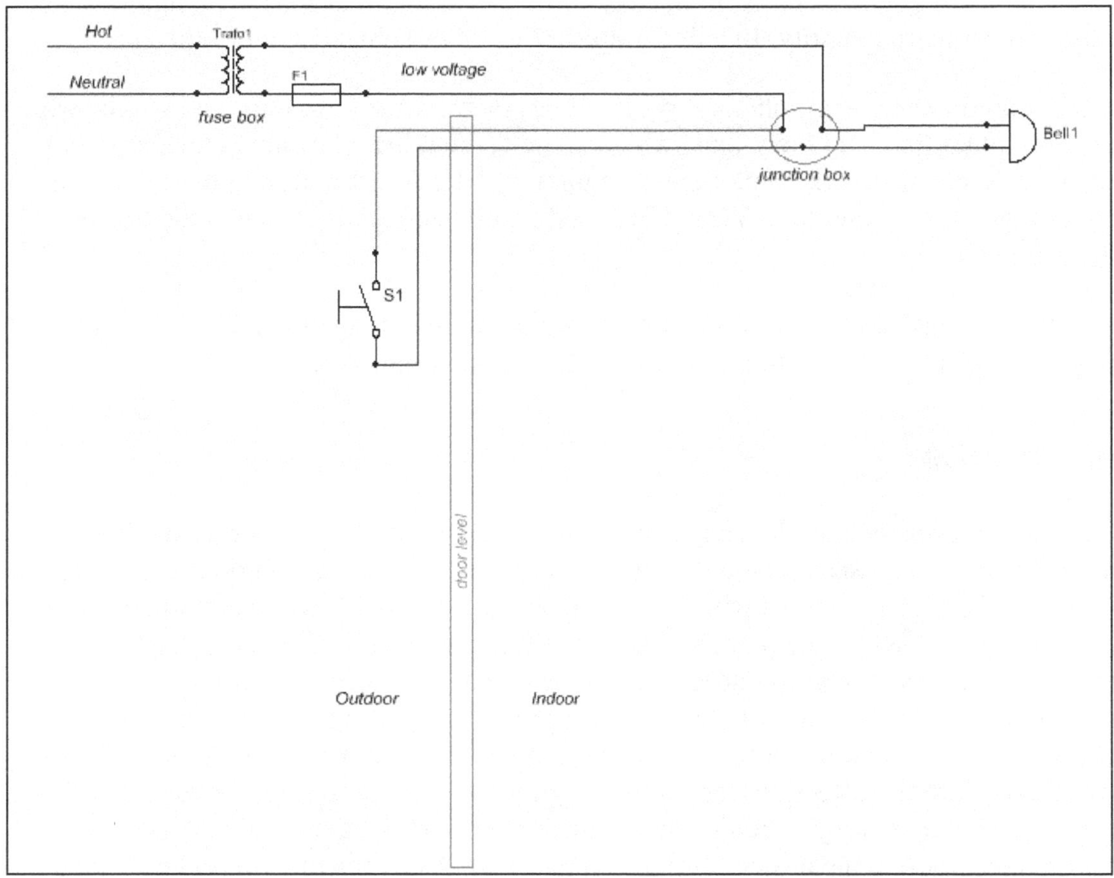

Figure 7-10 Low Voltage Doorbell Wiring Diagram. Source: Dmitry G. (2010). *Wikimedia Commons.* Licensed under CC BY-SA 3.0 (http://creativecommons.org/licenses/by-sa/3.0)

Guidelines for Using Diagrams

Principles to keep in mind when using a diagram are:

- Use labels. Since diagrams often depict very complex subjects, users need a guide to understand what they are seeing. Even if the diagram is simplified and abstract, the user will still need labels.

- If the subject matter is extremely complex, show an overview diagram and label the major sections or items. Then use a detailed diagram of each major item.

- Place the caption below the diagram.

GRAPHS

Graphs are popular ways to show and compare quantities. Bar graphs usually compare quantities at the same point in time, while column or line graphs typically compare quantities over regular intervals. In the cases of bar or column graphs, rectangular shapes are used to compare quantity. In a line graph, a line shows changes over time.

The bar, column, or line graph employs two lines to show the hard data: the x-axis, which is the horizontal line, and the y-axis, which is the vertical line. To show changes over time, always use the x-axis to plot the time intervals. The most common time intervals are years, months, or quarters. Yearly financial reports almost always include line or column graphs.

The terms "graphs" and "charts" are sometimes used interchangeably. Therefore, you may see bar graphs referred to as bar charts. Either one is correct.

Bar Graphs

The bar graph uses rectangular shapes in a horizontal orientation, as opposed to the column graph which uses rectangular shapes vertically. The bar graph on the next page attempts to show that students with debt are more likely to work while attending a 4-year college. It's very easy to see that there is an 8-17% difference in the percentages. The labeling is clear, and the graph does support the conclusion at the bottom of the x-axis: "Students with debit [sic] are likely to work more". The spelling error ("debit" instead of "debt") in the statement undermines the credibility of the graph creator. Another factor that detracts from the effectiveness of this graph is the confusing title: "Student Work Patterns vs Having College Credit Card Debts." The "versus" in the title is expected to show an opposition to a parallel item: this versus that. A clearer title might be: "Student Work Patterns and Student Debt." Or "Student Work Patterns: Students with Debt vs Students without Debt." The graph does support its credibility by stating its method of acquiring the data at the bottom of the graphic.

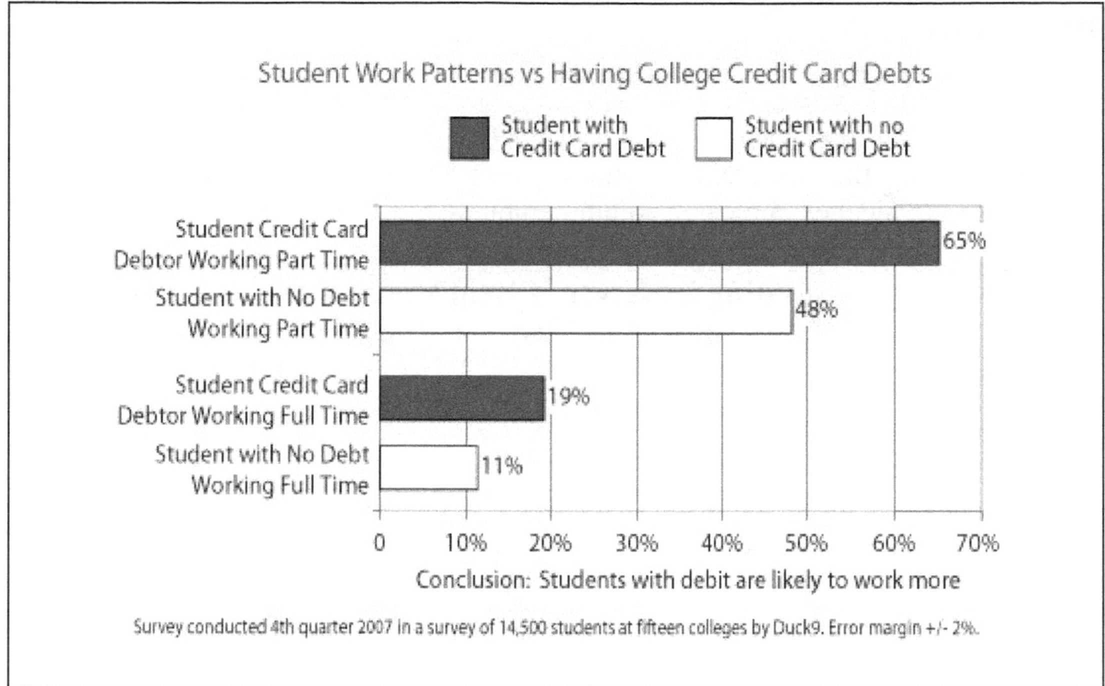

Figure 7-11 Bar Graph. Source: *Duck9.com* (14 April 2014). Used courtesy of Duck9

Column Graphs

The column graph below, found on the National Library of Medicine web site, shows the funding, primarily for grants and research, that the US government has approved from 2009-2013. Note that the time element is tracked on the x-axis and the money on the y-axis. This is very typical example of a column graph.

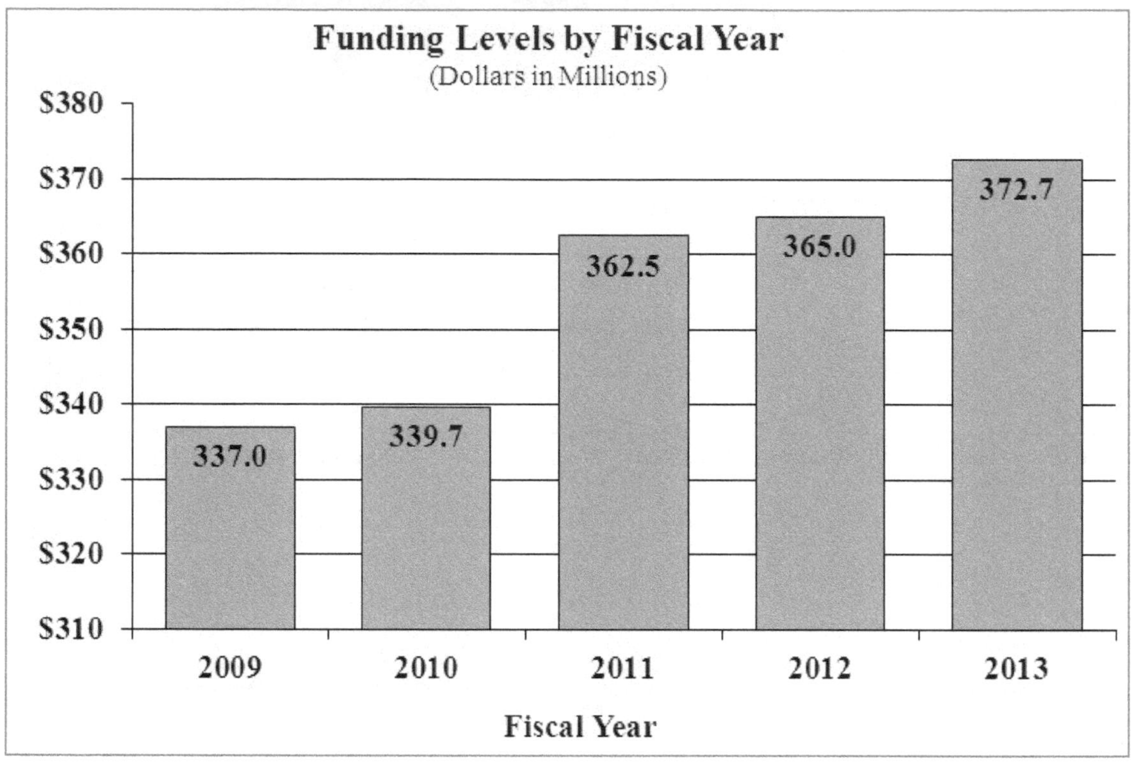

Figure 7-12 Column Graph. Source: U. S. National Library of Medicine. (2013). Public Domain.

The column graph below was created by the U.S. Centers for Disease Control and Prevention. It shows the percentage of people over 18 who report migraine headache, divided into male and female groups. The chart shows age on the x-axis and percentage on the y-axis. The web page where this chart appears gives the following interpretation:

> In 2004, the percentage of adults who experienced a severe headache or migraine during the preceding 3 months decreased with age, from 18% among persons aged 18--44 years to 6% among persons aged ≥75 years. In every age group, the proportion of women who experienced severe headache or migraine was greater than that of men.
>
> Source: CDC.gov (http://www.cdc.gov/mmwr/preview/mmwrhtml/mm5503a6.htm)

In this way, the text summarizes and clarifies the graph, helping the reader form a clear interpretation.

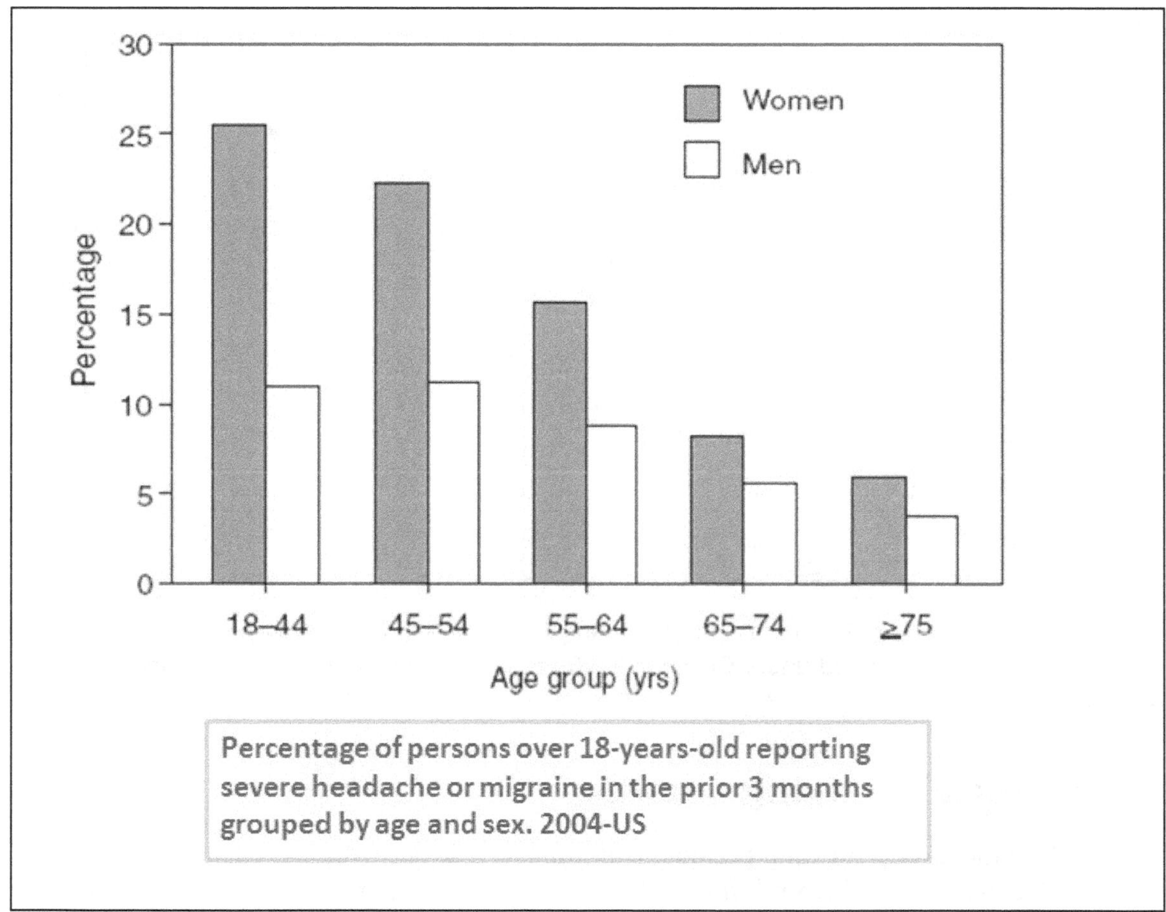

Figure 7-13 Column Graph. Source: U. S. Centers for Disease Control and Prevention. (2004). Public Domain.

Line Graphs

The line graph is an exceptional tool for showing several different items changing over the same period of time. Because it uses points in time, rather than space-consuming rectangles, it can handle more information.

The line graph below shows two trends at the same time—productivity rising and income falling—which is very effective way to demonstrate the point about the disparity between the two. Line graphs can handle many lines, but care must be taken to color-code the lines and label them clearly.

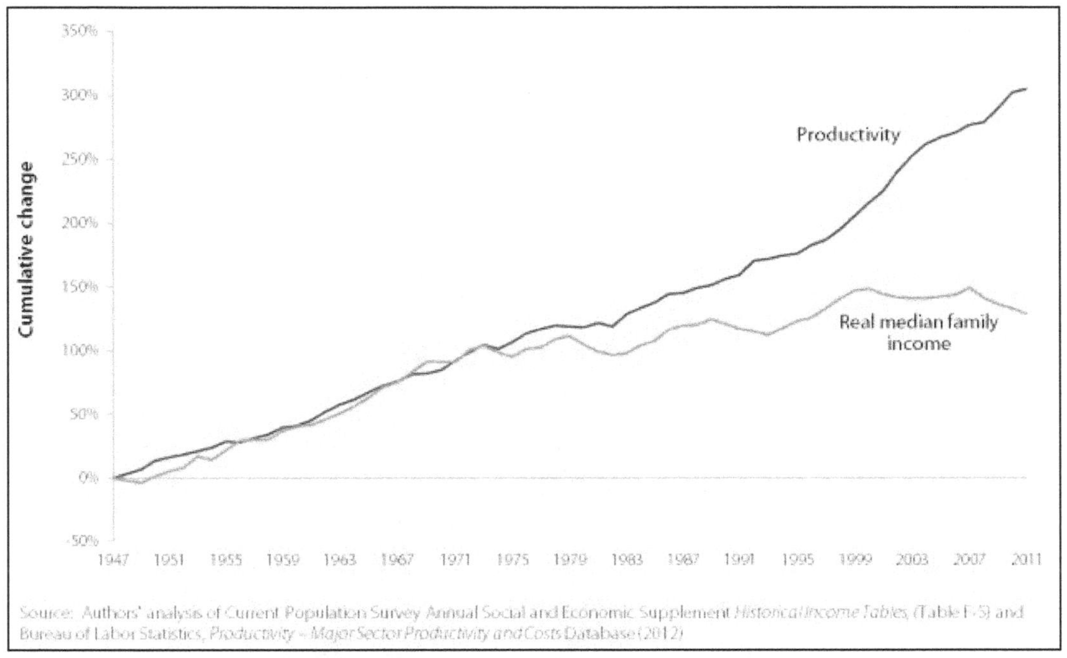

Figure 7-14 Line Graph. Source: State of Working America. Economic Policy Institute. *Wikimedia Commons.* (2009). Licensed under CC BY-SA 3.0 (http://creativecommons.org/ licenses/by-sa/3.0)

Guidelines for Using Graphs

- Use the x-axis for time periods, with the left side showing the earliest time period. Because we read from left to right, we visualize time moving from left to right.
- Money or other tangibles are usually tracked on the y-axis. We visualize the amount stacking up vertically.
- Keep the variables to a minimum. Don't let your graph carry so much information that your main ideas are hidden. Use more than one graph for complex material.
- Label each axis.
- Place a caption below the graph.

CHARTS

Charts are handy for showing percentages, process flow, progress, or organization.

Pie Charts

The pie (or circle) chart is the best method for showing how parts relate to a whole. Just like a pizza, or an apple pie, it's easy to understand the slice size because the whole pie is presented.

Pie charts are the most common way to show budgets and allocation of money. The pie chart below, about the 2014-2015 budget for the Michigan DEQ, shows how much of the budget comes from each funding source. The pie chart is easy to read, and doesn't require a key because the labels and percentages are included in the pie pieces.

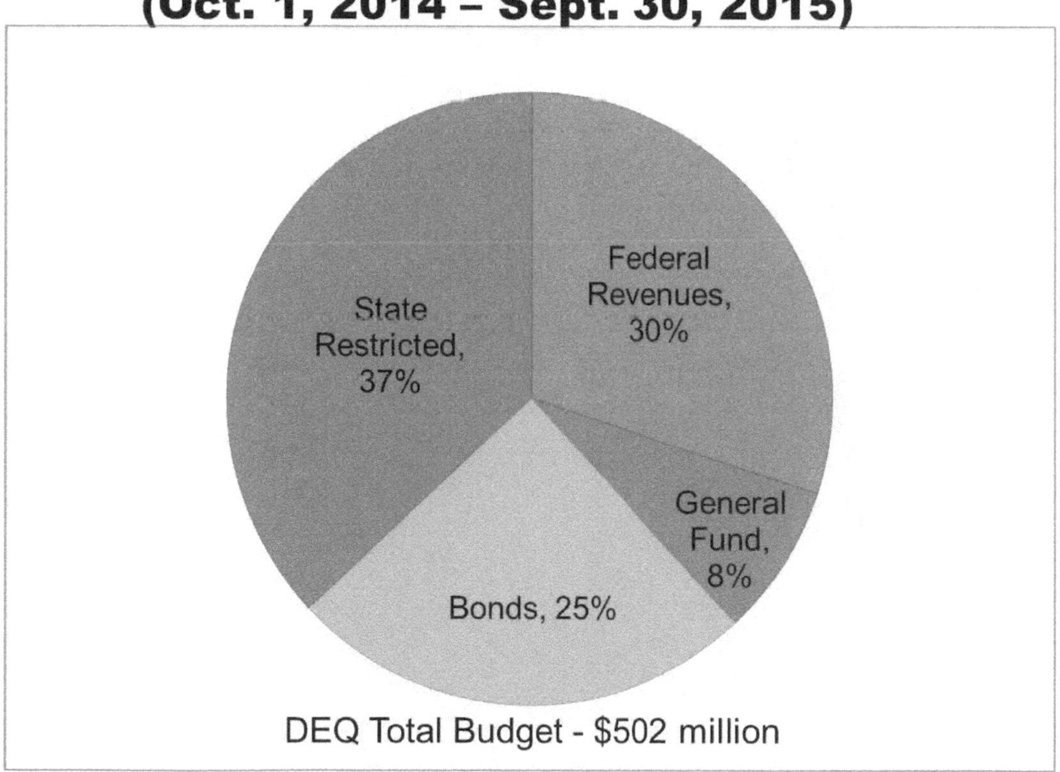

Figure 7-15 Pie Chart. Source: Keconfer. (2014). *Wikimedia Commons.* Licensed under CC BY-SA 4.0 (http://creativecommons.org/licenses/by-sa/4.0)

The biggest slices of the pie chart are usually shown on the left side. Pieces decrease in size as they are placed counter-clockwise around the pie. The smallest slices are often grouped in the upper right-hand area.

Pie charts can represent a limited number of "slices" with clarity, as differences in size become hard to differentiate when slices are small. For example, it is hard to see the difference between a 10% and a 15% slice. Therefore, labeling is extremely important. Pie charts that require more explanation are frequently paired with a table that gives much more detail. As you will see on pages 165-166, tables are the workhorses for showing a lot of information in an accessible manner.

Gantt Charts

Gantt charts look a lot like bar graphs, but they are very different in they way they are created and interpreted. Gantt charts are used to monitor progress for a project. Time is depicted across the x-axis and the various tasks involved with the project are listed on the y-axis. The duration of the task is shown as a rectangle, with the beginning and ending dates as the left and right sides of the rectangle, respectively. The part of the task that has already been completed is shaded.

An example of a simple Gantt chart for a software project is shown below.

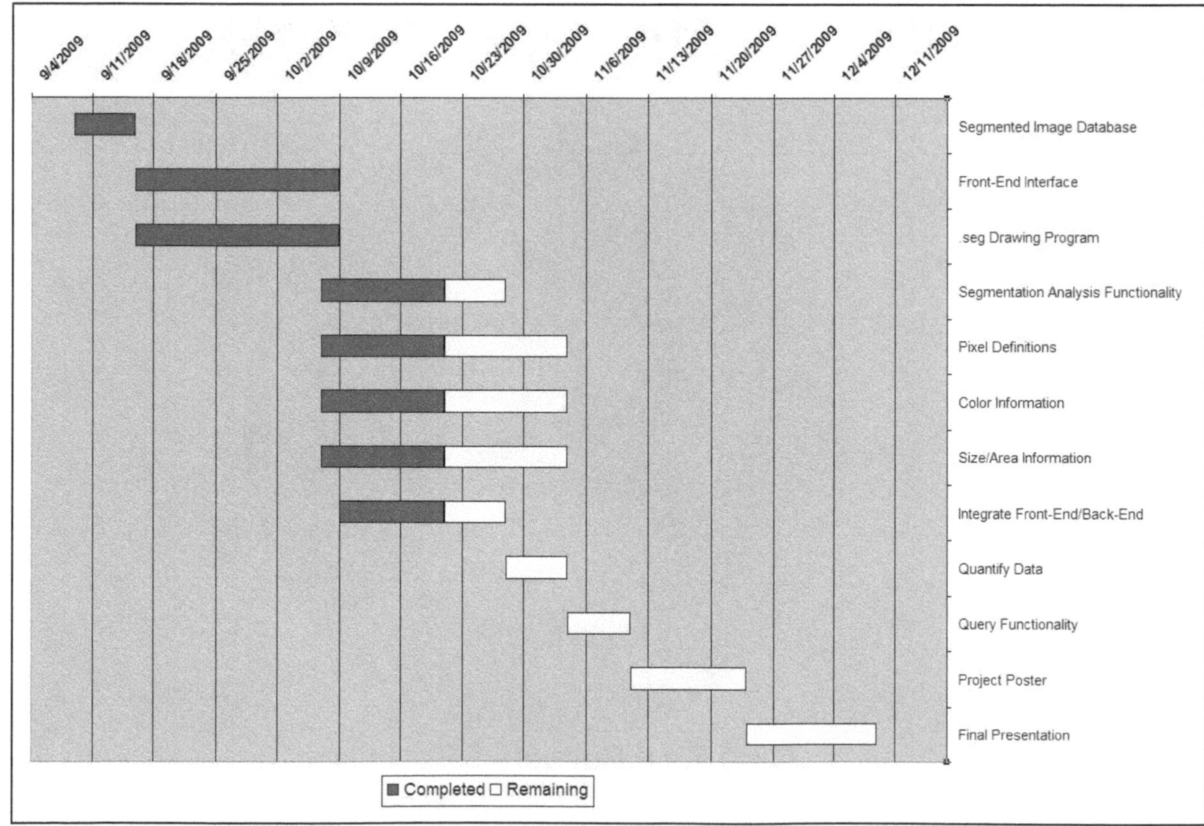

Figure 7-16 Gantt Chart. Source: Alex Thompson and Derrek Harrison (2009) *Wikimedia Commons*. Public domain.

Gantt charts are essentially timeline charts showing the progress of a project. Below is a timeline chart produced by NASA showing the progress of Mars exploration. In this chart, red indicates missions already flown, and orange are missions in development. The blue lines are the various goals of the missions. Note that the first two missions were about seeking water only; preparation for human exploration began in 2001.

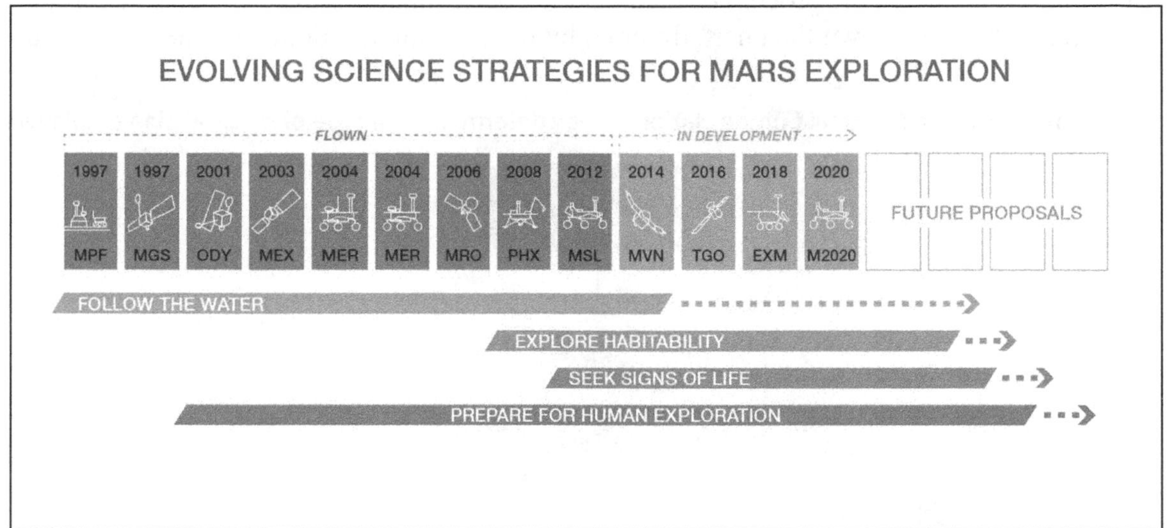

Fig. 7-17 Gantt Chart for Mars Exploration. Source: NASA (2013). *Wikimedia Commons*. Public domain.

Microsoft Excel has a Gantt chart tool that can be quickly learned to create a Gantt chart. A simple Gantt chart can also be produced through the table tool in various word processors. If you are ever in charge of a project, you will want to create a Gantt chart to help determine how long the project will take, what tasks are being completed on time, and what is the status of the project.

Flow Charts

Frequently, graphics such as flow charts are created to show the sequential steps that make up a particular process. Since a process, by definition, takes place over time, a flow chart is the perfect graphic choice to accompany the textual description. Figure 7-18 is a flow chart that shows the process of medical plan determinations. The process begins at the top and "flows" down the chart, diverted by the decision diamonds all the way down.

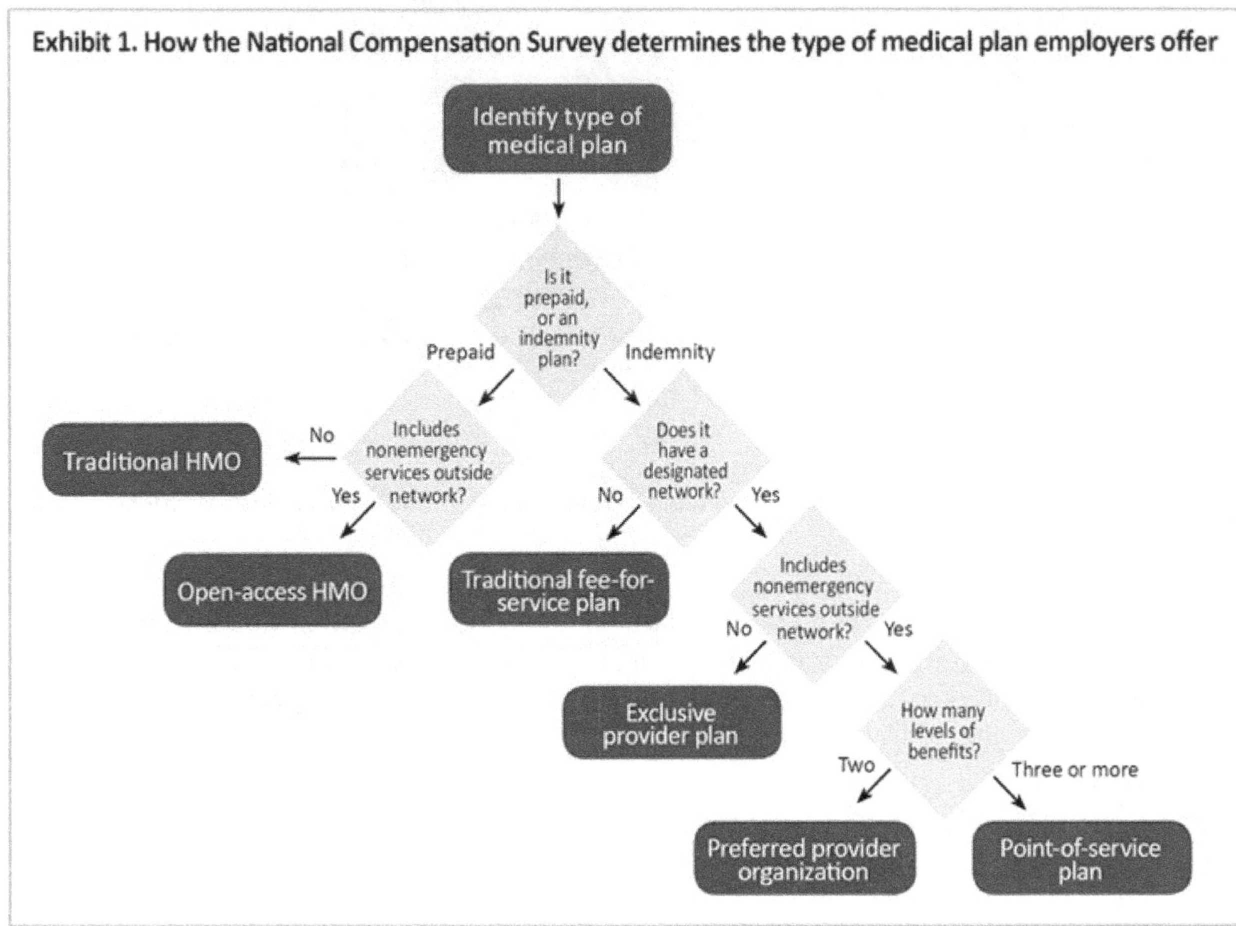

Figure 7-18 Medical Plan Flow Chart. Source: U.S. Department of Labor, Bureau of Labor Statistics. (2015). *BLS.gov.* Public Domain.

Figure 7-19 shows an example of a "swimlane" flow chart, showing the points where the process crosses into the responsibility areas (shown by the columns) of different groups for a customer order. Notice that the beginning and end shapes are rounded and that the major steps are rectangles. Flow charts such as this one are very helpful for pinpointing how groups work together, and where job duties and responsibilities lie.

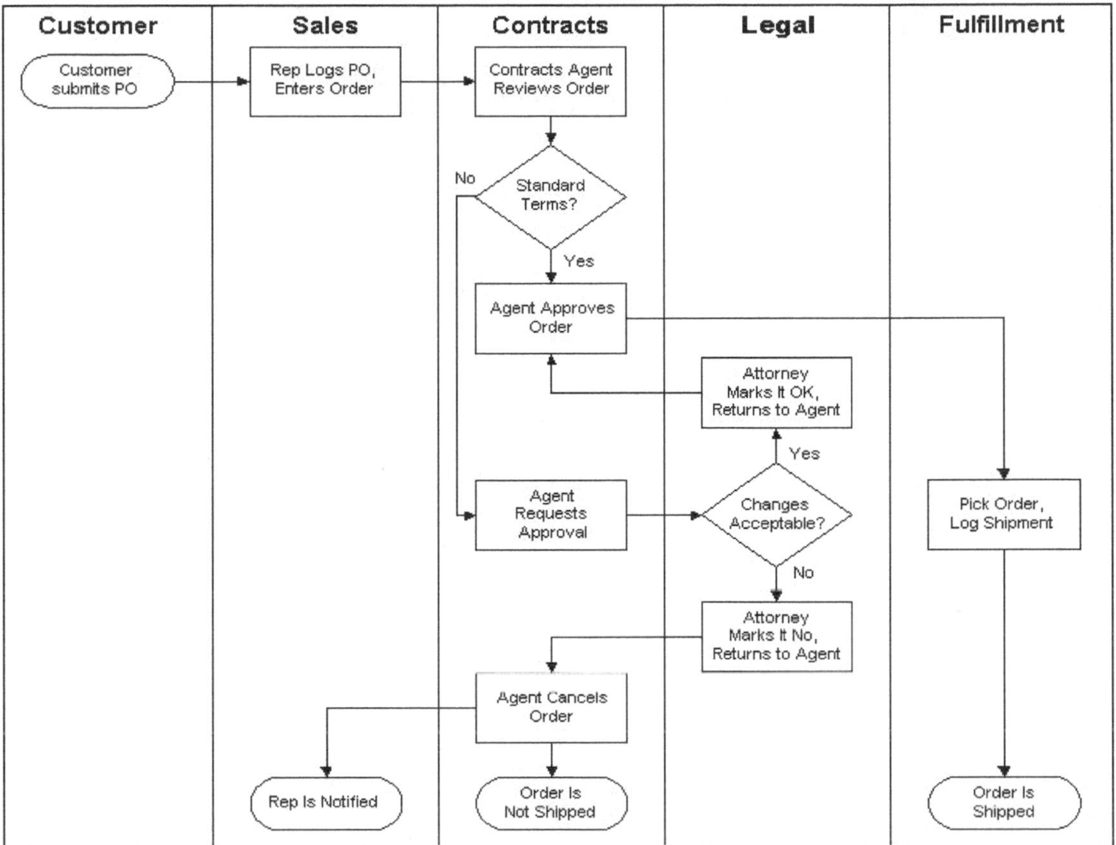

Figure 7-19 An Example of a "Swimlane" Flow Chart. Source: Paul Kerr. (2006). *Wikimedia Commons*. Public Domain.

Traditional flow charts use the following shapes:

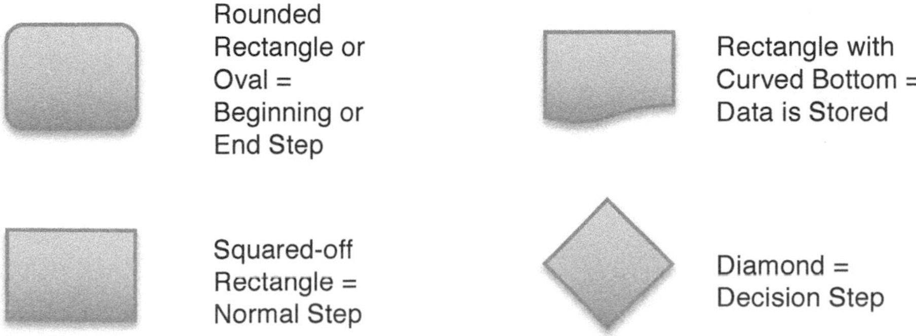

Organizational Charts

Organizational charts are the standard method to show hierarchy. They typically show the president or CEO and then branch downwards, showing all major work areas and departments. They are useful for showing who reports to whom. Newcomers to an organization can find them very useful for figuring out how the pieces fit together.

Figure 7-20 below shows an organizational chart for the Department of Defense. Notice that the chart includes the logo, increasing the credibility and assuring the association with the US Government.

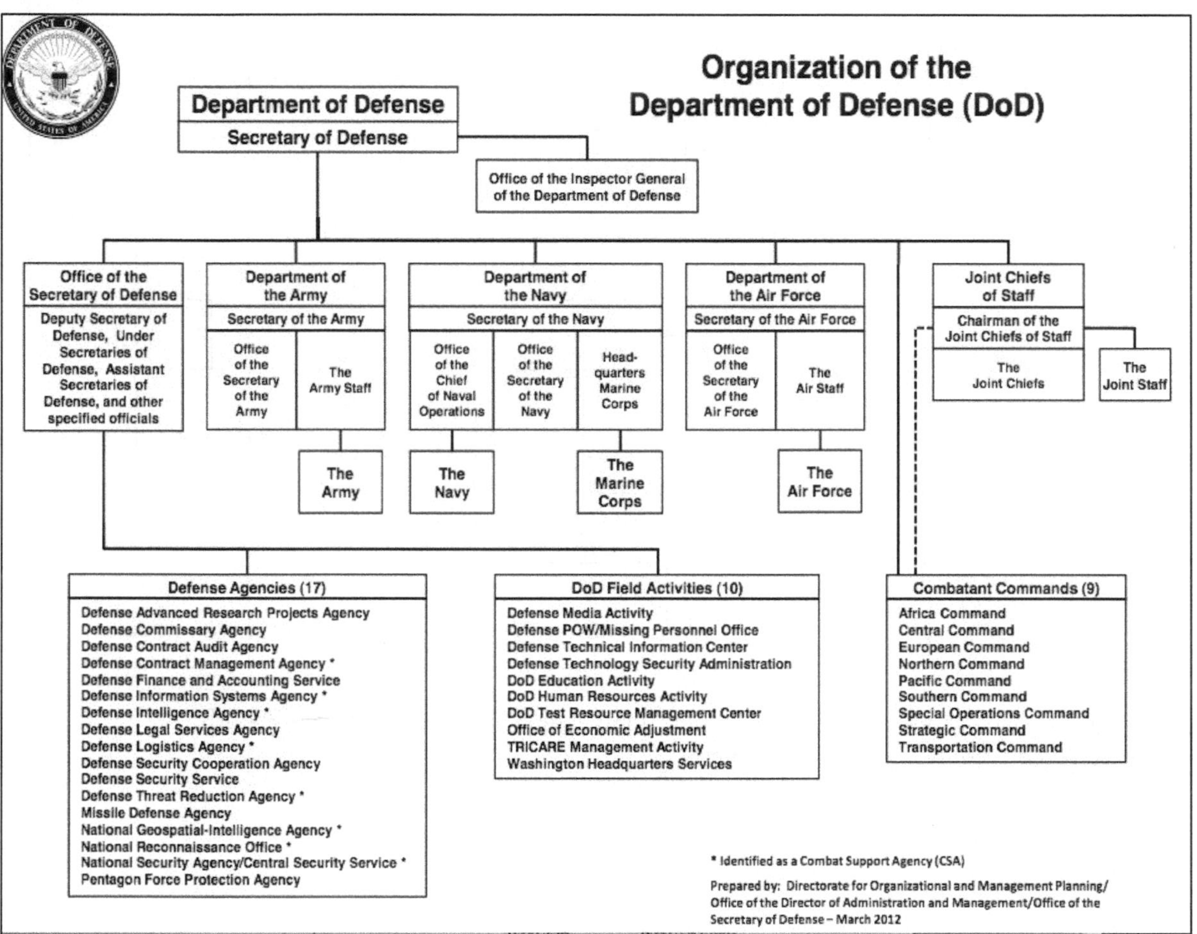

Figure 7-20 Organizational Chart. Source: Office of the Secretary of Defense. (2012). *ODAM.Defense.gov.* Public Domain.

A family tree, pedigree chart, or any other type of chart that shows derivation or relationship is considered an organizational chart.

Figure 7-21 below shows how the original research version of UNIX inspired other operating systems, including Mac OSX.

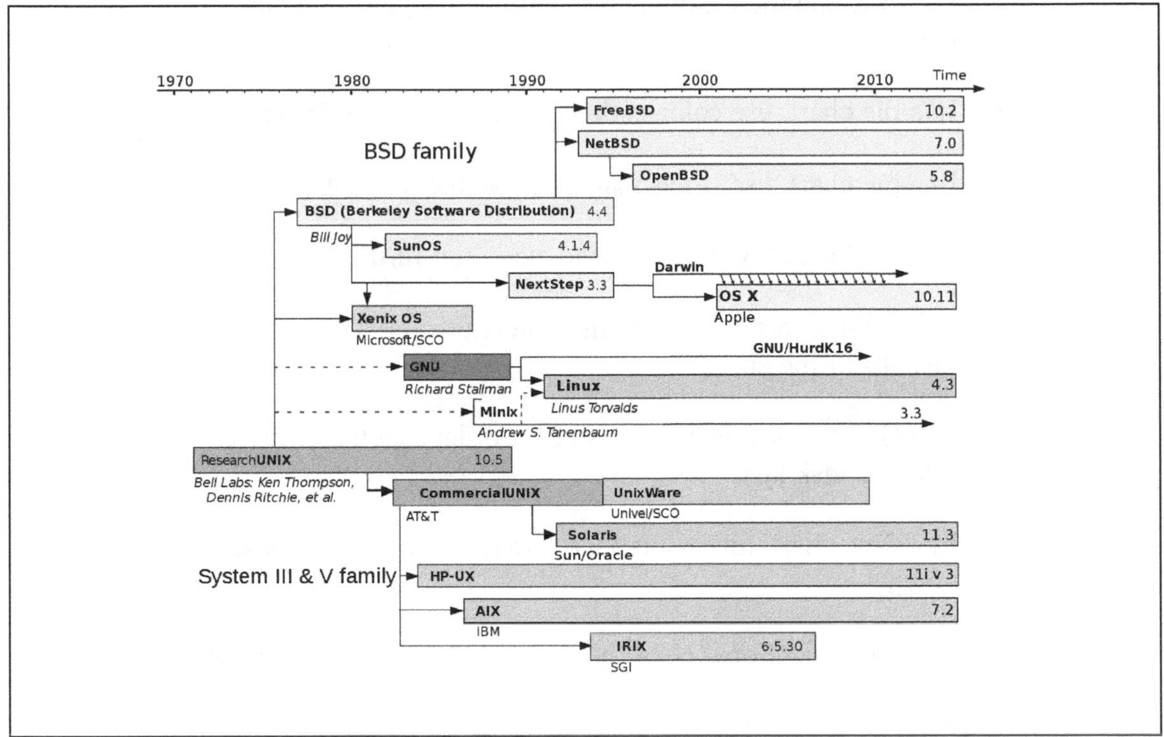

Figure 7-21 Development Family Tree. Source: Guillem, Wereon, Hotmocha (2009) *Wikimedia Commons.* Public Domain.

Guidelines for Using Charts

- Use pie charts to show percentages of a whole.
- In a pie chart, merge very thin "slices" into a bigger category whenever feasible, and then explain the group in a key, or in a table below the pie chart.
- In a pie chart, use color-coding so that each slice is clearly visible.
- In a pie chart, use labels that also give the percentages.
- Use a table below a pie chart to explain it further.
- In a Gantt chart, use equal time intervals on the x-axis so that readers can visualize time easily.
- In a Gantt chart, list the tasks in the order that they start no matter how long the task lasts.
- In a flow chart, make sure there are no continuous loops, or arrows that go nowhere.
- In an organizational chart, branch downwards or left to right.
- Place a caption below any type of chart.

TABLES

Tables are perhaps the most common—and easiest to create—of all the types of graphics. They can be used by themselves, or in conjunction with another graphic, adding hard data to a more visual depiction.

Tables use the x- and y-axis formula, except the x-axis items are called columns and the y-axis items are called rows. Each "cell," or box, in the table is determined by how the column and row intersect.

A good example of a common but fairly complex table, a bus schedule, is shown in Table 7-22. In this table, time is shown on both the x-axis and y-axis, but larger time periods such as the day are shown on the x-axis. To determine when the bus will arrive, the user must first determine the day and the general time of day on the x-axis and then find the specific times on the y-axis.

Notice that the table caption is **above** the table rather than below the table. Tables are the exception to the caption placement rule.

Table 7-1 Bus Schedule. Source: Oran Viriyincy. (2009). "Readable bus stop schedule mockup" *Flickr.com.* Licensed under CC BY-SA 2.0 (https://creativecommons.org/licenses/by-sa/2.0)

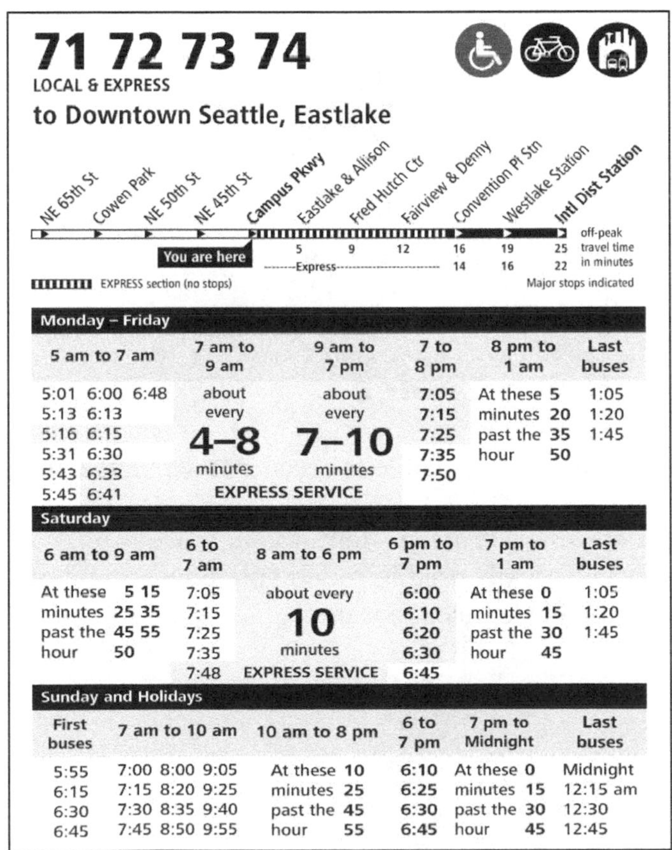

71 72 73 74

LOCAL & EXPRESS

to Downtown Seattle, Eastlake

NE 65th St, Cowen Park, NE 50th St, NE 45th St, **Campus Pkwy**, Eastlake & Allison, Fred Hutch Ctr, Fairview & Denny, Convention Pl Stn, Westlake Station, **Intl Dist Station**

You are here

	Eastlake & Allison	Fred Hutch Ctr	Fairview & Denny	Convention Pl Stn	Westlake Station	Intl Dist Station	
	5	9	12	16	19	25	off-peak travel time in minutes
Express				14	16	22	

EXPRESS section (no stops) — Major stops indicated

Monday – Friday

5 am to 7 am	7 am to 9 am	9 am to 7 pm	7 to 8 pm	8 pm to 1 am	Last buses
5:01 6:00 6:48	about	about	7:05	At these 5	1:05
5:13 6:13	every	every	7:15	minutes 20	1:20
5:16 6:15	4–8	7–10	7:25	past the 35	1:45
5:31 6:30			7:35	hour 50	
5:43 6:33	minutes	minutes	7:50		
5:45 6:41	EXPRESS SERVICE				

Saturday

6 am to 9 am	6 to 7 am	8 am to 6 pm	6 pm to 7 pm	7 pm to 1 am	Last buses
At these 5 15	7:05	about every	6:00	At these 0	1:05
minutes 25 35	7:15	10	6:10	minutes 15	1:20
past the 45 55	7:25		6:20	past the 30	1:45
hour 50	7:35	minutes	6:30	hour 45	
	7:48	EXPRESS SERVICE	6:45		

Sunday and Holidays

First buses	7 am to 10 am	10 am to 8 pm	6 to 7 pm	7 pm to Midnight	Last buses
5:55	7:00 8:00 9:05	At these 10	6:10	At these 0	Midnight
6:15	7:15 8:20 9:25	minutes 25	6:25	minutes 15	12:15 am
6:30	7:30 8:35 9:40	past the 45	6:30	past the 30	12:30
6:45	7:45 8:50 9:55	hour 55	6:45	hour 45	12:45

Tables can carry a substantial amount of information. The tax tables in the IRS tax preparation guide are a good example of a well-designed table. See Table 7-2 below. Notice how the table uses shading and white space to show the cells rather than a matrix of black lines. The table is clean and easy to read. Also, notice the reader-centered language in the header rows.

Table 7-2 Tax Table. Source: 1040 Tax Tables 2014. (2015). *IRS.gov.* Public Domain.

If line 43 (taxable income) is—		And you are—			
At least	But less than	Single	Married filing jointly *	Married filing separately	Head of a household
		Your tax is—			
2,000					
2,000	2,025	201	201	201	201
2,025	2,050	204	204	204	204
2,050	2,075	206	206	206	206
2,075	2,100	209	209	209	209
2,100	2,125	211	211	211	211
2,125	2,150	214	214	214	214
2,150	2,175	216	216	216	216
2,175	2,200	219	219	219	219
2,200	2,225	221	221	221	221
2,225	2,250	224	224	224	224
2,250	2,275	226	226	226	226
2,275	2,300	229	229	229	229
2,300	2,325	231	231	231	231
2,325	2,350	234	234	234	234
2,350	2,375	236	236	236	236
2,375	2,400	239	239	239	239
2,400	2,425	241	241	241	241
2,425	2,450	244	244	244	244
2,450	2,475	246	246	246	246
2,475	2,500	249	249	249	249

Guidelines for Using Tables

- Consider shading to enable the reader to separate columns or rows.
- Consider using a “narrow” font if your space is tight. For example, Arial Narrow is typically used in catalog price sheets and other complex tables for a clean, yet legible, appearance.
- Place a caption above the table.

LOGOS, SYMBOLS, ICONS, CLIP ART

Simple, single-message graphics are abundantly visible in stores, advertisements, on the Internet, and even on our clothing. These messages are a type of code because they are an abbreviated representation of a much larger message or entity.

Consider the Nike "swoosh," the American flag, or the logo for your college. All were designed to evoke a visual, immediate association.

Logos

A logo is a symbol of a company or organization. It appears on all products and communications that a company or organization sends or produces—from letterhead to car hood ornament. The word "logo" comes from the Greek "logos," which means "word." Logos are always copyrighted, and writers must not use any logos for which they are not authorized.

Logos are easy to associate with the company and product. When marketing and advertising specialists realized the advantages for logo usage in the 1970's, the revolution of logo use began. The rapid international expansion of markets and media has ensured that logos are part of our everyday lives, whether in New York City or Shanghai. Some of the most prevalent—and successful—logos include FedEx, Coke, Nike, Adidas, Mercedes Benz, and McDonald's.

Symbols

Symbols are characters that can stand for words or simple operations. The ampersand (&) is a symbol for "and." The percentage sign (%) is a mathematical symbol, meaning "divided by 100." The dollar sign ($) takes the place of "dollars." Below is a list of symbols found in Microsoft Word by using the Insert>Symbol command.

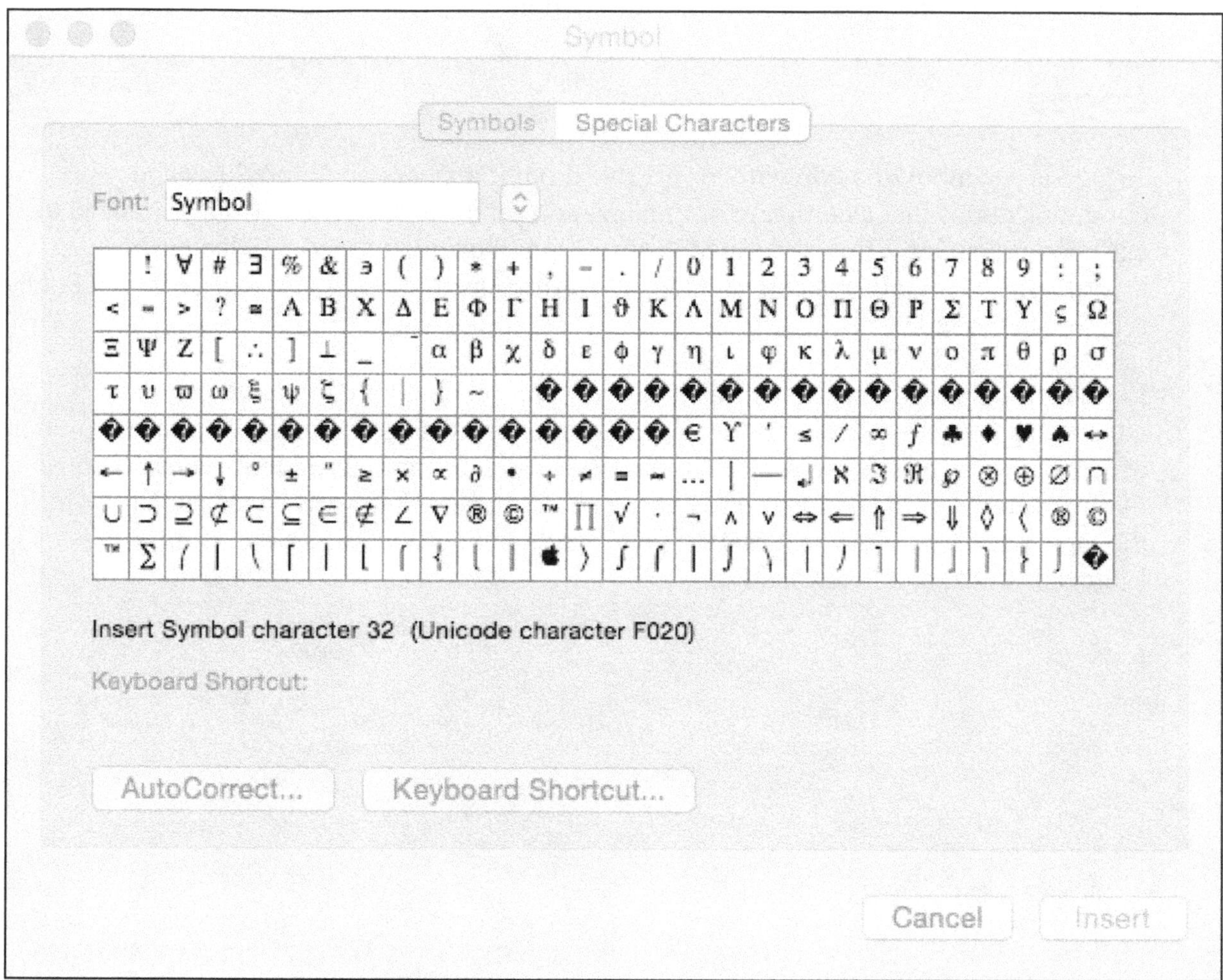

Figure 7-22 Microsoft Word Symbols Screen Capture

Icons

Icons are different from logos and symbols because they convey a single piece of information in a very simple, stylized manner. Because icons are so heavily used, they are considered "public domain" and do not need to show a source.

The icon for restroom is understandable by any member of our society.

An icon that is very useful in technical communications is the warning icon:

Another useful image for print and online communications is the icon for finding help:

Clip Art

Clip art can be used successfully to convey a single idea, mood, or tone. Clip art is readily available from hundreds of online sites. Always check the re-use information. In some cases, you are required to buy the clip art, and in most cases you are required to give the source.

Clip art must be geared toward the message and audience. The piece of clip art below, normally shown in green, was created to encourage consumers to "buy green," or be aware of how the choices they make at the grocery store affect the planet. It is included in a collection of clip art appropriate for Earth Day publications. It is meant to represent a shopping cart with items in it, and despite the lack of detail, the concept is very recognizable. Because the drawing is cartoonish and symbolic, the mood is light. This piece of clip art would be appropriate on Earth Day event flyers, web sites, and even with children. The piece of clip art would NOT be appropriate in a scientific report.

Figure 7-23 Clip Art: Buy Green. Source: Netalloy. (2012). *OpenClipArt.org.* Public Domain.

Guidelines for Using Logos, Symbols, Icons, and Clip Art

- If you are using someone else's logo or symbol, do so very carefully. Companies have special rules about how you can use their copyrighted images. Get permission.
- Icons that are universal do not require sources or permission. They are considered public domain.
- Clip art is easy to use, and dangerous. Be conservative with clip art choices and avoid the urge to "pretty up" a document with distracting images. Also, check the re-use rules.
- Clip art typically doesn't require a caption.

GUIDELINES FOR USING GRAPHICS

Below are some guidelines for placing graphics in documents, web pages, and presentations. Graphics can be amazingly helpful for the user, but you should use care.

- Because Internet graphics are relatively easy to find, and simple to copy and paste, there is an inherent danger with their use: failure to cite the source. Unless you created the graphic yourself, you must give the source. If you did create the graphic, you may cite yourself.
- Instructions rely heavily on graphics. Be generous with effective graphics, including one with each step, or at least with the most complex steps.
- Introduce your graphic before you place it. The graphic should go after the text that first refers to it. (The caption is not part of an introduction to the graphic.)
- Use a caption that includes the figure or table number, the title of the graphic, and the source. The word processing software will help you to automate the numbering and formatting.
- Place a caption below the graphic unless the graphic is a table. Captions for tables belong above the table.
- Size the graphic appropriately. Select and pull on the corner of the graphic to extend it to a size where the important detail can readily be seen. Miniature graphics are useless, and over-sized graphics take over the page. Provide balance.
- Use some white space around the graphic. Otherwise, it will look crowded.
- Be honest with the information in your graphic, just as you do with writing the textual components. Do not exaggerate or present the material in a way that the truth could be misconstrued.
- Be sensitive to international audiences. If you know that your document will be seen by people in cultures other than your own, do some research to find out what images are appropriate and what colors to use.
- Make color have meaning, if only to differentiate groups of items. Using color to "pretty up" a graphic reduces its value.
- Double-check the spelling in your graphic. Sometimes spell checkers won't include graphic text.
- Use a key to the information in the graphic if it's not very obvious what the colors, shapes, arrows, etc. mean.
- Zoom in. Take out detail that could detract from the central message.
- Go through the following table for choosing the correct graphic for your purpose.
- Go through the Graphic Checklist on page 173.

CHOOSING THE RIGHT GRAPHIC

To Show...	Type	Consider Using...
Appearance	Exact	Photograph
	Simplified	Drawing
Composition	Percentages	Pie Chart
	Parts	Diagram
	See Inside?	Cutaway Drawing
	See How Assembled?	Exploded View Drawing
Comparison	Of Quantities	Bar Graph
	Of Size, Shape	Drawing, Diagram
Concept	Commercial	Logo
	Other	Symbol, Icon, Clip Art
Organization	Hierarchical	Organizational Chart
	Of Components	Diagram
Change	In Appearance	Photograph, Drawing
	Of Quantity	Graph
	Exact	Line Graph
	Simplified	Bar Graph
	Of Progress	Gantt Graph
Relationships	Data	Bar Graph
	Things	Diagram, Organizational Chart
Process	Exact	Flow Chart
	Simplified	Diagram
Data	Exact	Table
	Simplified	Graph
Location	Exact	Map, Drawing
	Simplified	Sign, Icon, Symbol

GRAPHICS *Checklist* ✔

An Effective Graphic...	✔
Has a caption with figure number, title, and source	
Is placed after the text that introduces it	
Is the appropriate type of graphic for type of information, audience, purpose, format	
Has enough white space to not look crowded	
Is sized to be able to see important elements clearly	
Is accurate and consistent with regard to surrounding text	
Honestly portrays information	
Appeals to the audience	
Uses labels and a key where needed to explain important elements	
Uses correct grammar, spelling, and punctuation	

DISCUSSIONS

1. Find an example of an effective graphic on the Internet or in print. Share it with your class and explain why it is effective, using the checklist above.

2. Find an example of a graphic on the Internet or in print that fails to meet all of the criteria on page 173. Share it with the class and explain its strengths and weaknesses.

3. Respond to the following opinion: "Graphics on the Internet should not require a source. Anything I find on the Internet is free. Therefore, I shouldn't have to state where the graphic originated."

EXERCISES

1. **Write a progress report in hard-copy memo format** to your instructor describing your progress in the class. Include a Gantt chart.

2. **Create an 8-1/2" x 11" one-page flyer** for a lost pet. Include the most appropriate graphic choice.

3. **Match each item** on the left with the best graphic choice to depict it:

1. Stock fluctuation over a 3 year period.	a. Icon
2. Escaped convict	b. Table
3. NBA team statistics	c. Flow chart
4. Racial composition of the student body at your school	d. Bar graph
5. Steps in making paper	e. Organizational chart
6. Comparison of wages among 5 groups of wage-earners	f. Line graph
7. Chain of command in a major corporation	g. Diagram
8. Solar system	h. Drawing
9. Indication of whether or not smoking is permitted	i. Photograph
10. Names and locations of the warning lights on your car dashboard	j. Pie chart

4. Select a chart or graph from a current news source, such as *USA Today*, and analyze its effectiveness. What is it trying to illustrate? Is it ethical? How would you change the graphic to make it more accurate, understandable, or ethical? **Write a hard-copy memo report** to your instructor in which you evaluate the chart or graph and make suggestions for improvement.

8 - User Instructions

A set of instructions can be thought of as a process description written directly to the person who must carry out a procedure safely and effectively. Therefore, a very careful analysis of audience must be done. You must determine how much the reader already knows about the activity itself and about related skills, equipment, and tools.

The communication triangle for a set of instructions shows emphasis on the audience as shown in Figure 8-1 below:

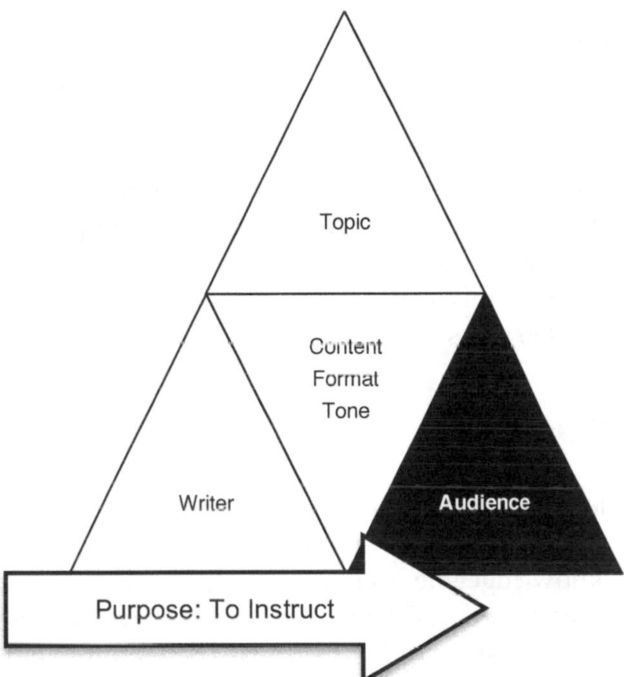

Figure 8-1 Communication Triangle for Instructions

ANALYZING YOUR AUDIENCE

You must find out how the audience will be using your instructions. Readers may just need to refer to certain sections from time to time, or they may need to follow your steps from start to finish to achieve success for complex sequential activities, such as assembling an IKEA table, programming an electronic device, or installing an icemaker.

You must know where the audience will be reading your instructions. Will people be driving a forklift? Will they be using a computer? Will they be outdoors? Knowing where your audience will be referring to your instructions will determine the format and materials you use. If your audience is learning how to pot plants, you might create laminated cards to have on the potting table, where dirt and water are likely to be present. Use the External Audience Worksheet on page 196 to carefully analyze your audience.

Vocabulary

You must be careful to use words that the audience already knows or else give definitions of new terms that the audience will need to know to do the procedure. You must use the same terms for the same items throughout. For example, using the term "set switch" in one sentence and "operating switch" in another for the same switch could greatly confuse your audience. Readers may go frantically to your list of materials or diagram of the device to find both items.

Sentence Structure

Begin each step with a verb in command form. "You" is understood and need not be stated. An example is: "**Bolt the oil pan** to the chassis." Or, you could use an introductory phrase and still begin with the command: "Using a hex wrench, **bolt the oil pan** to the chassis."

Avoid "recipe English." Recipe English leaves out important noun markers (articles) such as "the" and "a." These omissions can cause confusion. For example: "Ship sinks today" could be a command to crate up some sinks and send them to Ohio. In a completely different context, one might read this sentence as a statement that a ship has sunk or is scheduled to be sunk. "Ship the sinks today" is different from "The ship sinks today."

More than One Audience

If you have more than one audience, you may have to write on two different levels at the same time. One effective way to do this is to write simply, provide lots of helpful notes and graphics for the less knowledgeable user, and provide notes with more elaborate information for the more savvy reader. Or, you can write a "Getting Started" type of document in addition to the regular set of instructions. The Getting Started pages help the novice get somewhat familiar with the equipment, terminology, and fastest way to achieve some kind of success.

Important: A crucial point to remember in writing instructions is that most readers will not read the entire set of instructions before beginning; therefore, you must make sure that any necessary cautions or warnings are placed before the description of the step to which they pertain. Otherwise, your reader may get electrocuted/covered with glue/eviscerated or otherwise harmed, or even just embarrassed.

DETERMINING YOUR MAJOR SECTIONS

A set of instructions usually consists of the following elements:

- "How to" title
- Introduction
- Prominent safety info
- Bulleted list of tools and/or supplies
- Estimated time for completion
- Body of instructions with numbered steps and graphics
- Conclusion

Depending on the complexity of the set of instructions, you may also need:

- Table of contents
- Glossary
- Sections
- Steps with sub-steps
- Trouble-shooting table
- Customer support information
- Index

The general introduction of a set of instructions explains why the task should be performed, provides any warnings or safety measures that concern the whole set of instructions, estimates the time to complete the instructions, and describes or lists the tools and equipment that will be needed.

The body of the set of instructions is the numbered steps and graphics. Each step is written in the imperative mood (verb in command form with understood "you") and is sufficiently brief that the reader can perform the step without having to refer back to the step of the instructions.

If there are more than ten steps, break up the steps into major steps and sub-steps. People enjoy reaching smaller goals (major steps that include sub-steps) instead of keeping track of a very long list of individual steps. For example, instructions for washing and drying your family's clothes could be a literal "laundry list" of a hundred steps, or more. However, if you divide the steps into chunks that represent the smaller task, you can group steps under each one.

In a situation in which the step has only one sub-step, combine them into one step as shown below:

Example 1 - Incorrect: Step 1 with only one sub-step

1. Carefully remove the ink cartridge from its packaging.
    a. Tear the slot on the top of the ink cartridge foil.
2. Pull out and remove the orange tab in the slot on the bottom of the ink cartridge.

Example 2 - Correct: Step 1 combined with sub-step

1. By carefully tearing the slot on the top of the ink cartridge foil, remove the cartridge from its packaging.
2. Pull out and remove the orange tab in the slot on the bottom of the ink cartridge.

Figure 8-2 shows the correct way to depict steps and sub-steps. Notice that each major step has at least two sub-steps.

1. Gather the laundry.
    a. Go to the laundry room and get the large blue basket.
    b. Go to everyone's dirty clothes hamper and put the clothes in the blue basket.
    c. Go to the bathrooms and collect all hanging towels and washrags.
    d. Go to the kitchen and collect the used washrag and towels.
2. Sort the laundry.
    a. Make three large piles on the floor in the laundry room:
        - Multi-colored clothes
        - White clothes
        - Delicate clothes
    b. Check each pile to make sure it is not too big for the washing machine. If so, divide that pile into two equal-sized piles.

Figure 8-2 Using Steps and Sub-steps

The **conclusion** of a set of instructions usually sums up the procedure, and may include some helpful hints or alternate methods/uses. Customer Support information is usually found in the conclusion. Information in the conclusion is not critical, but helpful. Many kinds of instructions conclude with a troubleshooter's checklist, a table that helps the reader identify and solve common problems after the task has been completed.

Manuals

A manual is an extensive set of instructions, often bound into a book. Manuals can be classified according to function: procedures, reference, maintenance, and so forth. Manuals are generally written collaboratively because of their size and complexity. As is the case with instructions, writers must analyze audience and purpose carefully. The front matter of a manual generally contains a cover, title page, table of contents, preface, conventions (standard ways of referring to items), and how-to-use-this-manual section. The body is structured according to how it will be used. Two major types of long manuals are:

- **Reference manual**– Reference manuals depend heavily on the index. They are not meant to be read front to back, or even a chapter at a time. Users "dip into" the material, find what they need, and get back out. Repair technicians frequently use reference manuals.

- **Operational manual**– Operational manuals are meant to be read in a sequential manner, building the reader's knowledge and skill. Point of fact: very rare is the user who will read a manual thoroughly before or during the process of learning about the topic. Most users want instant results, to be "up and running" with as little reading as possible. For these users, graphics can be invaluable for demonstrating the general idea and major steps. Users' manuals are usually operational in nature.

Notes, Cautions, Warnings

When you are the writer of a set of instructions, you have an ethical and legal obligation to tell the readers where or how they can get into big trouble, either by hurting themselves or others, or harming equipment. In this area, assumptions can be lethal. Even if you are 100% sure that your audience is 100% sure that electricity is NOT being carried through the wires of the device you are instructing them to assemble, handle, or operate, you must always place a warning. Imagine that one of your readers had little sleep due to newborn infant care, or any other life event that could render even the sharpest individual a partial zombie, and place your warnings, cautions, and danger signs so that they cannot be overlooked.

> **Professionalism & Ethics**
>
> Providing notes, cautions, and warnings demonstrates that you care about your reader.

Notes are used for interesting details, hints for making the task easier, definitions, or any other type of extra information that is not absolutely necessary to the set of instructions. An example of a note in a software manual might be:

> Note: You can also use the Control + C command to copy your selected text.

Figure 8-3 Note

Notes can be placed before, after, or to the side of the material they pertain to. On the other hand, cautions and warnings should always be placed BEFORE the user has the opportunity to harm themselves or the equipment. Place them in a prominent position in your document, in highly legible type, and highlighted with red ink, if available.

Cautions are a type of advisory used for any situation in which the tools or equipment could be damaged:

> **Caution**: This laptop should be kept away from extreme temperatures (less than 32 degrees F, and more than 110 degrees F). Subjecting this laptop to extreme temperatures may cause equipment damage.

Figure 8-4 Caution

Warnings are a type of advisory used to let the user know that injury is possible through use or misuse of the equipment. Use the triangle with exclamation point icon as a graphical marker for any warning.

WARNING: Never use a knife or other metal instrument to remove toast from the toaster. You could receive an electric shock. Unplug the toaster and gently remove the toast.

Figure 8-5 Warning Icon with Text

Danger warnings are the most critical advisory because they let the user know that serious harm—or even death—could occur if the instructions are not followed correctly:

DANGER!!!!!!!

Do not stand on the top of the ladder.

Figure 8-6 Danger Warning Icon with Text

Some warning logos are specific to certain types of hazards. For example, the following international icon is used to advise of an electrical hazard:

Figure 8-7 Electrical Hazard Icon

If you are writing a set of instructions or a manual for a specialized group of people, make sure that you have access to the common symbols used among that group.

Graphics

Graphics are plentiful in a set of instructions. One of the reasons for this is that many people are visual learners. In other words, they prefer to learn by seeing rather than reading. Even those who prefer to read can use the graphics to confirm that they understand the steps.

Use the Choosing the Right Graphic table on page 172 to determine what types of graphics would be most helpful for your instructions. For example, if you are teaching the reader to hook up a computer system, you could show a simplified diagram of all the parts and connections. Also, refer to the Graphics chapter for more comprehensive information about how to use graphics.

PLANNING THE DOCUMENT CYCLE

Writing a set of instructions is one of the most difficult—and underestimated—projects. Its complexity comes from the fact that your audience must not only read and understand the document, but they must be able to precisely and safely perform a given task. Therefore, your document cycle for a set of instructions in many cases will include SME (subject matter expert) approval to make sure all details are correct. You must include a testing phase. (See Figure 8-8 below.) Why? Because your document is causing a tangible result: someone is going to do something and you must find out if they do it the way you intend for them to. Do not make the assumption that if it makes sense to you, it will make sense to your audience. You are not your audience.

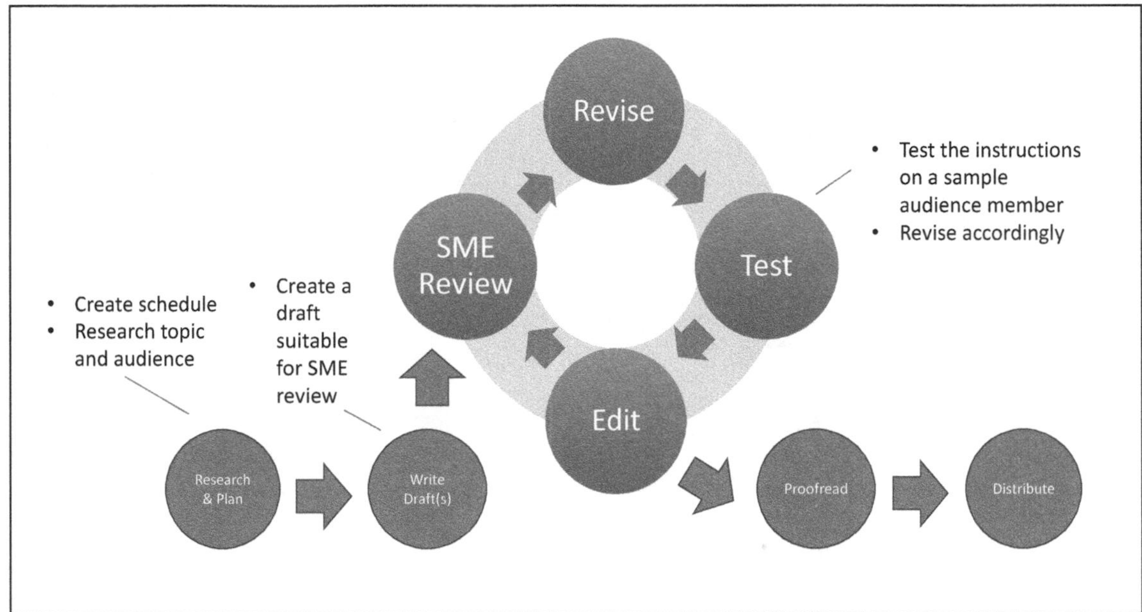

Figure 8-8 Document Cycle for Instructions

Basic User Testing

To set up a testing phase, add some time into your schedule after the second or third draft. You don't want to use a draft that is too primitive because the user will not have confidence that the information is correct.

To perform a basic user test:

1. If possible, choose a tester who is a member of your target audience.

2. Give the tester a copy of the instructions that looks professional and complete.

3. Set the tester with the equipment or products in the surroundings where he or she would be using the instructions.

4. Tell the tester that you will watch and take notes (on your own, separate set of instructions), but you won't answer questions. The tester should rely only on the instructions.

5. Ask the tester to "think out loud" as he or she ponders the meaning or intent of each part of the document. This is valuable information for you, and you must capture it in your notes, and use it for your next revision. If the tester comes to a dead end and is truly stuck, mark your notes exactly where the user stalled, and then give minimal information to get the tester unstuck. Emphasize that the problem is not his or her fault; it's a failure of the instructions. You don't want your tester to feel that he or she is being tested.

6. Thank the tester and then get busy making improvements to your document.

GUIDELINES FOR USER INSTRUCTIONS

In every type of instructions, whether a simple brochure for parking procedures on your campus or a 500-page user guide for repairing a complex electronic voting machine, the writing is simple and straightforward, with instructions written in the imperative (command form with an understood "you"). Graphics are plentiful.

When you write clear instructions, your reader can perform a given procedure without unnecessary difficulty or risk. You have the gratification that you've made things a little easier for at least one other employee or customer.

Basic guidelines for writing instructions include:

- Use "How to" in your title or subtitle to indicate that a set of instructions is to follow.
- Use commands. Example: "Turn the control knob to the ON position."
- Keep your steps simple. If a step gets too complicated, divide it into two or more steps.
- If your steps go beyond 10 steps, chunk the steps into sections or steps and sub-steps.
- Use at least two steps per section or two sub-steps per step.
- Use cautions, warnings, and danger advisories wherever necessary.
- Use notes sparingly.
- Use bullets and numbers correctly:
    - Use bullets for unordered lists. The items in an unordered list can be rearranged without affecting understandability.
    - Use numbers for steps or items that must occur in order.
- Use plenty of visuals. If you use photos, reduce the file size so that your file isn't too big for the document. If you use high resolution photos, decrease the number of pixels.
- Define any terms your target audience might not be familiar with.

Professionalism & Ethics

Always give the source for graphics in the caption. If you created the graphic, you may cite yourself.

- Use captions for each visual and refer to the visual in the step BEFORE the visual. If you didn't create the visual, cite the source in the caption.

- Test your instructions.

- Use simple language.

- Avoid "recipe English."

Applying all guidelines to a set of instructions would result in the following example shown in Sample 8-1:

Sample 8-1 Set of Instructions (simple), Page 1

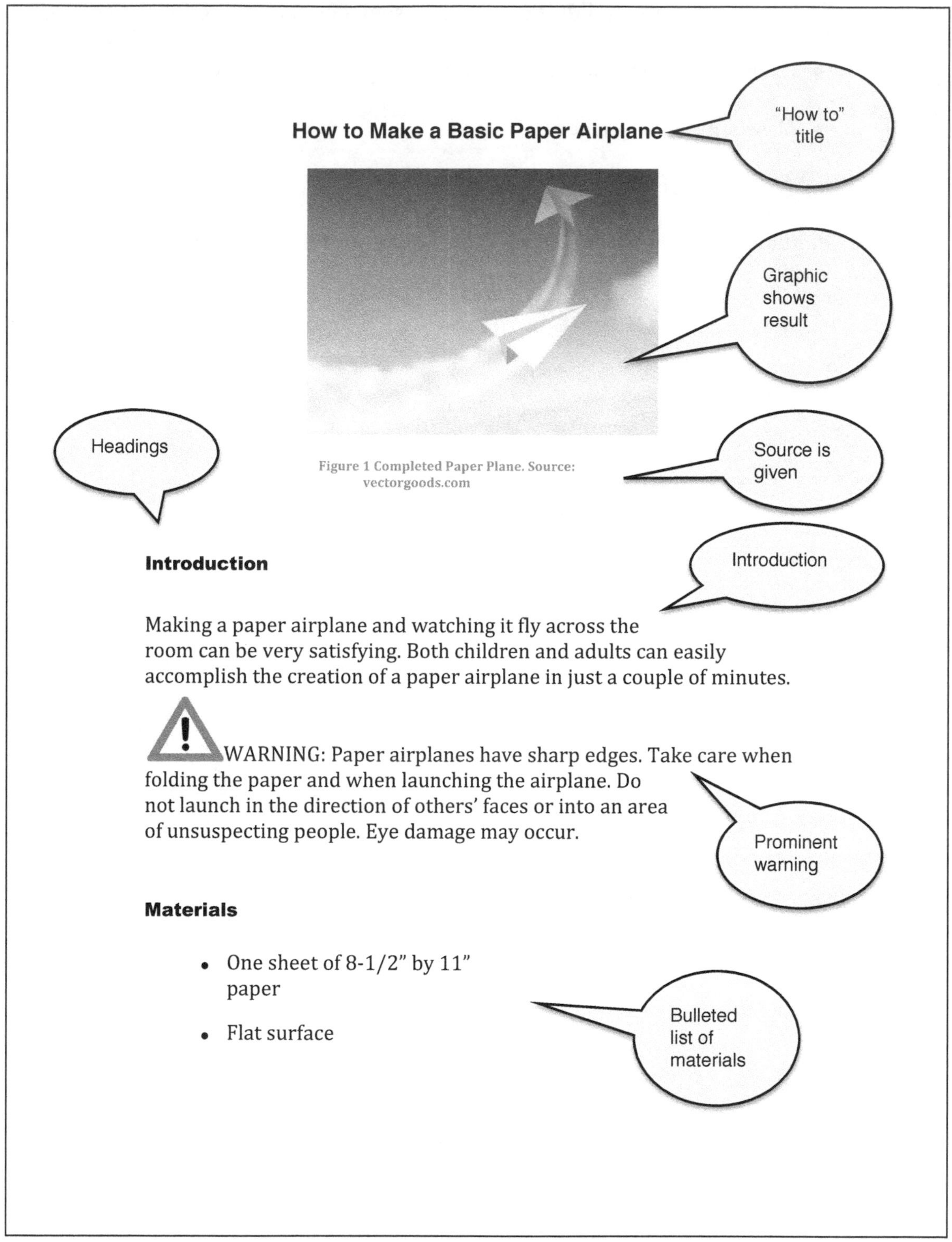
How to Make a Basic Paper Airplane
"How to" title
Graphic shows result
Headings
Figure 1 Completed Paper Plane. Source: vectorgoods.com
Source is given
Introduction
Introduction
Making a paper airplane and watching it fly across the room can be very satisfying. Both children and adults can easily accomplish the creation of a paper airplane in just a couple of minutes.
WARNING: Paper airplanes have sharp edges. Take care when folding the paper and when launching the airplane. Do not launch in the direction of others' faces or into an area of unsuspecting people. Eye damage may occur.
Prominent warning
Materials
One sheet of 8-1/2" by 11" paper
Flat surface
Bulleted list of materials

Sample 8-1 Set of Instructions (simple), Page 2

Instructions

1. Fold a sheet of paper in half and open it flat again. (See Figure 2)

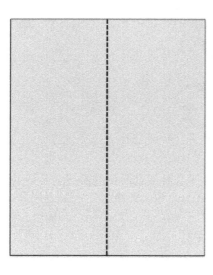

Figure 2 Sheet of Paper. Source: Nell Johnson

Sample 8-1 Set of Instructions (simple), Page 3

2. Fold the upper right and left corners toward the middle as shown in Figure 3.

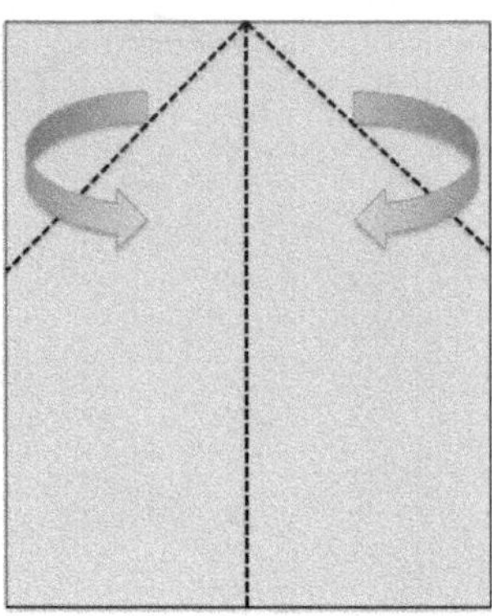

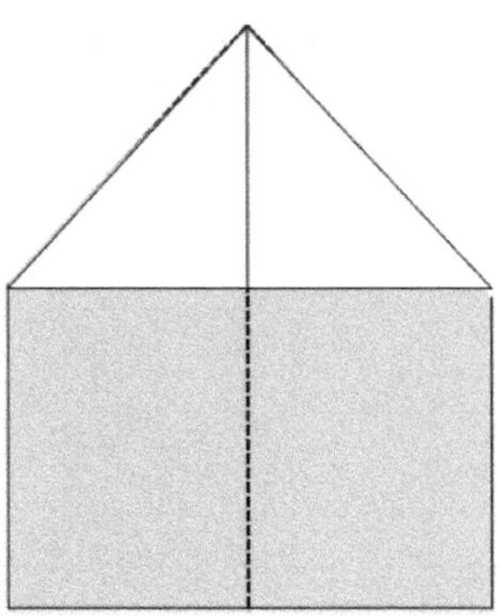

Figure 3 Fold the Corners In. Source: Nell Johnson

3. Fold the sheet along the diagonal from the top center to both bottom corners as shown in Figure 4.

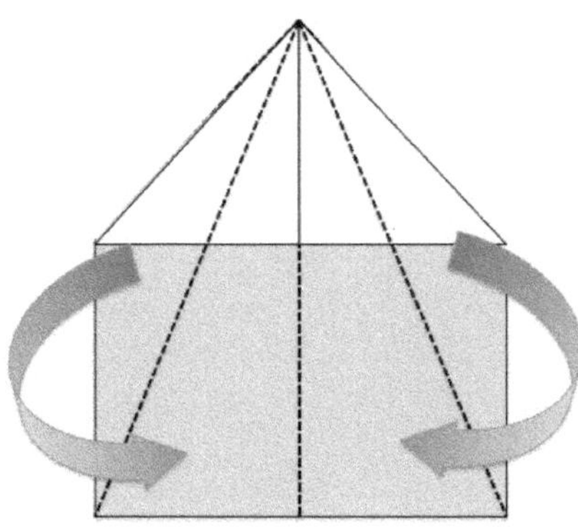

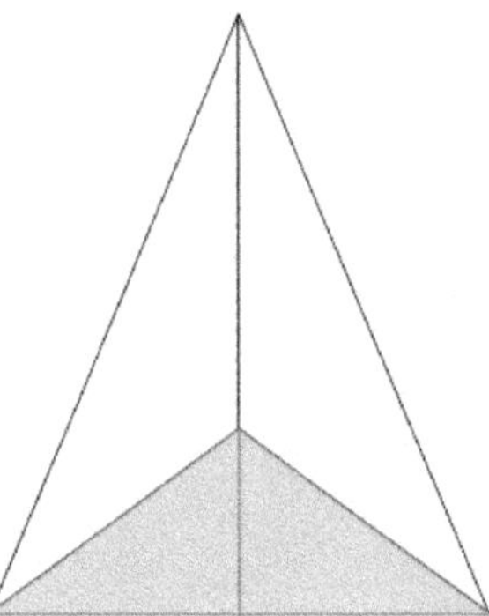

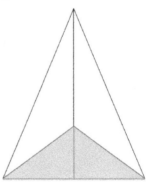

Figure 4 Diagonal Folds. Source: Nell Johnson

Sample 8-1 Set of Instructions (simple), Page 4

4. Fold the left side over to the right side as shown in Figure 5.

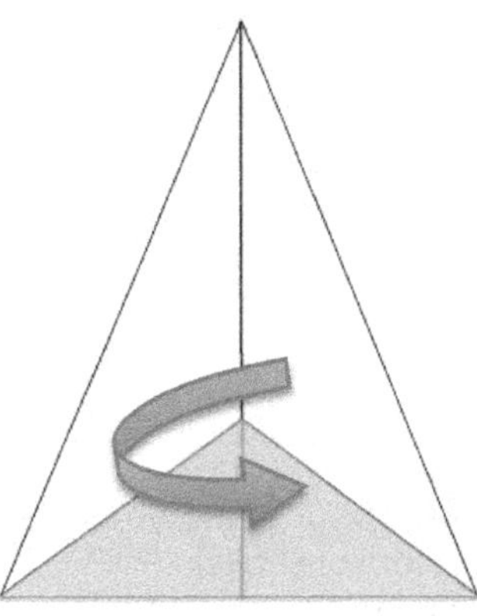

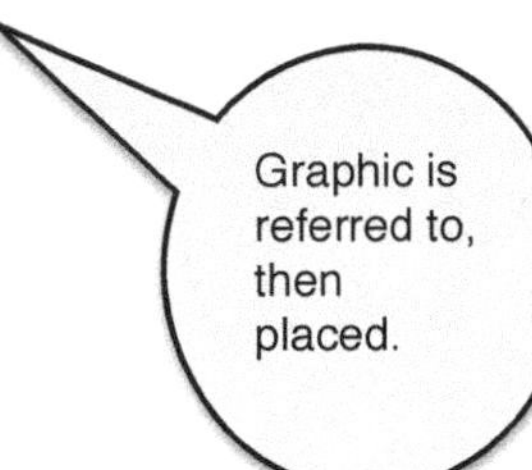
Graphic is referred to, then placed.

Figure 5 Fold Left over Right. Source: Nell Johnson

5. Fold each side in half diagonally toward the center fold as shown in Figure 6.

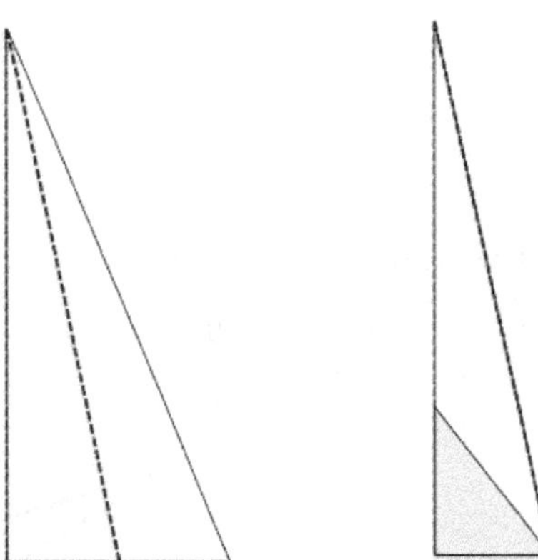

Figure 6 Fold Along the Dotted Line. Source: Nell Johnson

Sample 8-1 Set of Instructions (simple), Page 5

6. Fold the flaps down and the plane is ready to fly as shown in Figure 7.

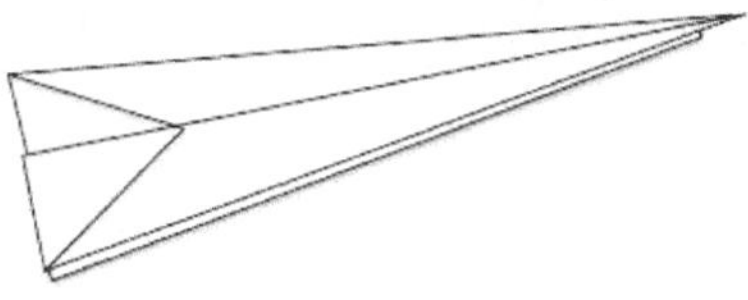

Figure 7 Ready to Fly. Source: Nell Johnson

Now that you have created your own basic plane, you can make adjustments to the flaps for some trick flying. Or you can create a fleet of flyers!

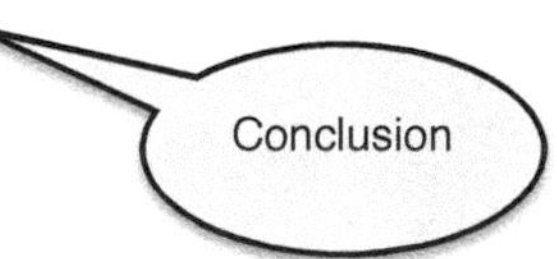

References

Completed Paper Airplane. [Drawing]. (2012). In *VectorGoods.Com*. Retrieved February 16, 2017 from http://vectorgoods.com/wp-content/uploads/2012/04/sky-vector.jpg. Licensed under Attribution 4.0 International (CC BY 3.0).

Johnson, Nell. (2014) Paper airplane drawings.

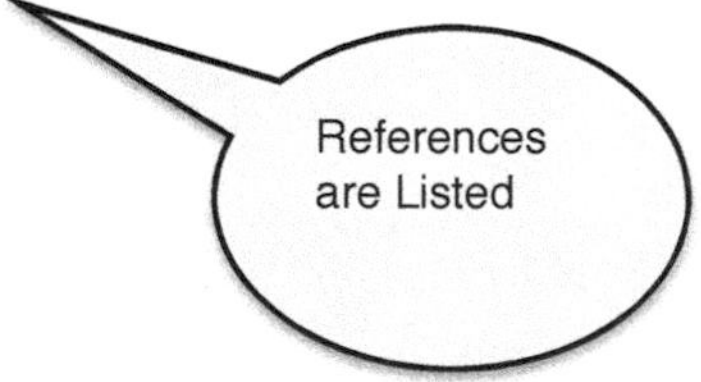

USER INSTRUCTIONS *Checklist* ✔

Effective User Instructions...	✔
Use a "How to" title	
Show a graphic of finished product; ample graphics throughout	
Use an attractive page design	
Begin with an introduction	
Provide a bulleted list of materials, supplies, skills required, time	
Include necessary warnings, cautions, and danger advisories	
Include helpful notes	
Define special terminology	
Use sequential numbered steps	
Use effective graphics, captioned, and sourced	
Appeal to the target audience	
Use appropriate tone for the audience	
Use natural English, language appropriate for the audience	
Use commands for steps (understood "you")	
Contain no more than 10 steps per section	
Are well-organized with headings and sub-steps, if required	
Use steps that are easy to read and understand	
End with a brief conclusion	
Use correct grammar, spelling, and punctuation	

DISCUSSIONS

1. Discuss use of videos as opposed to written instructions. Why are they popular? What are their advantages? Disadvantages?

2. Remember the last time you used a set of instructions. Perhaps you assembled an IKEA table, or put together a child's toy before Christmas. What do you remember about the experience? Were the instructions well-written? Do you think they were tested?

3. Discuss the testing of a set of instructions you have written for this class. Who did you recruit to do the test? What did you learn from the test? Did you change your set of instructions because of the test? How?

EXERCISES

1. **Write a set of instructions for a simple procedure you know very well.** Have an audience in mind who could lawfully use your set of instructions. (No instructions for illegal or imprudent procedures, such as demonstrating to your spouse how to load an assault rifle or showing an 8-year-old how to use dangerous equipment. Be able to fill the blanks for this statement:

   > The purpose of this set of instructions is to teach [AUDIENCE] how to [TOPIC]. Example: The purpose of this set of instructions is to teach my 13-year-old how to load the dishwasher; the purpose of this set of instructions is to teach a new employee how to fill out a timesheet.

   a. Write only 2-3 pages, and use your own words. Think about your audience and use words that they would understand. If you have to use a term they might not be familiar with, define it.

   b. Use a graphic for every step or every couple of steps. You can take digital photographs of someone performing the procedure, or you can draw your own basic diagrams. If you are instructing an online procedure, use screen captures as your graphics.

   c. Follow the pattern given in Sample 8-1 as much as possible.

   d. Test your instructions.

   e. Use the User Instructions Checklist on page 193 to make sure you have completed the assignment correctly.

2. **Write a set of instructions for another style of paper airplane.** Make your drawings in any software art program or draw them freehand. Give the instructions to a tester and perform a user test. Report your experience to the class.

3. Find a set of instructions on the Internet. **Evaluate the set of instructions** using the User Instructions Checklist on page 193.

4. Use the following step and **find an appropriate graphic** to illustrate it. Search the internet and find a graphic that will help a backyard gardener perform this first step of "How to Repot a Plant":

1. Gently pull the plant from the pot as shown in Figure 1.

   a. **Write the step, refer to the graphic, place the graphic, and then caption the graphic**. Use the automatic caption function in the word processing program. It's probably as simple as selecting the graphic and then Insert>Caption, but each program and version are slightly different.

   b. Follow the example of the captions in the Graphics chapter.

   c. Remember that you will need:

      - Figure number
      - Title of the graphic
      - Source

5. **Perform an audience analysis** using the External Audience Worksheet on the next page. Choose from the following scenarios:

   - You are to create a brochure for a "tiny house," a 100-400 square-foot home. The brochure will be handed out at home and garden expositions around the US. Visit web sites to find out more about tiny houses. Analyze your target audience.

   - You are to create a page of first 24-hour post-op care instructions for dog owners who are taking their dogs home from the pet hospital. Analyze your target audience.

EXTERNAL AUDIENCE *Worksheet*

Male? Female?
Approximate age?
Where do they live?
What is their income?
What is their education/reading level?
Is the audience computer-savvy?
What is their marital status? (married, single, widowed, etc.)
What is their occupation, or occupations?
What is their ethnic background?
What are their attitudes about my topic?
What are their beliefs about my topic?
What are their needs?
What are their wants?
What is their lifestyle?
What are typical behaviors?
What are their interests and hobbies?
Is the audience fluent in standard English?
What is the audience's most comfortable language?

6. **Perform an audience analysis** using the Internal Audience Worksheet on the next page. Choose from the following scenarios:

    - Scenario A: Your instructor has asked you to instruct class members how to participate in an upcoming technical writing contest. Only your class section will be invited to participate. **Analyze your target audience.**

    - Scenario B: Your supervisor has asked you to organize a scavenger hunt for your work **group** as a part of the company's 10-year anniversary celebration. Part of your task is to instruct members of your workgroup how to participate in the hunt. **Analyze your target audience.**

    - Scenario C: Your family needs to comply with a budget. You are going to create the budget and present it to your family, with instructions about how the budget will be followed. **Analyze your target audience.**

7. Use the audience analysis from Exercise 6 to **write a hard-copy memo,** presenting the choices you will make in writing for the target audience.

    - For Scenario A, **write a hard-copy memo to your instructor** in which you explain how you will instruct the members of your class. What choices will you make because of this audience? Why? What format will you use? Will you include graphics? What kind? Refer to the Choosing Format chart on page 36 and the Choosing the Right Graphic table on page 172.

    - For Scenario B, **write a hard-copy memo to your supervisor** explaining how you will instruct the members of your work group. What choices will you make because of this audience? Why? What format will you use? Will you include graphics? What kind? Refer to the Choosing Format flowchart on page 36 and the Choosing the Right Graphic table on page 172.

    - For Scenario C, **write a hard-copy memo to your instructor** in which you explain how you will instruct the members of your family. What choices will you make because of this audience? Why? What format will you use? Will you include graphics? What kind? Refer to the Choosing Format flowchart on page 36 and the Choosing the Right Graphic table on page 172.

INTERNAL AUDIENCE *Worksheet*

Who is the primary audience?
Who is the secondary audience?
Hierarchy position in relation to you: Below Peer Superior
What is their job function?
What are their attitudes toward your topic?
What are their needs and wants?
Do they prefer written or oral communication? What type?
What is their educational/reading level?
Are they fluent in standard English?
How much knowledge do they already have about your topic?
What reaction might you expect from your document?
Does your audience use the computer at work?

9 - Process Descriptions

Descriptions of objects, mechanisms, processes, and procedures are central to technical communication. A description may be a complete document or part of another document. This chapter discusses general description, but focuses on the process description, which is usually an extended description that covers a process over time. Process descriptions are used heavily in technical communication.

The purpose for any type of description is to inform the audience. The communication triangle shows emphasis on the topic as shown in Figure 9-1 below:

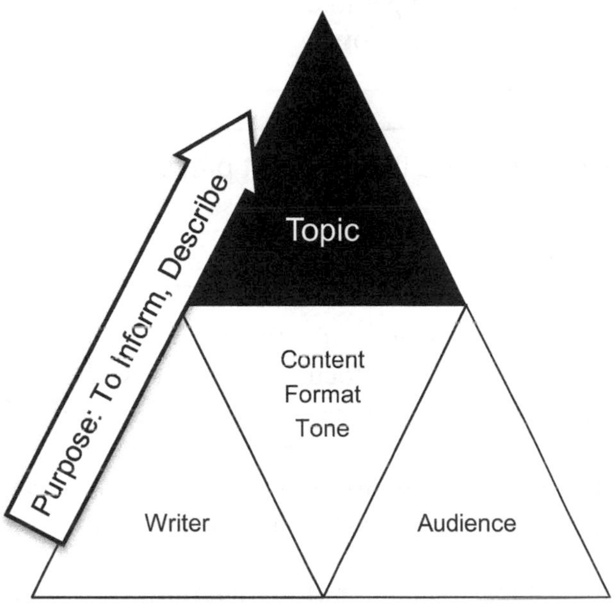

Figure 9-1 Communication Triangle for a Description

DEFINING YOUR TOPIC AND TERMS

To describe a process, you must be able to define it. Definitions are a crucial technique used in almost all kinds of technical communication, and especially in descriptions. Definitions can define objects, processes, and procedures. Definitions can be the building blocks, or they can be the entire building. For example, "Photosynthesis is the process by which plants use sunlight, water, and carbon dioxide to create sugar and oxygen." This definition can stand alone or be expanded into the process description. In any case, starting with a short definition gives the reader a very good overview.

Parenthetical definitions are often used because they can fit unobtrusively within a sentence, set off by commas, parentheses, or em-dashes. Examples of parenthetical definitions are shown below.

Example 1 - Parenthetical definitions

A croquet player uses a mallet (a wooden club) to strike the croquet ball.

A croquet player uses a mallet—a wooden club—to strike the croquet ball.

A croquet player uses a mallet, a wooden club, to strike the croquet ball.

Sentence definitions, more formal one- or two-sentence clarifications, follow the item = category + distinguishing characteristics pattern. An extended definition is a long, detailed explanation using techniques such as graphics, analogy, and history of the term. Definitions can be placed in the text, a marginal note, a hyperlink, a footnote, a glossary, or an appendix. An example of a sentence definition is shown below.

Example 2 - Sentence definition

Croquet mallets are wooden clubs that croquet players use to strike the ball.

DETERMINING SEQUENCE

A process description shows a particular sequence of actions or procedures that typically occur over and over with predictable results. The focus of the process description is the process itself, even though the audience must be considered carefully. Therefore, the writer must research and understand each step in the process in order to be able to describe it to an audience. Please note that this textbook will not differentiate significantly between process and procedure description. Both are informative chronological explanations.

A process description may contain steps, although **not instructional** steps. An important difference exists between the steps in a description of a process/procedure and instructions for a procedure. If you were writing a **description of the procedure** for ordering a cheeseburger, you might include:

1. The **customer** (actor and subject of sentence) waits in line until a cashier is available.
2. The **cashier** asks the customer what he or she would like to order.
3. The **customer** tells the cashier… and so forth.

Notice that in each case, the sentence uses active voice, beginning with the subject performing the action. We call this person or thing the "actor." Sometimes a description of a procedure will use actors as in the above steps or passive voice: "The customer is asked what he or she would like to order." See page 290 in "Resources - Grammar" for more information about passive voice.

Even though you include steps in your process description DO NOT use commands, as you would do for instructions.

Uses for Process Descriptions

Process descriptions are heavily used in the workplace, in the classroom, and even in the media. In the workplace, they can be used to plan operations, to define job duties, to show "hand-offs" (the point where a process changes hands from one job role to another), to examine existing processes for improvement opportunities, to teach employees daily workflow, or to show upper management and stockholders the basic processes and outcomes. Process descriptions are invaluable to the intelligent management of any workplace. With a clear idea of who does what, when, where, why, and how, work groups function effectively.

Some workplaces use Standard Operating Procedures (SOPs) to document the details of processes and procedures. SOPs are considered to be policy documents and must be strictly adhered to. In some fields, such as Project Management, the terms "process" and "procedure" have slightly different meanings. However, for our purposes they will be used interchangeably.

In the classroom, process descriptions are used to explain topics as varied as digestion, cloud formations, or the election of public officials.

In the media, process descriptions can be used to explain how a particular product is made, to gain an edge on the competition. For example, a dairy products company might advertise that their cows' milk comes from only well-fed, well-handled cows, and that the cows' milk goes through three stages of careful treatment and pasteurization. It could further state that the milk is maintained at a certain temperature for optimal freshness.

Benefits of Clear Process Descriptions

When you write a clear process description, your readers can understand all major aspects—the who, what, when, where, why, and how—of a given process. This understanding can:

- help internal audiences become more cooperative and successful employees;
- help students learn and apply their subject matter;
- help management find process problems and implement improvements;
- educate your customers and help them manage their expectations of you and your work.

You have the gratification that you've made things a little easier for at least one other employee or customer.

DETERMINING YOUR MAJOR SECTIONS

Process descriptions can vary greatly in complexity, from a one-paragraph explanation to a multi-page report. The content is determined by the complexity of the process, the purpose of the description, the level of detail needed, and the audience for the document. Consider these elements when creating a process description:

- Title that uses the word "process" (For example, "The Process of Photosynthesis")
- Introduction
- Overview of what the process does, why it is performed, how long it takes, how many elements are involved, etc.
- Prominent safety information
- Body of the description
- Sections with headings
- Numbered steps, or
- Paragraphs, or
- Combination of numbered steps and paragraphs
- Graphics, usually including a flowchart

Depending on the complexity of the process description, you may also need:

- Table of contents
- Parenthetical definitions
- Glossary
- Sections
- Steps and sub-steps (See Figure 9-4)
- Conclusion
- Index

Compare the steps and sub-steps in Figure 9-2 with the steps and sub-steps for a set of instructions from page 179 of the User Instructions chapter. Both refer to the same process, but one of them instructs the reader (the set of instructions) and the other describes the process (the process description).

1. The laundry is gathered.
    a. The large blue basket is retrieved from the laundry room.
    b. Clothes from the dirty clothes hampers are put into the blue basket.
    c. Hanging towels and washrags from the bathrooms are put in the basket.
    d. The used washrag and towels from the kitchen are put in the basket.
2. The laundry is sorted.
    a. Three large piles are placed on the floor in the laundry room:
        - Multi-colored clothes
        - White clothes
        - Delicate clothes
    b. Each pile is checked to make sure it is not too big for the washing machine. If so, the pile is divided into two equal-sized piles.

Figure 9-2 Using Steps and Sub-steps in Process Description

PLANNING THE DOCUMENT CYCLE

The document cycle is determined by the complexity, audience, and critical nature of the process description. For example, the process description for handling radioisotopes would require stringent review cycles by all of the subject matter experts involved in a nuclear medicine department.

In general, the process description involves the same major steps as any other important document, as shown in Figure 9-3. However, a complex process may require multiple simultaneous reviews to ensure accuracy. If there is a discrepancy in how different employees (subject matter experts, or SMEs) envision the process, consider this a success. Your description has uncovered an area ripe for process improvement.

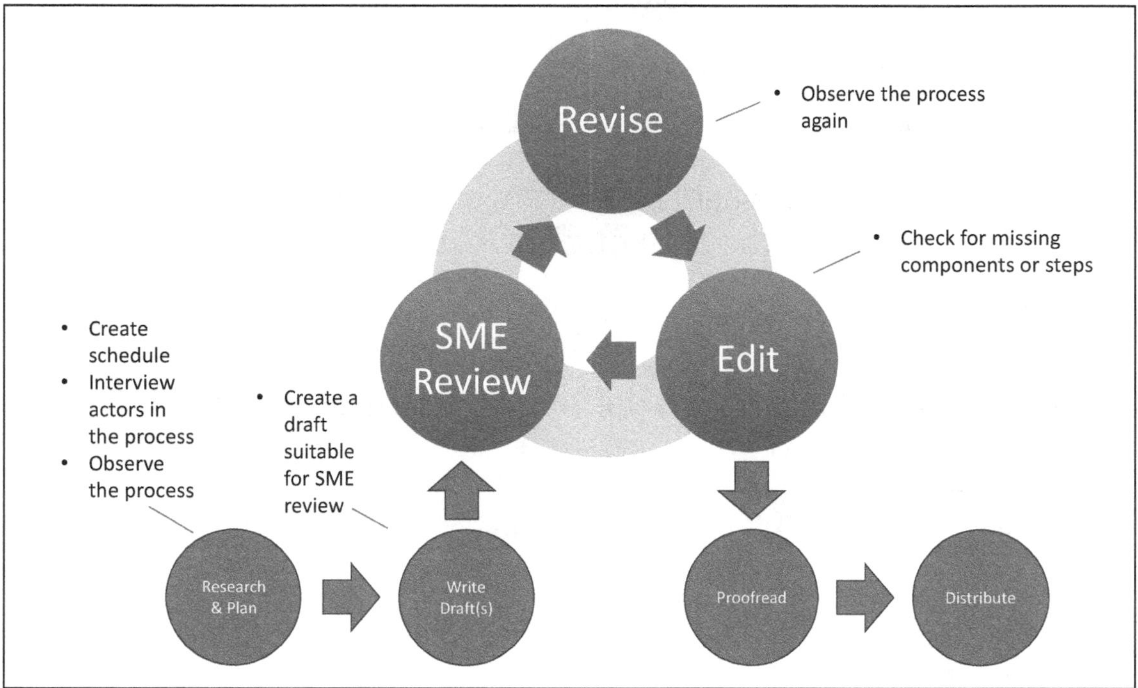

Figure 9-3 Document Cycle for a Process Description

GUIDELINES FOR PROCESS DESCRIPTIONS

Basic guidelines for writing a process description include:

- Use "Process" in your title or subtitle. It makes it obvious that a process description is to follow.
- Use declarative sentences or passive voice. Example: "The operator turns the control knob to the ON position" or "The control knob is turned to the ON position."
- Make the language match the audience.
- Describe any safety issues.
- Use bullets and numbers correctly.
- Use bullets for unordered lists. The items in an unordered list can be rearranged without affecting understandability.
- Use numbers for steps or items that must occur in order.
- Use a flow chart.
- Define any terms your target audience might not be familiar with.
- Use captions for each visual and refer to the visual in the step BEFORE the visual. If you didn't create the visual, cite the source in the caption.

Professionalism & Ethics

Always give the source for graphics in the caption.

Process descriptions can be very formal documents, used both for internal reference and also for policy and procedure—or even legal—compliance. For example, the process description on the next few pages (Sample 9-1) is written in a formal report with title page, table of contents, glossary, and approval table. In contrast, the process description in Figure 9-7 shows a much simpler—and somewhat humorous—process description with flow chart.

Sample 9-1 Process Description, Title Page

 **Moseley Computers - International Division**

Business Submission and Approval Process

Sales Department

Business Process.doc 1 of 6 11/10/2014

Sample 9-1 Process Description, Table of Contents

Table of Contents

Sample 9-1 Process Description, Overview

Process Overview

Purpose

The Business Submission Process tracks the roles and tasks involved in the submission and approval of new international computer products sales.

Scope

International accounts only.

Roles

- Customer
- Sales Rep
- International Sales Manager
- Shipping Department Rep
- Invoicing/Billing Rep

Supplies/Permissions

- International Sales Manager requires access to Franklin system

Policy

This process supports the Process Improvement Project, Policy 98.

Sample 9-1 Process Description, Detail

Process Detail and Flow Chart

Process Steps

1. The Customer notifies the Sales Rep that they wish to buy computer products or the Sales Rep contacts the Customer and presents product information and the Customer wishes to purchase.

   Note: If the Customer notifies another Moseley employee instead of the Sales Rep, that employee will notify the Sales Rep.

2. The Sales Rep determines if enough information is provided to confirm the sale.

   If YES: The Sales Rep goes to Step 3.

   If NO: The Sales Rep and International Sales Manager follow these procedures:

   a. The Sales Rep calls the International Sales Manager and provides the details of the proposed sale.

   b. The International Sales Manager determines if the details of the proposed sale meet current fiscal year profitability criteria.

      If YES: The International Sales Manager approves the sale.

      If NO: The International Sales Manager suggests that the Sales Rep present another purchase option to the Customer. Return to Step 1.

3. The Sales Rep notifies the International Sales Manager via e-mail of the details of the Bill of Sale.

4. The International Sales Manager enters the sale information into Franklin.

5. The International Sales Manager produces a sales packet and e-mails it to the Sales Rep.

6. When the packet arrives, the Sales Rep follows completes the sale:

   a. The Sales Rep contacts the Customer and verifies details.

   b. The Sales Rep contacts the Shipping and Billing Departments.

7. The Sales Rep notifies the International Sales Manager that the sale is complete.

END OF PROCESS

When the sale has been completed and the International Sales Manager receives confirmation, this process is complete. The next process, Order Fulfillment, begins when the Shipping Department receives the order.

Sample 9-1 Process Description, Flow Chart

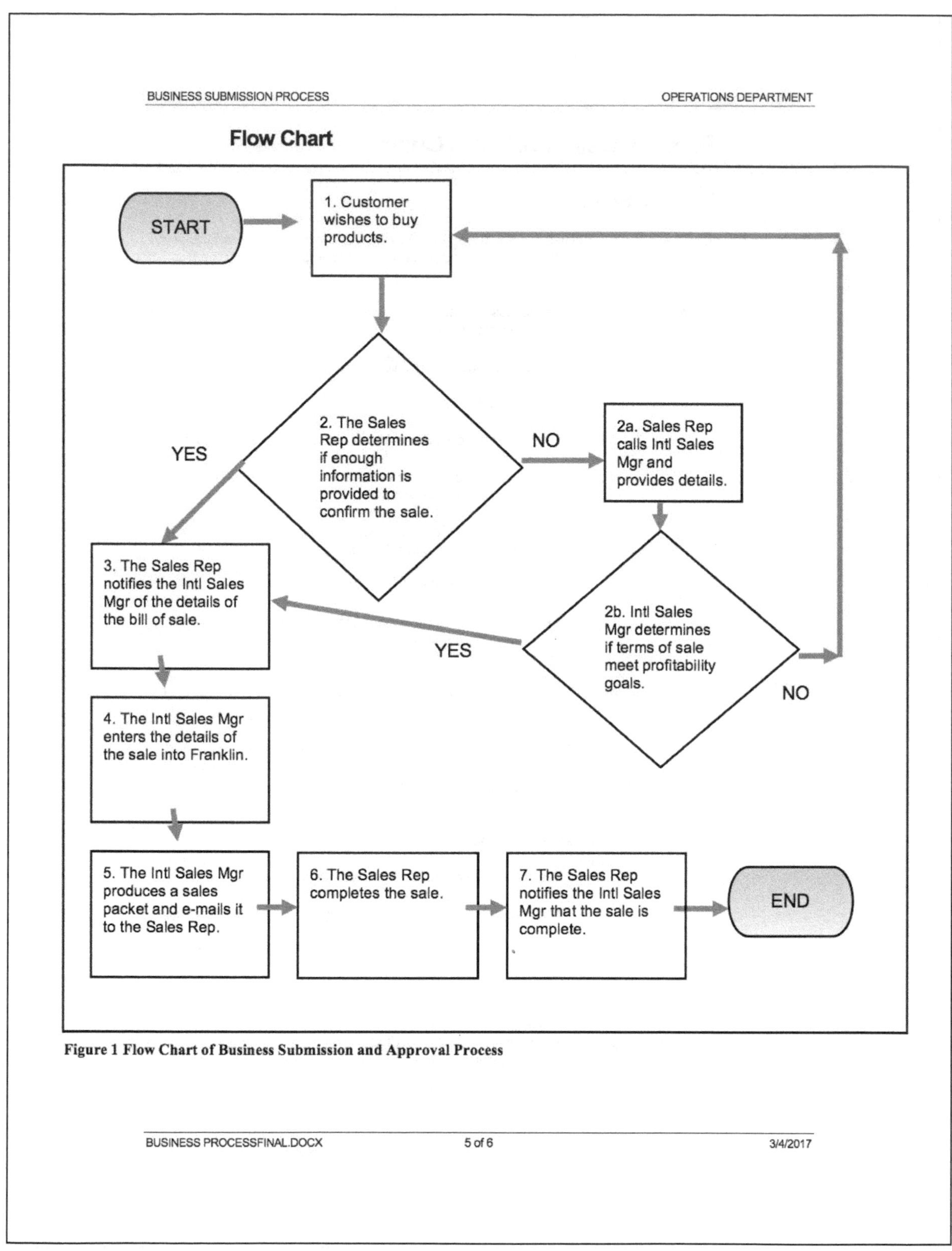

Sample 9-1 Process Description, Glossary and Approval Page

Glossary

Term	Definition
Franklin	Moseley's sales software for internal use

Approvals

The following individuals have reviewed and approved this process.

Role	Signature	Date
International Sales Director		
International Billing Department Director		
International Shipping Department Director		

Sample 9-2 Process Description (simple), Page 1

The Decision Process for Changing a Diaper

Prepared by: Charlene Whittaker

Introduction

The **purpose** of this process is to describe a fair and equitable process in which two parents can decide which one will change a diaper that is aromatically offensive. The **actors** in this document are Parent 1 and Parent 2; these are either the natural/adoptive parents or guardians of the child, or two people who are temporary caregivers of the child. The **audience** for this process are caregivers of small children who might appreciate an amusing yet valid method to decide who has to perform this duty. The process begins with the child indicating that he/she needs to have their diaper changed and continues to the point of assigning the parent to the task. The flowchart on page 3 (Figure 1) shows this process.

Process

Step 1: The child appears uncomfortable and the diaper is swelling.

Step 2: Parent 1 or Parent 2 determines if the child's diaper smells offensive.

- If Yes: The Parents go to Step 3.
- If No: The Parent checking the diaper goes to Step 12.

Step 3: Parents 1 and 2 determine if either will voluntarily change the diaper.

- If Yes: The volunteering Parent goes to Step 12.
- If No: Parent 1 and Parent 2 go to Step 4.

Step 4: Parent 1 and Parent 2 determine if either have any unused Diaper Points (DPs) – points earned by either parent, often from changing a particularly offensive smelling diaper, which allow the parent holding the points to compel the other parent into diaper changing duty.

- If Yes: Parent 1 and Parent 2 go to Step 5.
- If No: Parent 1 and Parent 2 go to Step 7.

1

Sample 9-2 Process Description (simple), Page 2

Step 5: Parent 1 and Parent 2 determine if the DP balance is tied.

- If Yes: DPs cannot be used. Parent 1 and Parent 2 go to Step 7.
- If No: Parent 1 and Parent 2 go to Step 6.

Step 6: The DP leader between Parent 1 and Parent 2 decides whether the DPs will be used for this diaper change.

- If Yes: The parent with fewer DPs goes to Step 12.
- If No: Parent 1 and Parent 2 go to Step 7.

Step 7: Parent 1 and Parent 2 begin the Rock, Paper, Scissors (RPS) tournament. The diaper changing RPS tournament rule consists of a maximum of 5 throws. The winning parent must win 3 out of 5 throws. See the *World RPS Society: Game Basics* (http://www.worldrps.com/game-basics) for the detailed rules of the game.

Step 8: Has either parent won 3 rounds of RPS?

- If Yes: The parents go to Step 9.
- If No: The parents go to Step 7 for the next round.

Step 9: Which parent has won the RPS Tournament?

- If Parent 1: Parent 2 goes to Step 11.
- If Parent 2: Parent 1 goes to Step 10.

Step 10: Parent 1 gets diaper duty and goes to Step 12.

Step 11: Parent 2 gets diaper duty and goes to Step 12.

Step 12: The parent changes the child's diaper.

Conclusion:

The diaper change decision process is quite important as parents become exhausted from lack of sleep, or if one parent has changed a disproportionate amount of offensive smelling diapers. This procedure should insure that diaper-changing duties are distributed fairly between both parents.

Sample 9-2 Process Description (simple), Page 3

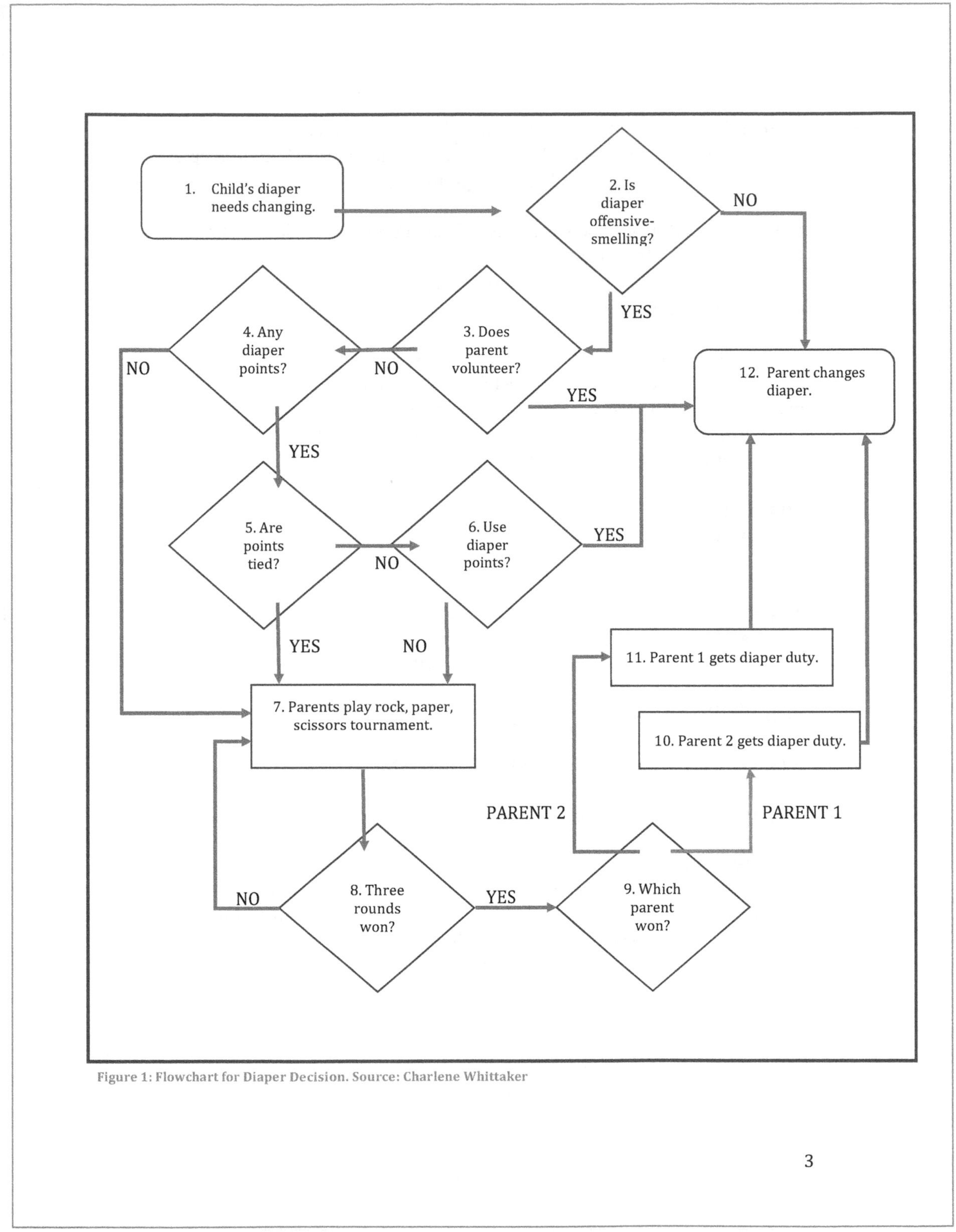

Figure 1: Flowchart for Diaper Decision. Source: Charlene Whittaker

3

PROCESS DESCRIPTION *Checklist* ✔

Effective Process Descriptions...	✔
Use a "Process" title	
Use a standard flowchart with caption, other graphics as needed	
Use an attractive page design	
Begin with an introduction	
Provide a bulleted list of materials, supplies, skills required, roles involved (if needed)	
Define special terminology	
Include necessary warnings, cautions, and danger advisories	
Include helpful notes	
Use sequential numbered steps	
Appeal to the target audience	
Use appropriate tone for the audience	
Use natural English, language appropriate for the audience	
Use descriptive steps (either third person or passive voice)	
Use present tense	
Are well-organized with headings and sub-steps, if required	
Use steps that are easy to read and understand	
End with a brief conclusion	
Use correct grammar, spelling, and punctuation	

DISCUSSIONS

1. Imagine that you are a work team manager. Each member of the team performs a different function, but they all must work together to produce one widget per day. Think of as many reasons as you can to make a case for documenting the production process with a process description. Why is it a good idea?

2. Use the space below to draw a simple flowchart of your process for either arriving to school to work. Include at least one decision point. For example, do you check the traffic reports to decide whether to drive Route 60 or the Interstate?

EXERCISES

1. Think of a process that you go through on a daily basis. It could be anything from brushing a child's teeth to logging onto a laptop. **Create a memo report** to your instructor describing the process. Write out the steps using third person (For example: 1. The dad picks up the toothbrush. 2. The dad applies children's toothpaste. 3. The child opens her mouth.)

2. **Draw a flowchart** (either in Microsoft Word or with a pencil and paper) that reflects the process you described in Exercise 1, with the same steps.

3. Review the reports and the flow charts in Samples 9-1 and 9-2. Notice the decision diamond and how it is used. Think of a process that you go through on a daily basis that contains at least one decision or option. Depending on the decision or option, your actions could be slightly or significantly different. **Write a simple process description** describing the process with steps and with flowchart, showing at least one decision step.

4. **Write a memo report, including a flow chart, to your instructor** describing a process for handling the weekly workload for this class. Use first or third person ("the student").

5. Think of a process that you would like to improve. It could be at work, at your college, at home, or even in your community.

    a. **Write a letter report** (for external audience) **or memo report** (for internal audiences, such as your college, at home, or at work) listing the current steps, in third person, using the job title, **with a flowchart.**

    b. **Describe the improved process with matching flowchart**.

10 - Proposals

A proposal is, essentially, any piece of writing whose purpose is to convince the reader to support a desired plan. The proposal often seeks financial support, but it may seek only approval. Companies often prepare proposals to pitch ideas for clients. Authors write proposals to publishers for new books. Workers may write proposals for changes in procedure or for new equipment purchases. Students write proposals for research projects or for scholarship funding. Scientists, artists, teachers, and community leaders, and others write proposals to obtain grants to support their work. Many organizations or individuals depend upon financial grants from outside sources for their continued research or even existence, so the ability to write a convincing proposal is an important skill.

Unlike reports, which may simply set out factual information or make recommendations, proposals are intended to persuade the reader to act.

The triangle below illustrates the relationship between writer and reader in a proposal.

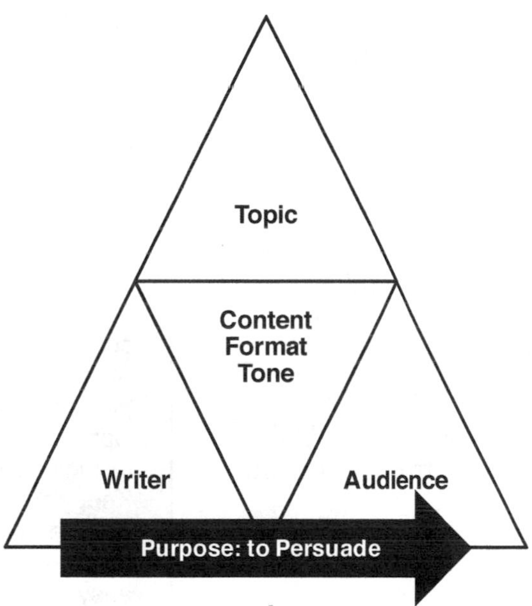

Figure 10-1 Communication Triangle for Proposals

CONSIDERING AUDIENCE

Since a proposal asks the audience to respond, not just read, proposal writers need to think carefully about their audience's motivations. Persuasion begins with an understanding of the readers' assumptions and priorities. Outside agencies, potential customers, and internal management will have differing interests, goals, and concerns.

Outside Agencies

If you plan to submit a proposal to a granting agency, it is important to consider that agency's mission. If you want support for an art project, the National Institutes of Health would probably not be the first place to apply—unless, perhaps, the art is part of a hospital complex or art therapy idea. If you are interested in clearing a forest to make way for a parking lot, Friends of Trees is not a logical grantor. Read the mission statement on the agency's website home page (if available), and also examine the fine print in the grant application itself. Some distinctions are subtle: some grants may be available only for starting projects, not continuing existing ones. Others may specify only certain endeavors within a broad category: painting rather than sculpture, for example. Grantors are also investors: they want to put their money to use in a particular way to achieve ends that contribute to their overall goals. Try to understand what those goals are.

Granting agencies sometimes offer examples of successful proposals on their websites for you to review. Take advantage of this helpfulness and educate yourself about previous successful grantees. The National Endowment for the Humanities, for example, includes valuable resources on its home page, such as a budget template and sample narratives from successful applications.

Customers

A proposal to a customer is normally written to encourage the client to buy a product or service (or both). Successful proposals consider the need or problem and provide a specific solution. Often, potential customers invite proposals or bids for work to be done. If you are writing in response to a formal request for proposals (RFP), read the original request carefully. It will contain a description of the project and important specifications. Successful proposals will not only meet the specifications and offer a

Professionalism & Ethics

Honesty and accountability at every step of the proposal cycle are essential. It is very tempting to overstate your case or exaggerate your capabilities. Remember that when a customer, company, or supervisor accepts your proposal, that you are ethically (and sometimes legally) obligated to fulfill it. Grants or RFPs often require updates, progress reports, or site visits to mark progress.

Take the time to figure out exactly how much material you need or hours that will be required to complete the job. Do not make a wild guess or deliberately underbid with the idea that you can ask for more funds or time later. Lies or half-truths can come back to bite you in the form of missed deadlines, lost business, and a ruined reputation. Contracts sometimes include fines for late deliveries.

When your proposal is successful—when you get the grant, or the project, or the schedule that you wanted—that means that your reader has placed significant trust in you. Carefully record spending, including receipts for purchases. Keep records of dates and work completed, including person-hours (even volunteer hours). It is easy to forget the specific requirements of a grant or RFP until reports come due, and very difficult to go back and reconstruct what happened and when. Be scrupulous with client or grant money and spend it on only approved purchases.

carefully. It will contain a description of the project and important specifications. Successful proposals will not only meet the specifications and offer a competitive price, but also, if possible, consider the customer's long-term needs and goals. For example, a proposal to set up a new computer system might include some assistance for the near future in training workers to use it.

Many business proposals are written less formally as part of day-to-day business. A landscaper, for example, might write a proposal while standing outside on the customer's property. A clearly organized form on duplicating paper is very helpful in those situations to standardize company bids and remind workers to give specific cost information.

Since customers usually compare bids from different providers, it is important to be as clear as possible about the work to be done and the price for doing it. A low bid, for instance, may not include the full scope of work of a higher bid, and the customer needs to be able to make accurate comparisons.

Readers in the Workplace

Occasionally, you may write a proposal within your own company to buy new equipment, institute a new procedure, or establish a new policy. You might propose a specific schedule for your own parental leave or for an innovative work situation you desire, such as online commuting. It is essential in all of these situations to consider not only the person to whom you give the proposal, but also the people he or she might share it with. Your original request might be a memo proposal, read by just your supervisor—but then passed on to upper management and the human resources department. Consider the concerns of both your primary and secondary readers.

ORGANIZATION

Your proposal should be easy to navigate and should not waste the reader's time with repetition. Avoid sections with overlapping functions, such as a summary and an abstract. Clarity is more important than exact copying of a format. But, pay careful attention to elements that are specifically required in the terms of grants or RFPs and make sure you meet those requirements, or your application may be disqualified.

Section headings in a proposal, as in any document, are important to guide your reader through the discussion, and experienced readers may skim over your proposal to look for those sections. Because there are many types of proposals, standard headings can vary widely. To make sure that your headings correspond to the various elements your readers expect, review grant documents and past proposals to determine what section headings are expected. Your company may have standard forms for bids or for in-house proposals; ask to see them.

Problem-Solution Structure

Think of the proposal as an extended narrative: present the issues or problems before proposing a solution. In a grant proposal, the writers need to show that they have an informed grasp of the problem before presenting a great idea about how to solve it. In a proposal for a business client, the problem may already be well known or specifically described, but a description of the issues involved is still appropriate to demonstrate the proposer's complete understanding before launching into the proposed solution.

The space required to establish the key points in the problem/solution narrative may vary according to the project. For example, you may need to work very hard on a statement of need in a grant application to persuade city commissioners to shift budget priorities and allocate funds for a new sidewalk. In writing a response to an RFP, on the other hand, your project description (the solution) will be more important than establishing need, as the need is a given; you would spend most of your time in that situation demonstrating that you understand the project's complexities and have a clear idea about how to manufacture the product, solve the problem, or provide the service in an effective way.

Proposal Sections

In a proposal, your audience should be able to see the whole story, without diversions or tangents that may cause them to lose focus. The sections of the proposal will vary in length and emphasis depending upon your audience and on the specifications of the grant or RFP.

The elements of any proposal should lead the reader through a logical flow of information to show how the particular need is to be fulfilled. A good proposal includes at least these general sections, although they may be named slightly differently depending on the requirements of the grant or RFP:

Introduction

Introduce the project briefly with a broad overview. This section is sometimes called "Purpose," "Abstract," "Summary," or "Overview."

Statement of Need

In a grant proposal, this is the section where you establish the need for your project. Making your case may involve researching specific background facts about the community that it will impact. For example, how much has the population grown since the old library was built? How many accidents have happened at the intersection in the last 10 years? How long was the temporary student housing intended to last? What problems or needs exist? In a proposal response to an RFP, this section might recap specifications to show an understanding of the needs of the client, discussing particular urgencies or areas of special concern. For instance, a proposal to produce a new packaging material might reasonably review the failings of other materials early in the document as background to the new idea. In this section, you may also present various possible alternatives, with their advantages and disadvantages.

Project Description

This section should be a narrative of the process of completing the project. You might begin with a summary of the work, such as "over a six-week period, we propose to clear Warehouse #4 of its contents, repair and paint the interior, and install a new lane-based organizational system." Then, detail the steps toward that process, describing the specific concerns and requirements of each stage. For a long, multi-phase project, this section might be very large and divided into sub-sections. A very simple project might include only a few sentences in this section. An RFP normally allows some flexibility in deciding how to complete the project—here is where you can allow your special plan for the project to shine.

Timeline

Using an easily-read table, show the proposed chronological progress of the project. The table may include actual dates (January 3, 2020), or relative time points (Week 3). For projects that require completion by a certain date, specific dates are best.

Budget

Using a table or column format, display all expenses related to the project, including labor costs and person-hours. Make sure that decimal points are lined up in columns for easy reference. If the project is to be completed with volunteer labor, include an estimate of the person-hours required, but note that they are to be fulfilled by volunteers. The time estimates will be useful later in determining accuracy and in reporting the results in the documentation that may be required to fulfill the terms of a grant or RFP.

Results Expected

In this section, describe not only the specific result, as in "new parents will be allowed two months of paid parental leave" but also the wider benefits: "the generous parental leave policy will not only benefit existing employees, but also improve employee retention and attract the attention of highly qualified applicants for new positions." Describe the anticipated effects of the completed project. Will the results include greater safety and therefore cost savings to the company? More convenient and thus faster access to records? A more educated and thus more useful worker?

Conclusion

This section provides a sense of closure for your document. It is also your final opportunity to remind your readers about the strength of your case. Provide a sentence or two reviewing the project and its anticipated benefits, if approved. The conclusion is the place to say that you appreciate the chance to make this proposal, that you appreciate the consideration, and that you hope to have a continuing and productive relationship.

Contact Information

The name of the person, organization, or company submitting the proposal should be clearly written on page one. Detailed contact information (mailing address, email, and phone number of a key contact person for the proposal) may be provided at the beginning or end, but it is essential. The name of the organization is not enough. Readers need to know the name of a person to contact. What if your bid was selected, but the message was lost in the wrong voice mail? Or, what if a key question went unanswered because readers could not contact a knowledgeable person, and thus went on to approve another application?

Qualifications

In many proposals, some information about the organization, community, or specialist is included to show the proposer's qualifications, such as a degree or certification (if required) or a list of other projects completed. In a grant application, the proposed grantee might detail their years of experience or area of specialization. This section is optional unless specifically required by the grant or RFP, but it can help to demonstrate readiness to accomplish the proposed task.

DOCUMENT CYCLE

The document cycle for a proposal is a multi-review process. Begin writing early so that you can give proofreaders generous time to review drafts. Figure 10-2, below, shows the review cycle of proposal writing. The graphic shows four drafts, but you may have more.

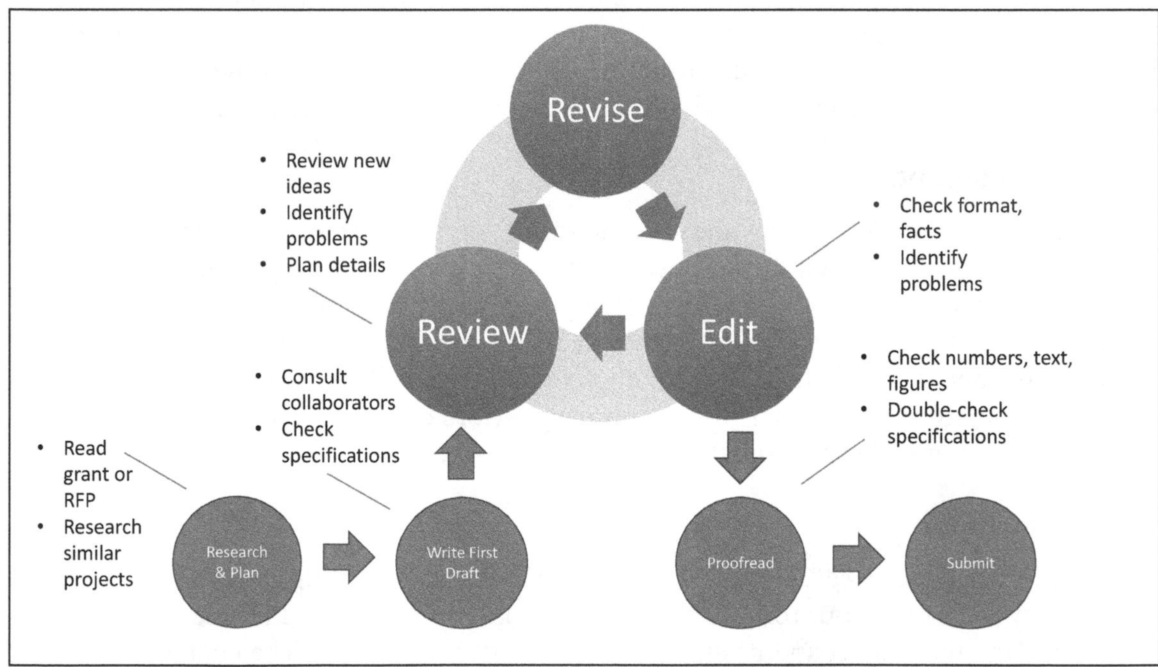

Figure 10-2 Document Cycle for Proposals

Deadlines

Proposal development is driven by deadlines. Work backwards from deadlines to determine your work schedule. For an in-house proposal, such as the purchase of a new copy machine, determine the date needed, and work backwards from that time point.

If you are responding to a call for proposals or grant, read carefully to identify all important dates. Sometimes an abstract may be due at a certain time and then a full proposal somewhat later. Note how the proposal is to be delivered: if submitted electronically, what file format is acceptable? If it must be sent by postal mail, when should it arrive?

When you are sure that you understand the deadlines your proposal must meet, plan the work for writing, reviewing, and editing your proposal.

Project Scope and Audience Concerns

This stage involves careful conversations, research and reading to determine the parameters of the project and the sensitive or complicated factors in its completion.

In-House Proposal Concerns

For an in-house proposal—changing a storeroom into a dedicated employee break room, for example—you need to talk to other employees who might benefit. Who wants it, and why? Research the costs and consider logistics. Most importantly, consider the concerns management may have. For instance, where will the supplies now filling that room be housed? Will employee hours be diverted for the project? Who will maintain this room? What costs will be involved? Will the new break room encourage employees to take longer breaks?

Customer Concerns

In a response to a potential customer's request for proposals, you will need to consider how your company's expertise fits the client's needs. What do you see as the tricky or problematic parts of the project? Do you see underlying risks? It may help at this stage to research similar projects and identify common strengths or problems. What is standard in the field? What can you do that competitors can't or won't? Has anyone in your company worked with this client before? If so, what are some typical issues that may arise, or paths that can be smoothed at the start?

Grant-Related Concerns

When writing a grant proposal, you may be working alone or with others. Even if you plan to write the proposal as an individual—such as one teacher's grant to purchase a microscope to support third grade science lessons—you should enlist the help of others in your field. Bounce ideas off others who know your subject and share your goals. These people, even if they don't become collaborators, will be helpful readers at every stage of the document cycle. Research your topic and find examples of ways that others have approached it. For the third-grade science teacher, this might mean finding out more about ways that teachers around the country have taught the same lessons. How have those successes been measured?

First Draft: Project Narrative

Think about your proposal as a story. Write the parts that help your reader understand your point of view, such as the need for third-graders to get a good grounding in science and your frustrations with accomplishing that. Or, write about your view of the reasons that some machine parts do not work correctly, leading into a discussion of your own specially engineered product. Even if you do not ultimately keep all of this narrative in the document, writing it will help you establish an authoritative and recognizable voice in the proposal. Readers naturally become engaged with a story and want to continue.

As you consider the project narrative, you can also be creating a tentative timeline for production. To create a timeline, work backwards from the delivery date using your best estimates of the time required for each part. Keep in mind that your estimates will change with your increasing understanding of the process involved in completing the project. Research the costs and start a budget spreadsheet to keep track of figures. Save the introduction and conclusion for last, after you have a better idea of the scope of your proposal.

First Review: Examine for Concepts, History

Share the first draft with others in your company or in your field. Encourage these people to point out missing pieces in the story, contribute institutional knowledge, or offer tips about their prior dealings with the client. Colleagues may know of better suppliers or easier ways of doing things. They may even have applied for the same grant in prior years. Take criticism gratefully and gracefully; the more constructive suggestions you receive, the better chance you have of being awarded the grant or the contract or getting the result you desire.

Do not expect your reviewers to get back to you the same day, but do let them know when you would like to hear from them. Two or three days is an optimal time period: long enough not to disrupt most people's work schedule but short enough so that your draft does not get lost in the work pile. The days that your document is in the hands of the reviewers also serve as a cooling-off period for you as a writer, allowing you to see it later with new eyes.

Second Draft: Organize, Research

Review the comments you have received from colleagues and incorporate them into the proposal as needed. Begin to organize the project story into recognizable sections. For example, part of the narrative may be useful under "Statement of Need" and part under "Project Description." Write a summary or introduction; research and fill out the timeline and budget sections. Make sure that all information is current and correct and that sources are cited appropriately. At the end of this stage you should have all required sections drafted, if not in final form.

Second Review: Check Facts, Numbers, Specifications

Share the second draft with colleagues asking for judgment about particular specifications, including labor estimates. A good reason for waiting until the second draft to confirm facts and figures is that costs can sometimes change from one week to the next. At this stage, you may wish to ask specific people to focus on certain sections. A supervisor familiar with estimating person hours, for example, may be most useful as a reviewer of the labor estimated in the budget. A mechanical engineer may be most useful in reviewing the specifications for a particular metal part. These people will be grateful for the time-saving if you direct them to the sections you wish them to review most carefully. And, they will be honored that you wish for their specific input. Give them a full copy of the proposal, however, so that they can refer to any section as needed. Two or three days is a reasonable turnaround time.

Professionalism & Ethics

Keep careful records. Be sure to keep careful notes about cost sourcing (as well as any other researched information). It will do you no good to know that widget C can be obtained for only $1.19, if you do not remember who offered that price. Making these notes will add to your professional knowledge base.

Final Draft

After you have confirmed factual information, you are ready to shape the final draft. Review the originating documents once again for deadlines and requirements, and make sure those have been met. Use the checklist for effective proposals at the end of this chapter. Construct tables or figures to make sure sums are correct and that decimal points are aligned in number columns.

Proofread!

Proofreading is so important that it deserves its own stage in the document cycle. Ask at least two people who are very attentive to detail to read it carefully. By yourself, read each sentence of the proposal, starting at the end of the document, to make sure that each one makes sense and contains no errors such as missing words or extra words. Run Spell Check. Then, check the document again yourself.

Tip: Word-Substitution Errors

Some common word-switching errors may be caused by your auto-correcting word processor. It is smart to run "Find" on these words that have no place in a professional proposal (you may start a list of your own frequent word errors):

begging (correct word: ***beginning***)

defiant (correct word: ***definite***)

incontinence (correct word: ***inconvenience***)

manger (correct word: ***manager***)

Have you spelled all names, including the names of organizations, correctly? People often overlook typos in titles. Are all titles, including figure titles spelled correctly? Are figures numbered correctly? Is your budget total correct? Add up the numbers one more time to be sure.

Submit: Cover Letter or No Cover Letter?

The purpose of the cover letter is to clarify purpose and establish polite communication. It should greet the recipient; tell him or her what is being sent and why; and provide the name and contact information of the sender.

When a proposal is sent by email, the email message should be a professional cover letter identifying the grant, RFP, or other purpose and establishing friendly contact. The proposal itself should be a downloadable attachment. If allowable, saving the proposal as a PDF (portable document format) file is preferable to preserve formatting and to protect proprietary information.

When you send a proposal by postal mail, a professional cover letter on company letterhead is necessary. Use business letter format. Just as in the email version, the letter should identify the grant, RFP or purpose and establish a friendly and courteous tone. Mail your proposal in a large manila envelope so that the pages emerge flat for best presentation.

Some proposals do not require a cover letter. For example, some are uploaded to a special website: scholarship applications are one type that is handled this way. In this type of proposal, there are usually other application elements, and a cover letter is not necessary; in fact, there may be no way to upload an extra document or write an extra message in these situations. When a bid is completed and handed to a customer in the field, such as for a minor home repair, a cover letter is not necessary. A smile and a handshake suffice.

The examples on the next pages show various types of proposals: Sample 10-1 is a grant proposal; Sample 10-2 is a memo proposal in hard copy format; Sample 10-3 is a bid sent via email.

Sample 10-1 Grant Proposal, Page 1

Proposal for Building a Garden Compost Structure

Ellsburg Community Garden

February 2015

Summary:

This proposal outlines a plan to construct an enclosure to contain and encourage composting at the Ellsburg Community Garden. Soil is an essential resource for successful gardening and can become depleted when the same plots are used year after year. Truckloads of purchased garden soil are expensive, and we have the garden material to produce our own compost on site. A sturdy and convenient compost structure will help us become more self-sufficient, as well as provide a learning opportunity for nearby elementary school science classes.

Background:

The Ellsburg Community Garden opened three years ago, in spring 2012, to serve the Ellsburg/Argon population. A dynamic and longstanding partnership between Ellsburg Presbyterian Church and Argon Elementary School enabled teachers, churchgoers, and community members to come together to build a planned garden of raised beds on an unused church-owned lot adjacent to the school. A grant from Ellsburg Garden Club provided money for the first phase of construction (eight 4' X 10' raised beds). By the end of the summer that year, we added eight more beds, thanks to a Portland State University student-led capstone project, for a total of 16 garden beds.

Metro Water Services donated a rainwater cistern and a pump and assisted in the placement of a water line to the garden, completed in the fall of 2013. Boy Scouts moved and refurbished a shed for garden use, and constructed a pump house. Last spring, schoolchildren designed and painted a mural on the cistern. We are slowly moving toward a visible role in the community and becoming a model for responsible use of resources.

Problem: We Need a Way to Manage Compost Successfully

The community garden generates a large amount of plant waste: grass clipping, weed pulling, and end-of-season garden bed clearing are rich sources of potentially compostable and soil-enriching materials. During the last two years, we have accumulated a large compost pile, but it is not producing compost for gardeners, as it is too massive to manage and turn correctly. Thus, the accumulating plant debris has become a useless and ungainly eyesore.

At the same time, we are now facing the need to replenish the soil in our garden beds. The soil level in all beds has settled to about half the depth it was three years ago, and the fertility of the raised beds has begun to decline. The garden is struggling to find the money to add more soil. A truckload of weed-free garden soil costs about $500 (Hudson

Sample 10-1 Grant Proposal, Page 2

Landscape Supply). Two bags of compost for each garden bed will run at least $125 ($3.92/bag from Lowe's, X 2 bags per bed X 16 beds). The annual rents for garden beds covers water and general field maintenance only.

Solution: a Permanent Compost Station

We propose to construct a multi-compartment slow-composting structure that will be easy to use and maintain, with one section available for new plant waste; one section actively composting; and one with finished compost. The area presently taken up by our loose compost pile is approximately 8' by 20.' The finished composting structure will be approximately 6' by 18', with 3 sections that are each 6 cubic ft., reducing and organizing the present space being used by discarded plant material.

The compost station will be set against the north fence, in an area where gardeners are currently dumping plant debris. The first step will be to clear the existing compost pile to make way for the permanent structure. After construction, the compost can be moved into the new bins. The aerial photo below shows the proposed location of the structure, against the fence. Trees in the area shade that location, making it unsuitable for gardening, but it is conveniently next to the path and close to the garden beds themselves:

Fig. 1: Aerial View of Community Garden showing general location of composting structure (map may not be to scale). Drawing by F. Sylwester, 2015.

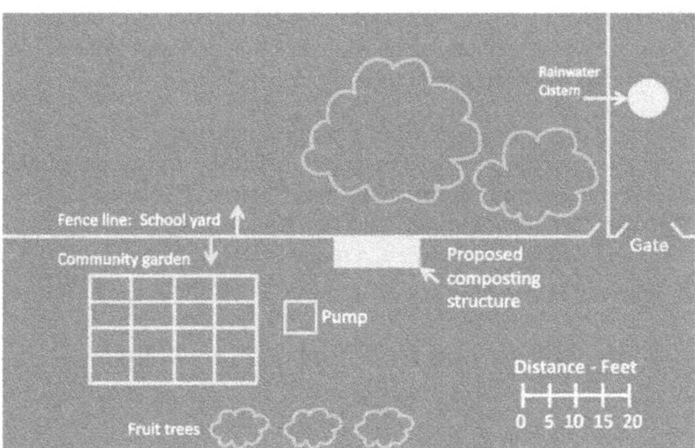

As the location, typical of northwest Oregon, is fairly moist and shady, the posts will be set in concrete to stabilize the structure and avoid rot. The walls at the front of each section will be made of removable, sliding planks to make removal and turning of compost easy. The illustration below, a photograph of a composting structure in place at Reedville Community Garden near Hillsboro, Oregon, shows a similar structure with removable boards along the front, to allow turning and removal of compost. One board is

Sample 10-1 Grant Proposal, Page 3

out of place in the photo, propped against the structure. Note that this structure is also along a fence, but includes four sections. Our plan is to include only three sections.

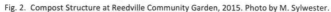

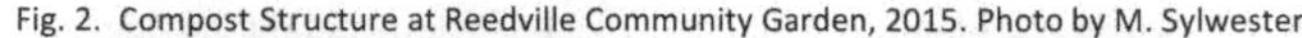
Fig. 2. Compost Structure at Reedville Community Garden, 2015. Photo by M. Sylwester.

Budgeted Materials:

Quantity	Item	Cost
6	2x4" X 10' Pressure treated lumber @6.97 ea Home Depot	41.82
8	2x4" X 12' Pressure treated lumber @8.57 ea Home Depot	68.56
18	2x2" X 8' Cedar @4.27 ea Home Depot	76.86
18	1x6" X 6' Common Board @ 2.87 ea Home Depot	51.66
2 rolls	½" mesh "poultry fence" cloth, 36" wide (comes in 25' roll at Home Depot, @ 19.77/roll)	39.54
6	3.5" zinc-plated butt hinges (2 per bin), 24 @ 1½" #8 screws) @3.97 ea., Lowe's	23.82
24	½x4" carriage bolts (+ nuts & washers); 25-count pkg =24.74, Home Depot	24.74
4 lbs.	2 -1/4" galvanized siding nails (5 lb. sold for $15.92, Home Depot)	15.92
1 lb.	plastic-cap aluminum roofing nails (sold in 1 lb. package, Ace Hardware)	8.49
8	4" flat corner braces + screws (4.59 for two-pack, Home Depot)	18.36
8	3" T-braces + screws @ 2.47 ea., Lowe's	19.76
1	bottle carpenter's glue, Lowe's	4.98
2 bags	gravel for setting posts @3.98, Home Depot	7.98
8 bags	quick-set concrete for setting 8 posts @ 4.98, Home Depot	39.84
Total Estimated Cost		442.33

Pricing information: Ace Hardware, Home Depot, Lowe's.. Jan. 2015 (prices subject to change)

Sample 10-1 Grant Proposal, Page 4

Budgeted Labor:

Volunteer Hours: 4 people X 24 hours = 92 hours. This project, including moving existing debris and leveling the area, is estimated to take three or four weekends of volunteer labor.

Timeline:

Date	Hours	Activity
May 17-18 (Weekend 1)	8	Clear and level current area for construction; move current compost pile to make room for construction and related activity. Mark planned location of compost station with stakes and twine.
May 24-25 (Weekend 2)	10	Prepare lumber to size. Set posts and construct compost station.
June 7-8 (Weekend 3)	3	Add existing plant material to new bins, signage to direct gardeners for deposits and withdrawals.
June 14 (Final Saturday)	3	Finish up any remaining work.

Anticipated Results:

The proposed permanent composting structure will enable us to supply the garden beds with self-composted soil and recycle the plant material we generate. If we can produce our own compost, we can also bypass the cost of replenishing soil in the future and also continue our mission of demonstrating a natural, self-sustaining garden and a healthy community. The composting station will also provide a teaching opportunity for the nearly elementary school in the earth science program there.

Conclusion:

The community garden is already self-supporting in terms of water and maintenance, from the cistern and rental fees. The only aspect of the garden that needs occasional outside funding is the input of fertile soil. This project can be completed in a few weekends by volunteer workers, and the materials should cost less than $600. This project is a wise investment in the future of the garden and in the health of our community.

Thank you for considering our application.

Sample 10-1 Grant Proposal, Page 5

References and Further Reading:

AceHardware.com. Ace Hardware Corporation. 2015. Web. 24 Jan. 2015.

"Build a Compost Bin." *OregonMetro.gov*. 2015. Web. 31 Jan. 2015.

"Composting Structures." *University of Minnesota Extension*. University of Minnesota. 2015. Web. 3 Jan. 2015.

HomeDepot.com. Homer TLC. 2015. Web. 29 Jan. 2015.

Lowes.com. LF, LLC. 2014. Web. 27 Jan. 2015.

Martin, Callie. "Home Composting 101." *SkagitCounty.net*. Skagit County, WA Solid Waste Division. 11 June 2009. Web. 12 Jan. 2015.

Contacts:

Patty Evenwood (503-111-2222) - Garden Coordinator
pevenwood@gmail.com

Mark Eckert (503-888-2002) - Committee Chair
mseckert@comcast.net

Ellsburg Community Garden
c/o Ellsburg Presbyterian Church
1595 NW 21st Ave.
Ellsburg, OR 97123
503-214-1234

Sample 10-2 Memo Proposal in Hard Copy Format, Page 1

Carson Medical Devices, Inc.

MEMORANDUM

Date: November 3, 2015

To: Terry Lancaster, Food Services Manager

From: Marshall Feinstein, Assembler

Subject: Proposed "Healthy Option" Menu Changes

Summary

The following memo proposes menu changes to the current cafeteria offerings. These changes are recommended based on health benefits and more diverse food options.

Background

As an employee of Carson Medical Devices for twelve years, I frequently eat in the company cafeteria. It provides a fresh, hot meal at a reasonable price. I know that the cafeteria has been in operation for 14 of the 15 years this company has been in business, and always operates at a profit according to the company reports.

Currently, the cafeteria offers many delicious options, but most are also high in animal fat, processed carbohydrates, processed meat, and high fructose corn syrup. For example, today's menu offerings are:

- Fried chicken (fried with white flour and pork lard) with potato salad (high in fat in the form of mayonnaise)
- Hot dogs (processed meat with white bread bun) with French fries (high in salt and saturated fat)
- Pizza (white flour crust topped with processed meat)

There were no low-fat options or fresh fruit and vegetables.

Sample 10-2 Memo Proposal in Hard Copy Format, Page 2

According to the USDA website (http://www.choosemyplate.gov/men-and-women#sthash.9mITdgdI.dpuf), diet is an important part of maintaining a healthy lifestyle:

> "Adults of all ages have different nutrition and physical activity needs as their lives and bodies change. A strong and healthy body can provide many benefits. As you age, maintaining healthy habits is an important way to lower your risk for cancer, diabetes, heart disease and hypertension. Make your food and beverage choices a priority and be physically active to feel and look better.
>
> **Eat a healthy diet**
>
> Fruits, vegetables, whole grains, and fat-free or low-fat dairy products are healthy choices. Include protein foods such as poultry, fish, beans, eggs, nuts and lean meats. Choose foods that are low in saturated fats, sodium, and added sugars."

Need

Employees at Carson Medical Devices need to have healthier choices for the lunch menu. Providing healthier choices can contribute to the overall health and well-being of our employees.

Project Description

I suggest that we begin by adding one healthier option for each lunch. For example, today's menu could have been:

- Fried chicken with potato salad
- Hot dogs with French fries
- Broiled fish and asparagus

As employees become accustomed to seeing one "healthy" item on the menu, they will expect to have that choice day after day. The demand for the healthier items may increase.

Timeline

Since there will be some training and supply chain challenges, I propose that the "Healthy Option" program begin after a month of research. If needed, I volunteer time to helping the cafeteria staff find the suppliers for the healthier food. As for training, I don't believe this is an issue. The healthier food requires less cooking because the food is simpler and doesn't require large vats of hot oil.

Sample 10-2 Memo Proposal in Hard Copy Format, Page 3

Budget

If there are any expenses involved in the introduction of the Healthy Option, it could be added to the cost of the new menu items and spread over the course of a year. Or, if Carson Medical Devices wants to support this proposal, perhaps some of the miscellaneous operating funds could be used. After all, having healthier employees can only benefit the company: fewer sick days, fewer health costs.

Results Expected

If the Healthy Option is implemented, all employees at Carson Medical Devices will have a food choice every day that is delicious and healthy. Some people who bring food from home or go out to lunch may begin to eat in the cafeteria because of the menu changes. The cafeteria could see an increase in patronage.

Conclusion

As a company that provides prosthetic devices to the medical community, we would be going one step toward improving our image, both to outsiders, and employees. Our business is health-related; our company should be health-conscious.

Thanks for reading this proposal. Feel free to contact me for further discussion of this proposal. My phone number is 555-5555, extension 6. My email is m.feinstein@carson.com.

Sample 10-3 Bid with Emailed Cover Letter, Page 1

From:	**Ellen Armstrong <armstrongphotos@gmail.com>**
Subject:	**Sinclair/LeRoq Wedding Video**
Date:	**March 22, 2017 2:02 p.m. PDT**
To:	**Amanda Sinclair <amanda25@hotmail.com**

Hi Amanda,

Thank you for stopping by my studio. I enjoyed talking with you this morning about your upcoming wedding!

Attached is a detailed price quote that reflects the plans we discussed.

Your date of August 30 is available in my schedule right now. Please let me know as soon as possible about your decision so I can hold that day for you. You can call me any time at (503)111-2222.

I appreciate the opportunity to help you preserve your beautiful wedding day memories, and I look forward to hearing from you soon.

Sincerely,

Ellen

Ellen Armstrong, Owner

ARMSTRONG WEDDING VIDEOS

503-111-222

armstrongphotos@gmail.com

Sample 10-3 Bid with Emailed Cover Letter, Page 2

armstrongphotos@gmail.com 503-111-2222
1145 Kirkegaard Lane Portland, OR 97100

PRICE QUOTE

Client: Amanda Sinclair

Date: 3/22/17

Project: Sinclair/LeRoq Wedding

Date of Wedding: August 30, 2017

Location: McMenamin's Grand Lodge, Forest Grove, OR

Project Description: Video of wedding from 2 hours pre-wedding through three hours of reception, including candid shots of wedding party before and after the ceremony.

I use only the best equipment in order to offer you excellent results. I have two assistants and will be on-site for 8 hours. Editing and adjusting the video for quality is part of the job. Within two weeks after your wedding, you will have a beautiful video on archival DVDs to remind you of your special day.

Thank you for your business!

Sincerely yours,

Ellen Armstrong, Owner

Description	Qty. @ Unit Price	Cost
Setup for stable and roaming video with Sony PMW-EX-3 XDCAM and Wireless Lavalier Microphones	1 day @ $450	$450
Assistant Camera Operators' Labor, 8 hrs.	1 day @ $240/day per operator, 2 operators	$480
Editing, Adjusting Color/Sound (includes notes, disc menu setup)	6 hrs. @ $50/hr.	$300
Archival DVDs	3 DVDs @ $20	$60
Total:		$1,290

IMPORTANT: A 10% deposit will save the date for you.

PROPOSAL *Checklist* ✔

An Effective Proposal . . .	✔
Is written in the appropriate format: email, memo, letter, report, or an example/template provided by the agency	
Begins with an introduction or overview	
Establishes or reviews the problem or need	
Provides specific qualifications or background of proposer (may not be necessary in workplace proposals)	
Provides an easy-to-follow project description	
Shows a clear timeline	
Offers a well-researched and itemized budget in readable form; gives details about resources needed (people, hours, skill sets, etc.)	
Presents alternatives wherever possible, and explains their shortcomings	
Describes the specific results expected	
Relates specific results to the larger picture	
Sums up the project narrative in the conclusion	
Expresses appreciation	
Gives contact information	
Uses natural English, language appropriate for the audience	
Uses correct grammar, spelling, and punctuation	

DISCUSSIONS

1. You are the manager of a small, struggling manufacturing firm. A colleague tells you of a grant that is available for projects your firm is perfectly suited for doing. In reading the grant, you notice that your company does not meet every qualification specified. However, you are confident that you can do the work, and do it well. Should you apply for the grant? What do you recommend?
2. In writing up a bid for a customer to do some remodeling, you notice that the job may require some re-wiring to be performed prior to starting the project. You will not know for certain, however, until the walls are opened up and the work has begun. Should you write the cost of the wiring into the bid? Going too high may cause you to lose the job.
3. You work with several women who are breastfeeding; they normally express milk on their breaks in the restroom and store it in the office refrigerator. You think that your workplace needs to designate a lactation room with its own refrigerator. What might be the obstacles to this proposal and whom do you need to convince? Suggest strategies for getting this project approved.
4. In your experience, either in work or in life, what kinds of suggestions have you made that were unsuccessful? In retrospect, what could you have said or done to make approval more likely?

EXERCISES

1. **Write a brief proposal in hard copy memo format for an improvement to your own household,** such as the purchase and installation of a household appliance or the implementation of a new chores schedule. Specify the audience for your proposal and include all essential proposal elements. Maximum length two pages.
2. **Design a one-page form for a service company** (such as landscaping or housecleaning) that employees can use in the field to write up bids for customers. Make sure that spaces for important elements are included so that employees do not forget anything.
3. **Research and report about business practices in a country outside the U.S.** and present your findings to the class. Provide documentation for your report. Are there ways that proposals might be read in that country that are different from expectations in the U.S.?
4. **Write a formal proposal for a project that will benefit your community, and that would require less than $5000 to complete.** Designate a specific audience, such as a community group, city committee, housing association, or other community organization. Plans, budget, and timeline should not be just made up; research the expenses and labor required, and document your sources for that information in the proposal. Include plans for maintenance or continuation.

   Sample ideas for Exercise 4 proposals :

   - Co-ops of various kinds (childcare, tool-sharing, book-lending, food-buying)
   - Community gardens
   - Youth mentoring organizations
   - Shared repair/craft spaces, car sharing
   - Anything else you can think of that would have long-term benefits and can be created cheaply

   Use the Budget Estimate Worksheet on the next page to keep track of pricing estimates for your project.

BUDGET *Worksheet*

Budgeted Materials			
Item & Provider	Price per item	Quantity	Total Price
		Materials Subtotal→	
Budgeted Labor			
Activity	Cost per hour	Hours	Total Price
		Labor Subtotal→	
Other Costs (overhead, mileage)			
Other Costs Subtotal			
Materials + Labor+ Other = Total Estimated Cost			

11 - Writing for the Web

Almost everyone in our society goes online, perhaps daily, mining the Internet for information. Rather than referring to encyclopedias in bulky printed volumes, or going to the library and searching for books or articles on your topic, you have probably gotten used to using a search engine such as Google to quickly look up answers.

Because **Internet** (the "web") material is easy to access, cheap to produce, and extremely popular, it has become an integral part of doing business in the US. Therefore, you may be tasked with writing for your company's publicly accessible website or for your company's **intranet** site, which is accessible only to employees and other authorized readers. Or, you may create your own website, which is very common for entrepreneurs who wish to have a web presence. The daunting task is made much easier now using applications that keep the HTML (hyper-text mark-up language) hidden. In other words, you don't have to software code your way onto the Internet.

As easy as it may be to produce material for the web, it's not easy to produce good, effective material. Knowing how to present information and how to be persuasive are learned skills for web writing. Here are some important considerations to think about before planning and writing a web page or article:

- Who is my target audience and how do I reach them?
- What is my purpose in writing the web page or article?
- What are my ethical considerations? Where does my information originate? Is the source reliable? Have I cited the source?
- What graphic elements will I use?
- How will I design the page?
- What do I want/need to say, and how do I say it?
- How can I organize the information for the reader?
- How can I make the web page as readable as possible?
- Do I have enough time to do a good job? Do I have a proofreader? Do I have a tester available before I "go live" with this page/article/site?
- For websites only: Do I have enough time to maintain this website once it has launched?

PURPOSE AND AUDIENCE

Just as with printed documents, online pages require that you carefully examine your purpose and audience. Every web page isn't meant for everyone. Using choices in design and content, web page creators use every way possible to appeal to their target audience.

For example, notice the differences between the two examples below. Figure 11-1 shows a US Government website intended for adults. The people who might be interested in going to this site might be trying to find out general information to get started with a recycling program. Or maybe they just want to find out if they should be recycling. In any case, the reader will probably be citizens who want to do their part to recycle and find information about how to get started easily.

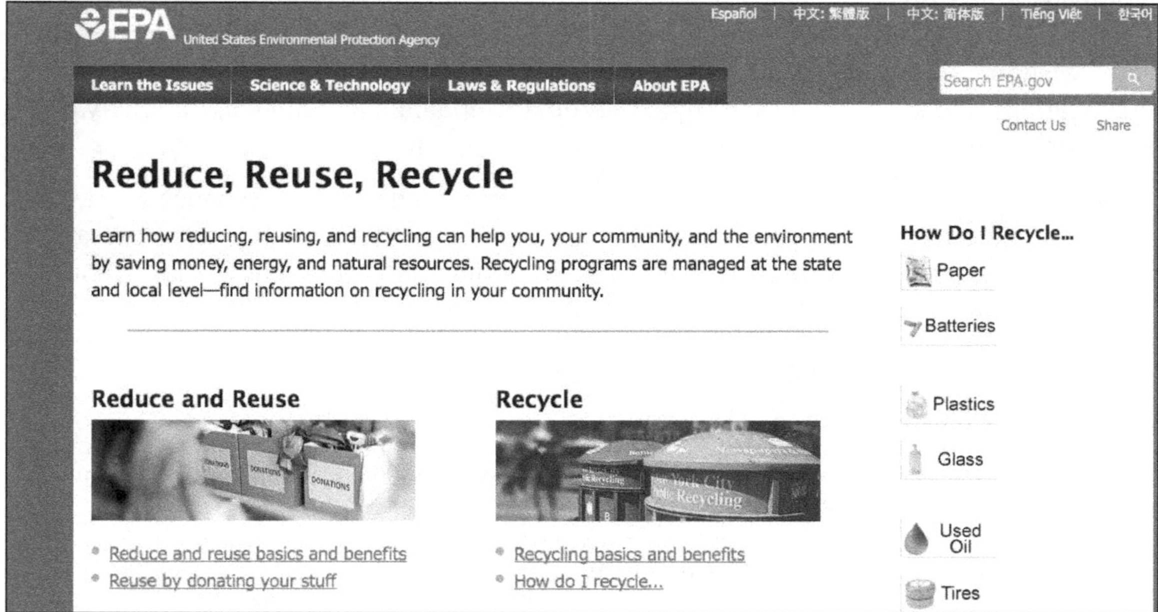

Figure 11-1 EPA Recycling Website for Adults. Source: www2.epa.gov

The webpage has a clean, understated, modern look. It appeals to both women and men, as evidenced by the lack of photographs depicting any particular gender. Both photos highlight the recycling containers, rather than the people who are recycling. The page makes it easy to click on the tabs, the menu at the right, or the links below the pictures. This webpage would be a good introduction to the world of recycling for the average American adult.

In contrast, take a look at Figure 11-2, showing another recycling web page for a different audience: children.

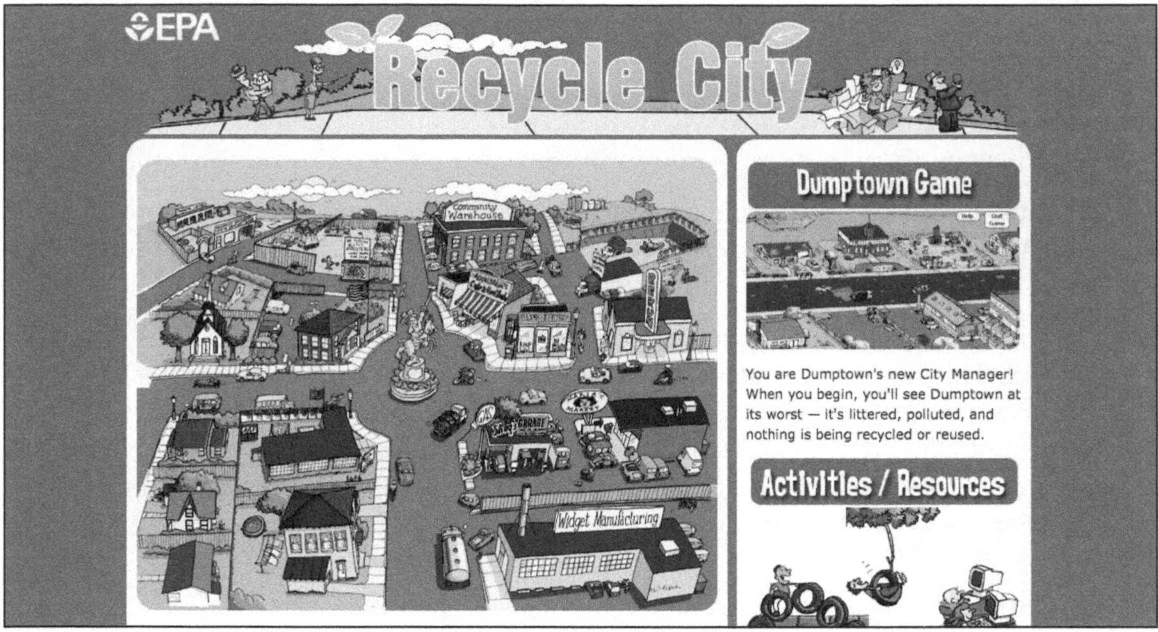

Figure 11-2 EPA Recycling Web Page for Children. Source: www3.epa.gov

This web page uses bright primary colors. When you place your cursor over the large graphic, the message "Click here to get started" appears. This allows children a very easy way to get to the second level of the website, which shows the quadrants of the city: Northeast, Northwest, Southeast, and Southwest.

Each page is an activity, allowing children to do a lot of clicking on colorful icons to learn various aspects of recycling.

The two examples above show how web designers and writers zero in on their target audiences. Every choice is conscious.

ETHICAL STANDARDS AND CULTURAL SENSITIVITY

More information is available to more people in the world than ever before in human history. However, more disinformation is also available. Anyone with access to a computer and the Internet can write or post just about anything. Opinion can be masked as truth; even intentional lies can appear to be truth. You cannot believe everything you read online.

As a writer, your goal is to ensure that everything that you post to an intranet or the Internet is clear, honest, and factual. The penalty for posting information that is not true ranges from losing credibility to losing thousands of dollars in a libel lawsuit. If you publish information that is untrue or malicious on your corporate intranet, you will certainly be reprimanded and may lose your job.

Avoiding Cultural Bloopers

Another area where web content can go wrong is not taking into consideration the potential for cultural problems. You may be able to zero in on your target audience very well. But don't do it at the risk of alienating another audience. Remember that anything posted on the Inernet is available worldwide to diverse cultures, and not just to your target audience.

An example of how a very good marketing idea can turn detrimental is an ad run by Absolut Vodka in Mexico City several years ago. Even though the ad appeared as a billboard and print, the image swiftly went around the world on the Internet.

The ad shows the area that was part of Mexico before the Mexican-American War of 1846-1848. This image upset some people in the United States who thought that there was a movement underway for Mexico to take back the area it lost (California, Nevada, Utah, most of New Mexico and Arizona, and parts of Colorado and Wyoming). Many websites encouraged United States citizens to boycott Absolut and to send messages to their corporate office. Absolut issued an apology and withdrew the advertisement.

GRAPHICS ON THE WEB

In general, the same principles for print media apply to web media in terms of graphics. The key to successful graphics use on the web is to control the urge to add too many graphics, too much color, and distracting motion just because it's "free." When the Internet first came into the workplace and home, websites were typically cluttered and over-engineered. Logos would spin, music would play, bright colors were used indiscriminately, and it was much like a digital three-ring-circus.

When writing or designing for the web, keep the number of graphics to a minimum and make absolutely sure that each one contributes effectively to the content. You may use a graphic to draw the attention of the reader, but use a heading below the graphic that informs the reader and invites further reading. Or you may use one as a background, providing a pleasing backdrop for the landing, or home, page.

The next two graphics show how a landscape photo adds interest and unites the various elements of official state web pages.

Figure 11-3 below is the official web site for the State of South Carolina.

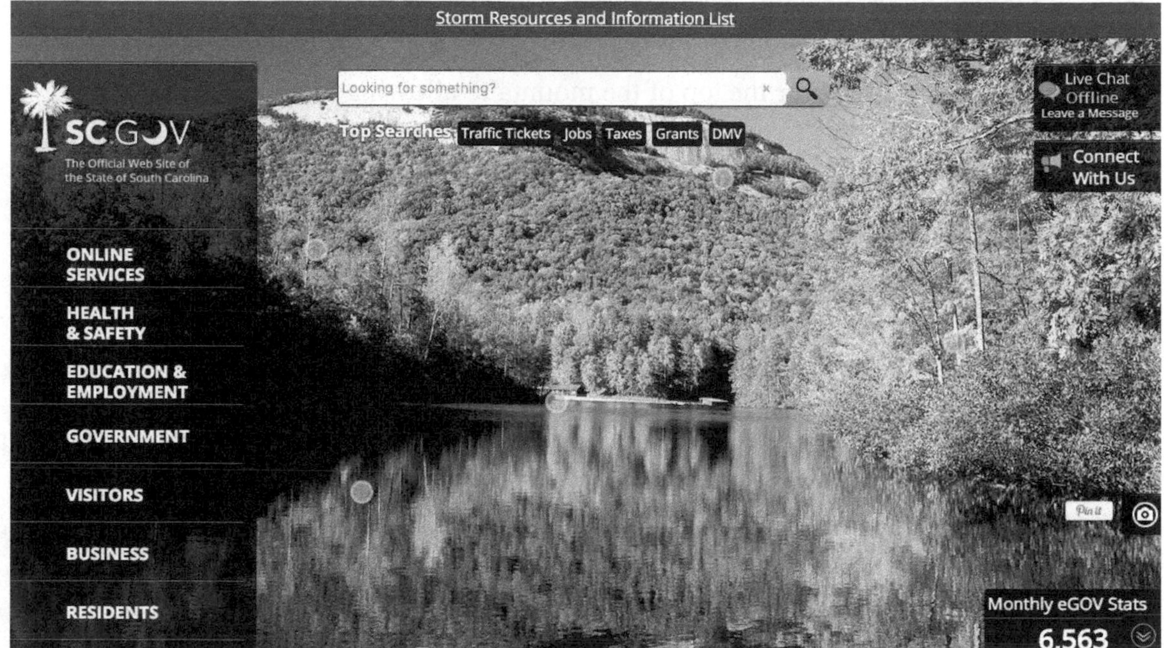

Figure 11-3 South Carolina Website. Source: http://www.sc.gov

This web page takes advantage of South Carolina's beautiful scenery. However, there are distracting orange circles (such as the one clearly seen in the water just to the right of the left-hand column) sprinkled over the graphic. Each orange circle has a news blurb about South Carolina, such as which town is particularly inviting to new business, or a balloon festival in another town. There is a prominent search box, but it's obscuring the top of the mountain in the distance.

One the plus side, the links at the left offer easily navigation. However, the apparent random placement of the items on the right give the web site an unfinished aspect.

Figure 11-4 below shows a more pleasing layout for a web site. It uses a breathtaking photo of Oregon natural beauty as a background and offers easy links to the side and below. The menu at the top contains a comprehensive list of information about Oregon.

The search box doesn't cover the top of the mountain, allowing the reader to enjoy the vista.

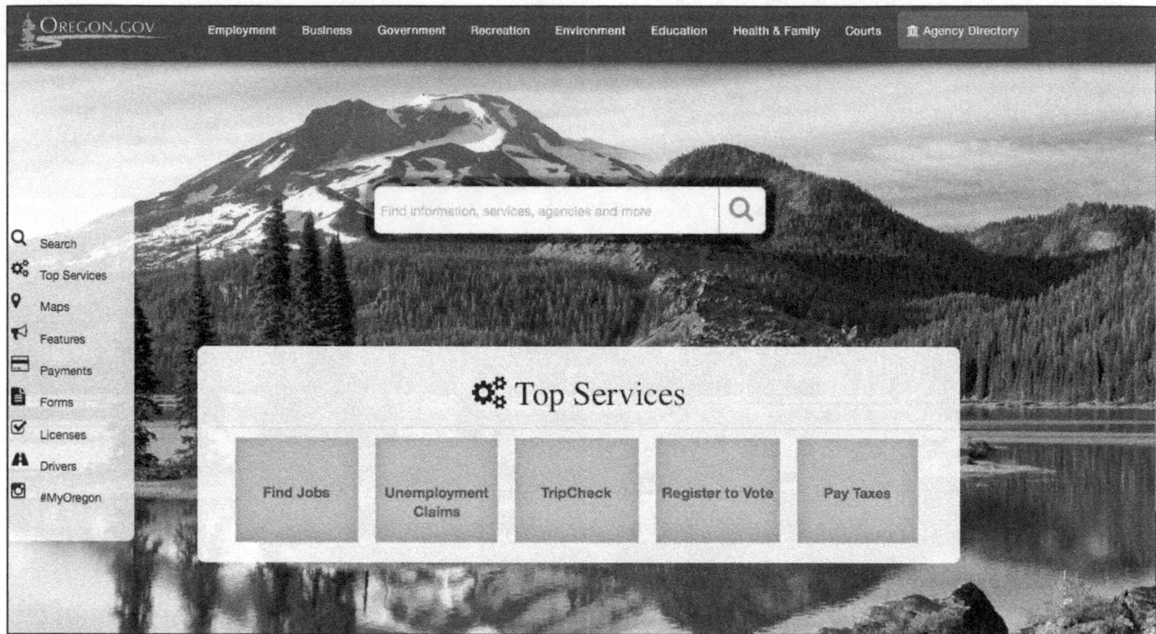

Figure 11-4 Oregon State Website. Source: www.oregon.gov

Although both state websites are commendable, the Oregon site handles graphic elements more gracefully. It is balanced and pleasing to the eye.

PAGE DESIGN

As the web matures, more and more research points to the tendency for readers to prefer simple, very legible pages. Since the possibilities for creating complex and colorful pages are endless, writers and designers must show restraint.

We now know that most **readers don't read web pages**. They scan, looking for headings and links. They want to retrieve quickly or link to another page. If the page requires careful reading, and the reader is motivated, such as for mapquest.com driving instructions, the reader will usually print out the material.

Taking into account that the audience will scan the page, headings, sub-headings, and bullets play an even more important role than in print media. You can think of these organizational items as equivalent to signs on the freeway. The user is speeding through the page and needs to see quickly where he or she is (page header = highway number) and what options are available (billboards = headings, subheadings, bullets). Alternate routes or destinations (links = exits) are clearly marked.

Home Page

The home page, or landing page, is the first page you see when you go to a website. It serves as a table of contents for the rest of the site and also communicates the image for the product or service. An example of a very usable home page is seen in Figure 11-5. Travel Portland is a website developed by a private non-profit organization that promotes the city of Portland, Oregon as a tourist destination.

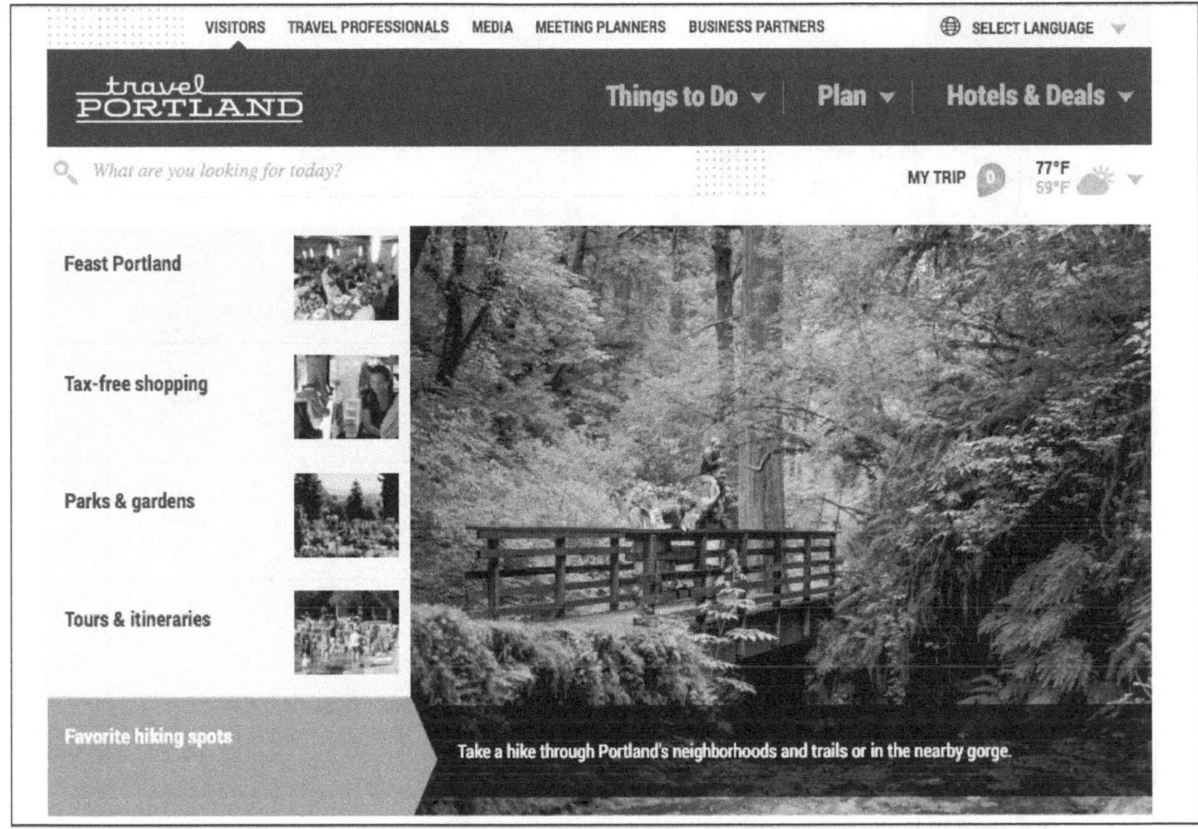

Figure 11-5 Travel Portland Home Page. Source: http://www.travelportland.com/

Notice how the home page highlights one large graphic at a time, by automatically scrolling through the major sections on the left. The website is extremely versatile, allowing the user to choose his or her role (top menu: visitors, travel professionals, media, meeting planners, business partners) and language.

The use of text is minimal, and the headings on the left serve as links.

Content Page

A content page is a page that is accessed from the home page. It gives some detail about one of the topics chosen on the home page. Web content consists of web copy, or text, but it also includes graphics, videos, sounds, animations, blogs, etc. A content page may be very general and provide links to web content for further detail. In this manner, the user can make choices to find the exact topic and format he or she is looking for.

Using the Travel Portland example, we see in Figure 11-6 a content page for the "Favorite hiking spots" heading.

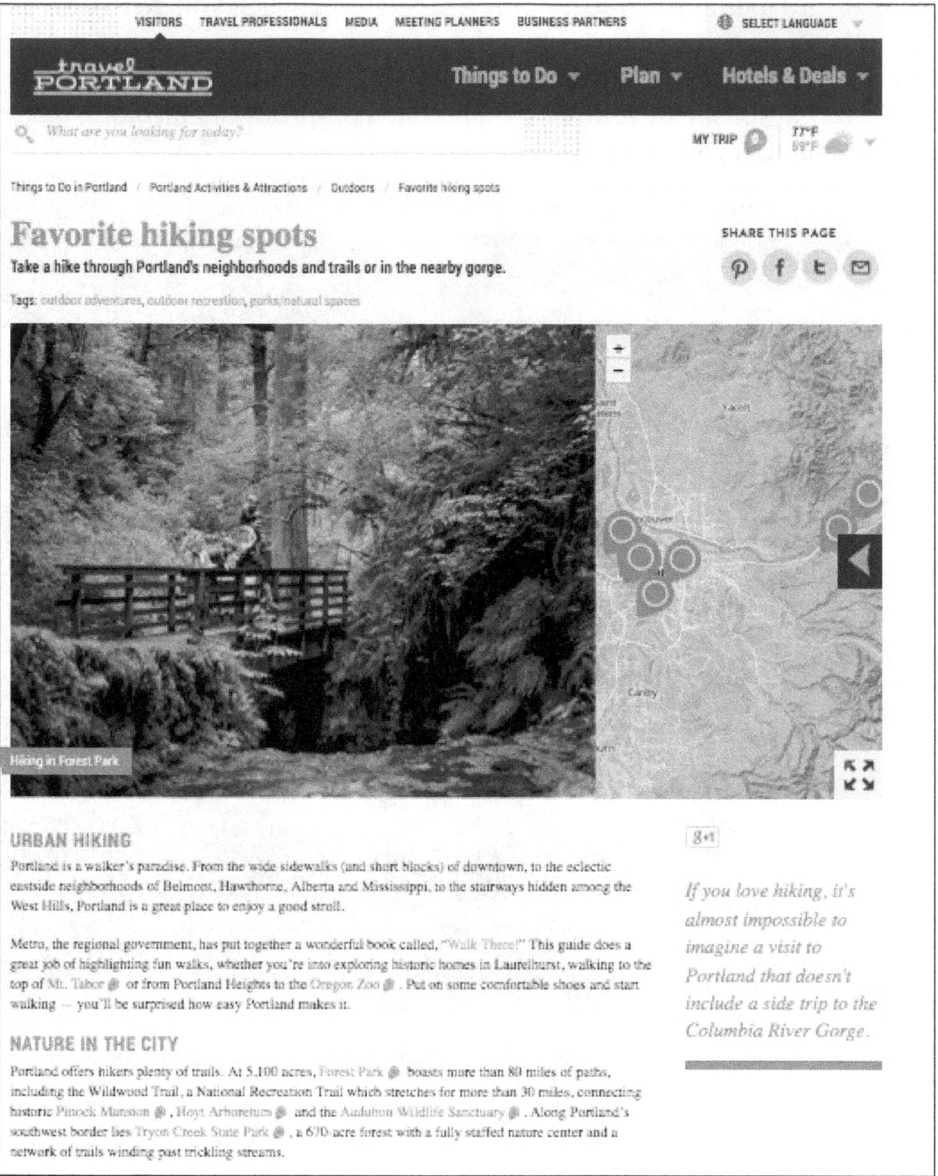

Figure 11-6 Travel Portland Content Page. Source: http://www.travelportland.com/article/favorite-hiking-spots/

This content page repeats the graphic from the home page, using it as a marker to let the reader know that he or she has reached the intended page. A map to the right helps the Portland tourist find the recommended hiking areas. Subheadings are used to divide the content into types of hikes, and links are used within the paragraphs to allow the user to go directly to any options of interest.

The Travel Portland website is an example of how the principles of web page design can be applied effectively. The paragraphs are short and the sentences have a simple structure. The overall look of each page is attractive and informative. Readers can dip in and find what they need quickly. The image of the City of Portland is enhanced by the professionalism of the website.

Formatting Choices

In general, the same formatting choices for printed text apply for web pages. These include:

- Left-aligned text
- White or very light background
- Black or very dark text
- Limited use of font families

Unless you are a very experienced web designer, it's best to stay away from "dark" web pages, in which the background is dark and the text is light. It's a difficult combination to pull off effectively, and may ruin your chances for readability.

Some formatting choices are especially tailored for web pages:

- Underlined links (no other use of underlining)
- Narrower margins (shorter lines of text)

CONTENT: HARD COPY TO WEB COPY

In most cases, material that is chiefly created for hard copy (magazine articles, for example) is placed on the web without restructuring the content. This type of content is intended for serious readers who are motivated to read the online page as they would read a hard copy version. Even so, the text for online reading is likely altered somewhat, unless the content is a PDF. The column width may change, the space between lines in a paragraph may increase, the graphics may be placed in a slightly different place, etc.

The most important difference between a print article and an online article is the ability of the online format to allow for linking to other parts of the site, or other sites on the web (hyperlinks).

The following example (Figure 11-7) shows how a magazine article can be adapted to the web. Notice the prevalence of hypertext (the text in the article that has a link) and how these links add to the usability of the article. Readers can go into further depth on any hyperlink.

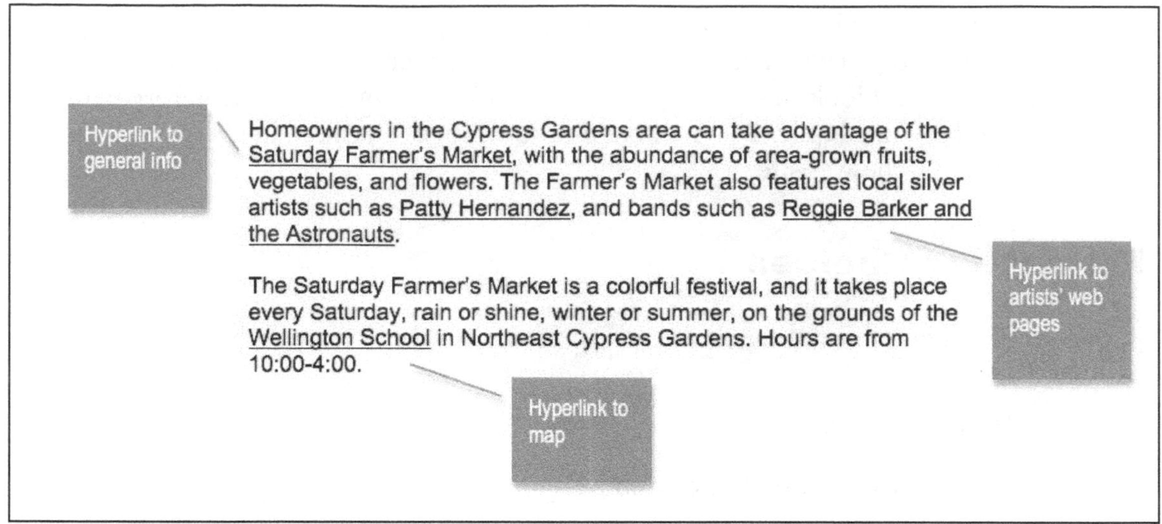
Homeowners in the Cypress Gardens area can take advantage of the Saturday Farmer's Market, with the abundance of area-grown fruits, vegetables, and flowers. The Farmer's Market also features local silver artists such as Patty Hernandez, and bands such as Reggie Barker and the Astronauts.

The Saturday Farmer's Market is a colorful festival, and it takes place every Saturday, rain or shine, winter or summer, on the grounds of the Wellington School in Northeast Cypress Gardens. Hours are from 10:00-4:00.

Figure 11-7 Example Text with Hypertext and Hyperlinks

Otherwise, the adapted article follows the basic guidelines of good page design and clear writing. Paragraphs can be longer than 50 words, as happens frequently in printed material, and sentences can be complex. The audience for the particular piece determines tone, word choice, sentence and paragraph length.

BLOGGING

Blogging is a special kind of web writing that involves serial contributions to a website. "Blog" (short for web log), like newsletter or editorial columns, showcases a personal voice and can be used to promote, inform, inspire, instruct, market, complain, or virtually any purpose the writer desires.

This emphasis on a personal voice with an identifiable perspective is unusual in technical writing, but has become a dominant form of web writing, and it is the reason that this form is so variable. Some blogs are simply the writer's personal expression and vary from day to day; others focus on one topic, such as politics or parenting, and attract interested readers.

Bloggers interested in making money from their efforts have advertising on their sites. In these blogs, traffic on the site becomes important to the blogger, as advertising dollars can fluctuate accordingly.

Some blogs are included in company newsletters to employees or customers; those directed at customers are often marketing tools for product or company promotion.

Audience

If you are asked to write a blog, remember that an awareness of your target audience is crucial.

Readers of a blog are attracted both to the topic addressed and, significantly, to the personality, credibility, or ethical stance of the writer. They often leave comments at the end of a blog post, and the blogger frequently replies. The combination of the blog and comments creates the sense of a like-minded social gathering, similar to that found in social networks. The difference, of course, is that the blog topic and blogger are the central focus.

Strategies

Because blogs depend on the writer's persona, they are normally written in the first person (using "I"). Because they inherit the "log" tradition, they are also usually dated and presented chronologically. Topics may vary by season or with trends or world events.

Bloggers and others who are interested in web traffic engage in search engine optimization (SEO). SEO is the strategy of adjusting vocabulary and content to bring the website to the top of a user's search engine results list. For example, a blog that refers to creating art or photo pages to memorialize events will probably attract more readers if the word "scrapbook" is used, as that is a word likely to be used in searches.

The title of the blog helps bring readers to the site, just as a headline once upon a time sold newspapers. So, bloggers analyze their audience carefully and write titles accordingly: what are the audience's needs? concerns? interests? pleasures? Here are some sample titles from actual blogs in 2015:

- Finance Girl
- Dream Green DIY
- Remodelaholic

Users do not usually type specific titles into their browser search engines. More often, they are looking for certain topics and type in words that are important to them. You can easily see that "remodel" may bring up one of these; "DIY" + "green" will bring up another, and "finance" + "girl" may find the first. Search engines of course seek key words in the articles within a blog as well, but the title of a blog, like any other document, is the first opportunity to signal what it holds.

Professionalism & Ethics

Since a blog implicitly encourages readers to depend on your words, it is very important that you consider those words carefully. If you recommend a product or give instructions, it is very important that you check facts carefully and include cautions or safety measures where appropriate. If you recommend actions in the social or political sphere, make sure that these actions are ethical, legal, and reasonable.

WEB PAGE *Checklist* ✔

An Effective Web Page . . .	✔
Is geared to the audience (See the Web Audience Worksheet on page 46)	
Fulfills the purpose	
Contains factual information; follows ethical standards; is credible	
Demonstrates cultural sensitivity	
Uses graphical elements well; contains no distracting elements that detract from the purpose and audience's understanding	
Has a pleasing, uncluttered page design	
Uses concise, direct, plain language	
Enables the reader to find what they want without reading everything	
Makes use of effective headings and subheadings	
Limits paragraph length to 50 words or less, unless adapted from hard copy or intended for in-depth reading	
Uses simple sentence structure	
Uses correct grammar, spelling, and punctuation	

DISCUSSIONS

1. Your supervisor has asked you to write a report with graphics for the corporate intranet summarizing the progress of his or her "pet project." You write the report using complete factual data and present it to your supervisor for approval. Your supervisor reads it and asks you into the office to privately discuss showing only the favorable data, leaving out any project problems. How would you handle this?
2. For an online discussion, find a web article that seems to provide opinion masked as objective reporting. What clues do you see that make you think the material is misleading? Provide the URL for the article so that others may refer to it.
3. Research some web bloopers and report them to the class.
4. Discuss the differences between the following websites advertising bridal gowns:

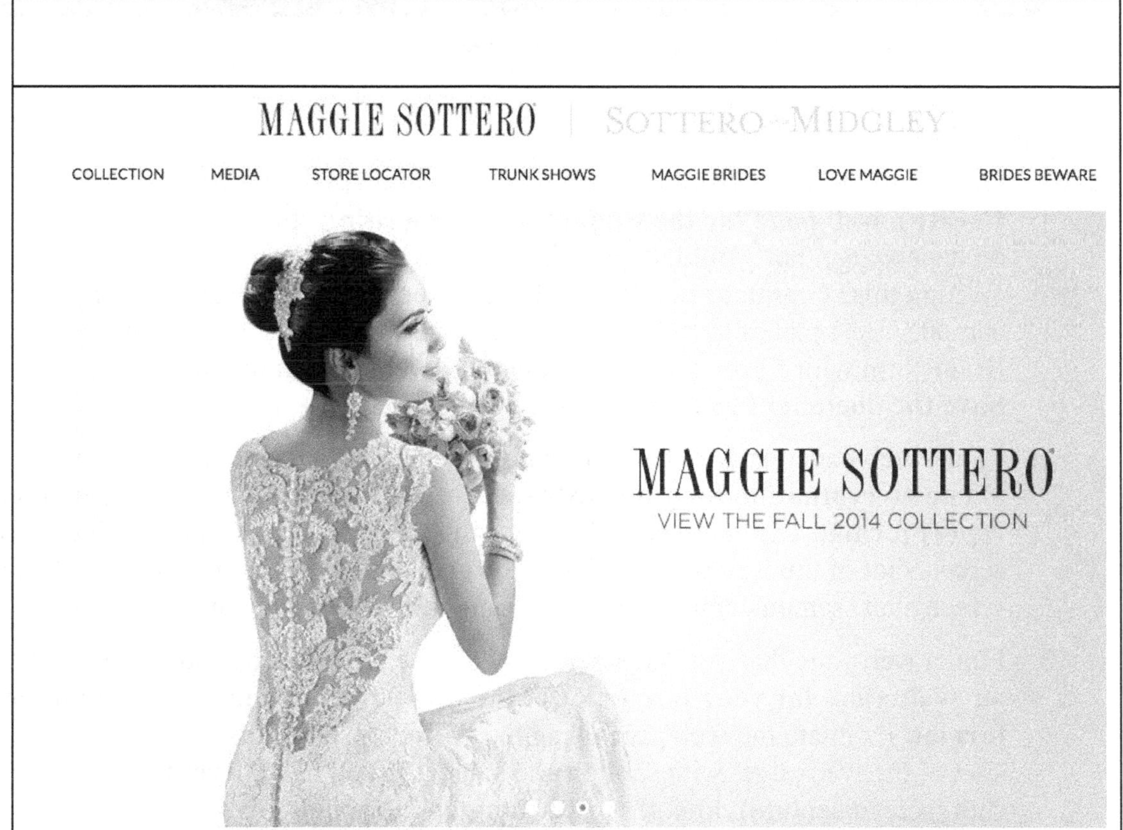

Figure 11-8 Maggie Sottero Wedding Gown Website. Source: http://www.maggiesottero.com/

Figure 11-9 Bridal Website Mock-up. Source: Anonymous

EXERCISES

1. **Create a web page for the students in your writing class.** What could you put on a web page that would interest the members of the class? Software tips? Writing tips? Grammar rules? Sample documents? Cheap restaurants close by the campus? Best places to park? Bus and rail lines? Best coffee on campus? Brainstorm with a group and then design the web page individually or as a group. **Save the document as a web page.**
2. Find a web page that you have determined to be poorly written and designed. **Write an evaluation for your instructor of the web page in an internal memo report format.** Evaluate the web page using the Web Page Checklist. Include a screen shot of the web page, with caption and source. If you have never taken a screen shot (screen capture), look for instructions online about how to do it.
3. Find a web page that you have determined to be well written and designed. **Write an evaluation for your instructor of the web page in an internal memo report format.** Evaluate the web page using the Web Page Checklist. Include a screen shot of the web page, with caption and source. If you have never taken a screen shot (screen capture), look for instructions online about how to do it.

12 - Job Application Materials

You probably already have a resume on hand and have applied for jobs in the past, sending a cover letter or email along with the resume. You might not realize how important these materials are. They are the first impression you offer a prospective employer, and they make that impression in a matter of seconds. A hiring manager may have hundreds of applications to go through, and you must make a good impression to keep yours in the "keep" pile.

Job application materials are unique in professional writing, as the point of view is personal. In nearly all other workplace or technical writing situations, your topic is a product or a company or a customer or a process, and you as writer are present only in your business role. Technical writers are almost never acknowledged in the documents they prepare. In a job application, however, you are putting yourself forward as the topic to be examined. When you compose a resume or cover letter, you are writing about yourself. Your experience and personal qualities are the evidence presented for persuasive consideration.

The figure below shows the emphasis on writer and topic in this persuasive writing situation.

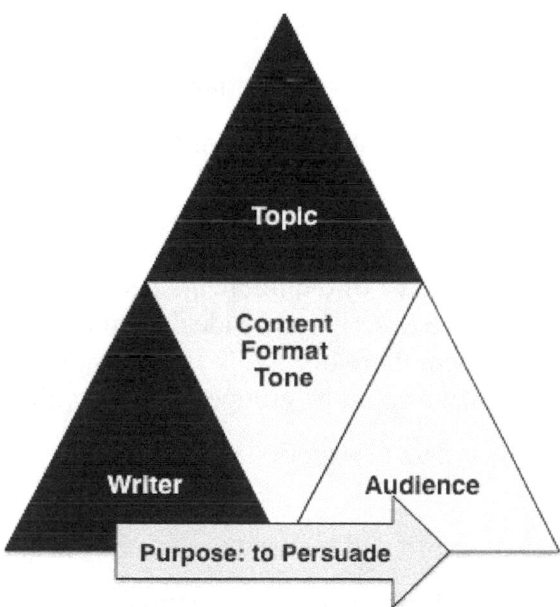

Figure 12-1 Communication Triangle for Job Application Materials

JOB ADVERTISEMENT ANALYSIS

First, read the job advertisement carefully. Highlight key words used in the job description. The simple example below shows the organization of a typical job ad.

Sample 12-1 Job Ad

Restaurant Manager

Job Description: This person is responsible for creating a positive experience for customers; ordering food and maintaining documentation of inventory to ensure freshness; hiring, training, and overseeing staff to make sure the operations run smoothly; and monitoring the cleanliness of the restaurant at all times.

The ideal manager will

- have at least three years of managerial experience in the restaurant industry, including management of inventory and staff
- understand profit and loss statements
- be familiar with health and safety standards for food and kitchen
- be a strong leader and a creative problem-solver
- be willing to work evenings and weekends

Read critically. Rather than scanning the list of requirements needed and trying to match them to your resume, analyze the parts of the job description or ideal attributes, and organize them for yourself so that you can understand them more deeply. In the example above, notice that the various responsibilities and requirements could be grouped into four different categories:

- **Quantifiable requirements** (years of experience, nights and weekends of potential work)
- **Knowledge** (familiarity with profit and loss statements, health and safety regulations)
- **Skills** (documenting inventory, hiring and training staff)
- **Personal strengths** (leadership, creativity, positive attitude, problem-solving)

Reviewed in this way, the job ad becomes less a checklist and more a usable guide to presenting yourself. Which aspects do you think somewhat negotiable, which are easily learned, and which are most important and non-negotiable? For example, knowledge of financial statements and safety regulations is crucial, but that knowledge can be learned, and the job is much more than just reviewing spreadsheets and checklists. This job involves monitoring products, people, and places. And, to do that, a person needs to be able to keep track of details in a systematic way. A resume that reflects your ability to organize and present information clearly, then, will be very important.

Normally, a job application includes two items: **a cover letter and a resume (or CV).** Some job postings may require other materials, such as school transcripts, proof of citizenship, visa documents, or even answers to essay questions. Your application may be submitted by postal mail or, more usually, by email.

COVER LETTER

The cover letter is more than just a shipping receipt for the resume. The goal of the letter is to get you an interview, so take a lot of care in preparing it. Demonstrate your professionalism, make yourself interesting, and show that you are right for the job. This letter should get the reader to consider you as a real candidate, not just a list of skills and work experience. Highlight your unusual qualifications or your enthusiasm about certain parts of the job: "I recently completed a fascinating internship with ABC company, helping design sewer lines for developing countries, and I am eager to expand my experience in civil engineering."

The letter also allows you an opportunity to reassure your reader about parts of your resume that may raise questions: gaps in your work experience, apparent demotions, or unusually brief positions. Address these directly, without appearing to avoid or hide from inevitable questions. For example, "During the last year, I have been caring for my elderly grandfather; now that he has moved into hospice, I am again seeking full-time employment."

Email is the usual medium for job application letters, but some employers may request a printed application. Whether you write in a digital or paper format, the letter should demonstrate your professional standards: complete sentences, formal salutation, reasonable paragraphing, and a formal closing. Make sure you have the correct email address for the recipient; check the job ad for the specific individual or department who is receiving the applications. The date (normally part of standard letter format) is assigned by the email program itself. See Sample 12-3 on page 262, Emailed Cover Letter, for an example.

When the recipient opens the email, he or she should immediately see the text of your letter. Do not send a blank or minimal email message with the cover letter as attachment. Consider that your reader may be going through 100 application emails, and an email message that says only "Here is my application for the nurse's aide position" will be easy to skip. Hook the reader with an engaging letter immediately. Your resume should be the only attachment.

Cover Letter Format and Structure

Subject Line

The subject line is your first chance to make sure that your letter is read in the appropriate context. Recipients look at subject lines to determine (1) whether they should open the file (is it spam?) and (2) what topic it involves. Companies may have more than one open position, and so recipients may separate emails into different folders in the email stream. The subject line should identify the position and convey its professional intent. Do not write a friendly or personal note in the subject line ("Hey—just wondering") as it will jettison your letter into the spam folder or (at best) show that you do not know how to write professional emails.

Salutation

If the job ad instructs you to reply to a particular person, name that person in your salutation (Dear Mr. Johnson:). *Never* address your reader by his or her first name; maintain professional standards of courtesy. If no person is listed, but you are instructed to reply to a certain department, or perhaps just an email address, you may write "Dear Hiring Manager." "Sir or Madam" is somewhat old-fashioned, and "To Whom It May Concern" is downright generic.

Professionalism & Ethics

You may have heard it said that you should dress for the job you want to have; you should also write in the same professional mode that will be expected of you should you be hired. Aim for a cordial tone—pleasant but appropriately formal. Avoid begging for the job. Employers do not hire the person who seems neediest or funniest; they hire the person who seems to have the right qualifications and to be a good fit for the business. The person reading your letter and resume will try to imagine how you would function as part of the existing team.

Three-Part Body

Your letter should be limited to one page, but it is a good idea to divide it into paragraphs, even if each one is fairly brief. The white space between paragraphs signals a new thought and allows the reader to renew his or her focus. Three paragraphs usually will do the job very well, each covering a different topic. You may use more than three paragraphs, but think about the letter in terms of three general parts: the introduction, details, and closing.

1. **Introduction.** Tell what position you are applying for; where you saw the advertisement or heard of the job opening, and say something about why you are capable of doing the work.

2. **More about you and why you are well suited to the job.** Why do you feel that you are particularly well-qualified? Summarize your work experience or special qualities. Do not list everything you have done here (that's what the resume does); pull out just a couple of the most-relevant experiences to highlight. In this section, you can give more detail about those experiences and say how they have influenced you or prepared you. In this paragraph you can also detail how the position you are applying for fits your current goals and life circumstances.

3. **Conclusion.** Refer to the resume that you have attached or enclosed. Thank the reader for the chance to be considered, and ask (politely) for a chance to discuss the job further (interview).

Closing

At the end of your letter or email, choose a courteous and respectful closing line ("Sincerely" or "Best regards" are good choices). In a printed letter, leave space above your printed name for your penned signature. Your typed name should be followed by your current title (if you have one), and contact information such as phone number and email. Remember, the hiring manager cannot call you for an interview if he or she does not have your phone number.

Sample cover letters are shown on the next two pages. Sample 12-2 is a printed cover letter, and Sample 12-3 is an emailed cover letter.

Sample 12-2 Printed Cover Letter for Job Application

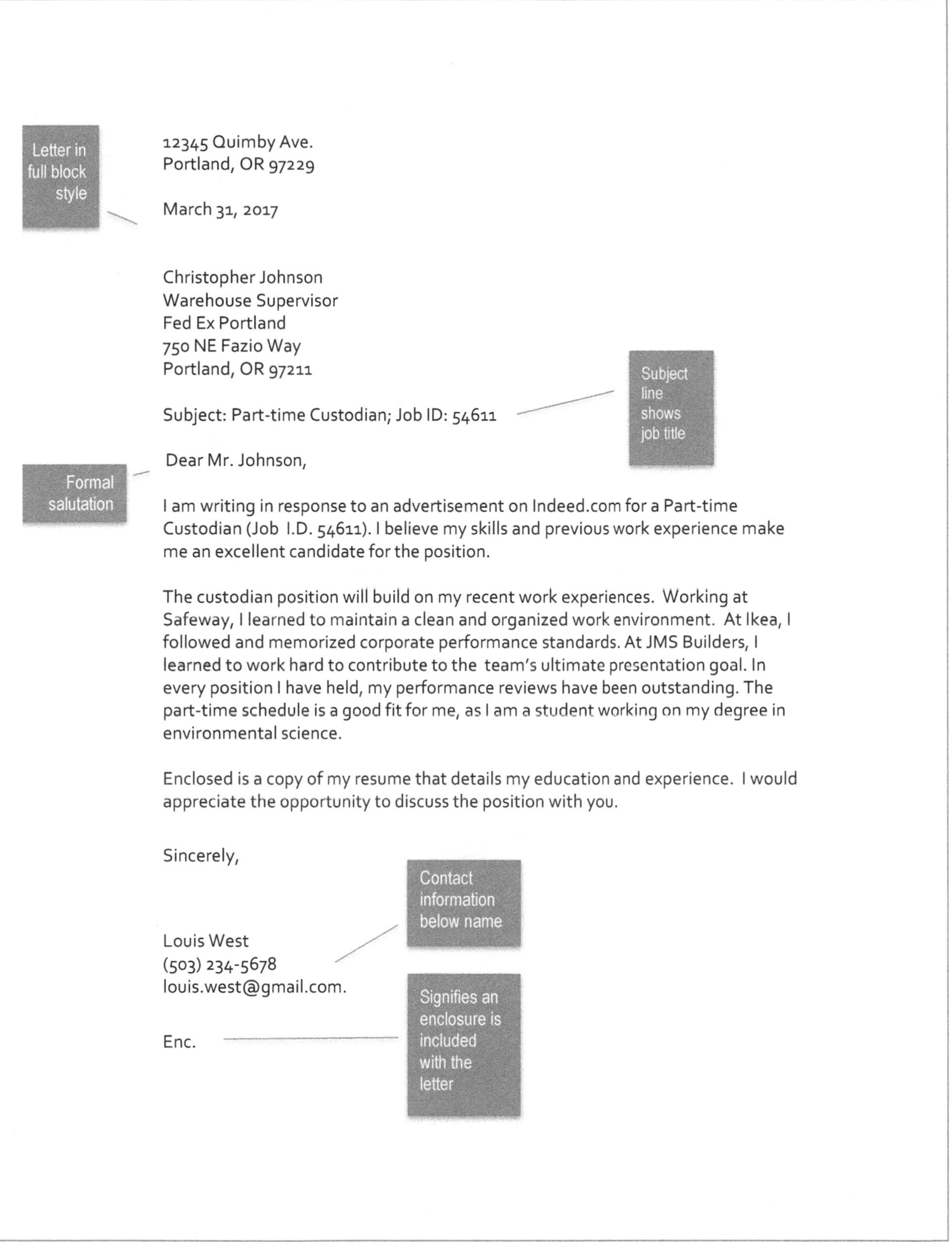

12345 Quimby Ave.
Portland, OR 97229

March 31, 2017

Christopher Johnson
Warehouse Supervisor
Fed Ex Portland
750 NE Fazio Way
Portland, OR 97211

Subject: Part-time Custodian; Job ID: 54611

Dear Mr. Johnson,

I am writing in response to an advertisement on Indeed.com for a Part-time Custodian (Job I.D. 54611). I believe my skills and previous work experience make me an excellent candidate for the position.

The custodian position will build on my recent work experiences. Working at Safeway, I learned to maintain a clean and organized work environment. At Ikea, I followed and memorized corporate performance standards. At JMS Builders, I learned to work hard to contribute to the team's ultimate presentation goal. In every position I have held, my performance reviews have been outstanding. The part-time schedule is a good fit for me, as I am a student working on my degree in environmental science.

Enclosed is a copy of my resume that details my education and experience. I would appreciate the opportunity to discuss the position with you.

Sincerely,

Louis West
(503) 234-5678
louis.west@gmail.com.

Enc.

Figure 12-2 Emailed Cover Letter for Job Application

From: jromero@yahoo.com
Subject: Day Shift On-Call Phlebotomist position
Date: March 31, 2014 9:32 PST
To: linda.tellez@stmaryshosp.org

Dear Ms. Tellez:

I am writing to apply for the day shift On-Call Phlebotomist position. I heard about the open position from my friend Karen Witters, who works at St. Mary's Hospital in the phlebotomy lab. I am very interested in the job, and I feel that my education and experience make me well qualified.

I am a Certified Phlebotomist (ASCP) and am currently working at Helvetia Health Care as a laboratory assistant. I completed the intensive Medical Laboratory Technology program through Portland Community College, which included a clinical internship.

I am often the technician who can draw blood when others cannot. The secret, in my view, is to establish a calming personal rapport with patients. Even a small thing such as addressing people by name can put them at ease. Listening to patients' concerns and informing them about procedures is very effective, I have found, in enabling them to relax.

Helping people monitor and manage their healthcare is my ultimate goal. I am interested in working full time as a phlebotomist, and an on-call position is perfect for me, as I thrive on a varied schedule. I admire your hospital's impressive record of high quality patient care.

Attached is my resume, detailing my qualifications and experience. Please call me so that we can discuss how I might contribute to the organization.

Sincerely,

Jessenia Romero
(971) 987-6543
jromero@yahoo.com

RESUME

The **resume** presents your educational qualifications, skills, and work experience. It is usually one or two pages long. The purpose of the resume is to demonstrate that you have the appropriate qualifications for the job *and* that the trend of your career shows interest and potential. Remember that your reader knows nothing about you, and that your resume will be read among documents submitted by other well-qualified applicants.

You should not necessarily supply the same resume for every job application. The best resumes are those that are reviewed and reshaped frequently and customized for a particular job application. Even if you do not have new skills or experience to add, you will probably discover that you need to write some parts slightly differently—emphasize different skills, for example—for different jobs.

It is a good idea to keep a composite resume on hand and update it as you add to your work experience or qualifications. Some jobseekers, applying to jobs in widely-varying fields (e.g. welder and human resources professional) keep separate resumes for their progress in the different areas.

The resume should show that you have appropriate qualifications for the job you are seeking and that you can present information in a professional and well-organized way.

Resume, Resumé, or Résumé?

All three spellings are commonly found in English. The unaccented version (resume) is preferable in digital communication.

The main argument for using the double-accented spelling (résumé) is that it is faithful to the (borrowed) French word. Except, English speakers generally pronounce the first "e" as "eh" rather than as the French *accent aigu* demands ("ay"), so that spelling is not helpful.

The singly-accented spelling (resumé) differentiates the word from the verb "resume" ("We will now *resume* coverage of the Olympic games"), but in English can be misinterpreted as an emphasis (rehzehMAY).

The spelling without any accent marks (resume) has the advantage of being easy to type on an English keyboard, but it makes readers depend on context for pronunciation and meaning. Confusion of resume (noun, rehzehmay) and resume (verb, rehzoom), however, is unlikely, as they appear together only in the most contrived contexts ("Now *resume* working on your *resumes*").

The most important reason for choosing "resume" as the preferred spelling of this word is that when scanned or otherwise read by an English-reading data system, accent marks can be misinterpreted or replaced by unintended symbols. So, accent marks can introduce complications in digital communication. Unless you have an excellent reason for including non-standard characters, you should avoid them. Resume it is.

CV (Curriculum Vitae)

A CV, or *curriculum vitae* (Latin for "the course of one's life"), is used primarily in educational and research settings and covers education and experience in detail, including publications. A CV may be many pages, depending on the length and productivity of an individual's career.

This distinction between "resume" and "CV" is particularly American. Outside of the United States, the term "CV" is more generally used than "resume." In fields where individuals move frequently across international borders, such as science, the term "CV" covers the summaries of education and experience for everyone from the hourly lab technician to the researcher in charge.

Resume Sections

Name and Contact Information

Include your first and last name. There is no reason to reveal gender if your name is gender neutral and you prefer to remain so. If your first name is gender nonspecific *and* you wish to be identified as male or female, save potential employers from an embarrassing gaffe and include your middle name if it is revealing, such as Dylan Anne Jones or Lynn David Anderson. You could also include a courtesy title (Mr./Ms.) somewhere in the application package, perhaps in the cover letter.

Contact information on the resume should absolutely include a phone number and an email. A mailing address is a good addition, but some people prefer to omit the physical address, particularly when submitting a resume to an online job site where it may be visible to thousands of people. You should at least include your city and state (and country, if you are applying for a job abroad).

Professional Objectives

Include this section only if your work experience and education do not necessarily point to your goals: for example, if you are changing careers or just graduating from school, this section may be useful. Delete this section if you are only using it to fill in the name of the job you are currently applying for.

Education

List degrees, certificates, or diplomas in reverse chronological order (most recent first). This section will be brief. If you have completed a degree in higher education, you do not need to include your high school diploma. It is important to include the year of graduation, even though you may worry that the year will reveal your age. Omitting the year stands out as unusual, and will create a red flag. If you feel insecure about your educational background but confident in your work experience, put work experience first on the resume to emphasize it. The example below demonstrates one way to include the year of graduation or certification in your education section.

> **Tip: Key words**
>
> Some employers, particularly those who receive hundreds of applications, may scan your resume, searching for key words. Be sure that your resume includes some of the terms used in the job ad, if they fit your experience. Do not risk being discarded for creative terminology!

Example 1 - Education listing by date

B. A., University of Oregon, 2007

A.A., Portland Community College, 2002

Architectural Design and Drafting Certificate, Portland Community College, 2000.

Work-Related Skills

If the job advertisement requires competence with certain software, systems or procedures, you should mention those skills specifically on your resume. Many jobseekers list skills in a separate section, usually above the work experience section for greater prominence. Some resumes build skill lists into job entries.

Work Experience

Organize work experience by date, with most recent first. There is no need to write the exact day that you began or ended a job; month and year are sufficient. Include the responsibilities involved in the work you have done, in addition to the title you had. For example, the position of "Floor Manager" becomes much clearer when you describe the actual duties involved. Use present tense for current activities, and past tense for those you are no longer doing.

Example 2 - Work experience listing by date

Sept. 2012-present: Assistant Manager, Manikins Boutique, Portland, Oregon. Oversee sales staff; restock inventory, handle end-of-day deposits.

April 2000-August 2012: Sales Associate, Macy's, Seattle, Washington. Assisted customers in selecting and purchasing women's clothing items; refolded and organized inventory.

People sometimes have large, noticeable gaps in their work experience. For stay-at-home parents or those caring for elderly relatives, this gap may stretch to many years. If you have become unemployed in the recent bad economic times, your resume may show large gaps as well. If you have these kinds of gaps, your reader will imagine all kinds of reasons for your unemployment that are unfavorable to you (laziness, jail, a job you were fired from), so you will need to address them in both the resume and the cover letter. If you do have a reason for the gap that is negative—a prison sentence, for example—the best approach is to reveal it and say what you have learned and how you are moving forward. Do not excuse or defend your prior actions. Acknowledge and move on.

The best strategy for addressing gaps is to write about your activities and skill-building during those times. What did you manage? What did you practice? If you have been learning or volunteering —taking computer classes, learning Spanish, or supervising children, for example—you can write about what you have done. Write about your activities in a straightforward and unapologetic way in the resume, including them as part of your experience, skills, or volunteer service:

Example 3 - Unpaid work experience listing

2006-2013: Stay-at-Home Parent. Managed activities, education, entertainment, and nourishment for four children.

Activities and Volunteer Service

In this section, include activities that you have participated in outside of work or school that help show your potential. Coaching and sports participation are good to include here (dragon boat team, soccer coach), as are community-building roles (master recycler, volunteer English tutor). If volunteer experience has been filling a gap in your work history, then include it in your work experience, noting that the position was unpaid. Do not include personal hobbies (model trains, scrapbooking). Include political or religious activities only if relevant to the job, as they are potentially divisive.

Honors

If you have earned significant honors in your personal, student, volunteer, or work life, include those in this section. These include honor society memberships, Dean's List or President's List, and significant scouting or club awards such as Girl Scout Gold and Silver Award, or Eagle Scout. Military honors may also be listed here.

References

Write "References on Request" at the bottom of your resume rather than list names and phone numbers. By withholding the names and phone numbers of your references until requested, you are preserving their privacy, as well as giving yourself the opportunity to notify your references that they may be receiving a call, ensuring that they are able to recall information about you quickly when asked.

Professionalism & Ethics

Your references should be individuals who have supervised you or are well qualified to testify about your character. Friends or relatives are not good references, from an employer's point of view. They are not impartial, and may even have their own reasons for exaggerating a good reference (they want you off their couch, perhaps).

Include or Exclude?

Some activities or information should be left off the resume. For example, listing political causes or protest activities may cause your audience to picture you holding a sign outside their door.

On the other hand, some personal responsibilities suggest your work ethic, trustworthiness, or team spirit, and are worth including. The chart below lists some common information and activities, separated into "exclude" vs. "include."

Table 12-1 Exclude vs. Include? Facts in Resume

Exclude from Resume	include in Resume
Overly personal details (e.g., age, race, sexual orientation, marital status)	Military service, including continuing National Guard or Reserves duty
Political affiliations (e.g., Democrat, Republican, Green Party)	Community service (e.g., coaching, tutoring, volunteering for social causes)
Religious affiliations listed for their own sake (e.g., Christian, Muslim, Jewish)	Positions that show trustworthiness (e.g., Temple Treasurer, PTA Secretary)
Home responsibilities unless to explain work gap (e.g., home-schooling, caring for elderly parent)	Involvement in sporting activities (e.g. teams, competitions
Achievements that are simply routine (e.g. "perfect attendance")	Notable honors or achievements (e.g. Eagle Scout, Dean's List)

Consider how your information seems from a prospective employer's point of view. The idea is to include experiences and activities that make you seem interesting, intelligent, and a good addition to the work team. Avoid including details that suggest that you would be unavailable or cause disruption.

Chronological vs. Functional Resumes

Chronological

Most job-seekers list their job experience in reverse chronological order, with the most recent job listed first. In this format, the Work Experience section begins near, or very near, the top of the resume. This structure emphasizes job experience, particularly the progress of the jobseeker through progressively higher-level positions. For those who have been in the same general field for a long time, this can be a very impressive structure. See Sample 12-4, page 268, for an example of a resume organized chronologically.

Functional or Skill-Based

For job-seekers who are new to the field, who are switching careers, or who have gaps in their work history, a functional resume structure can be useful. This kind of structure emphasizes knowledge, skills, or education at the top of the resume. Job history may appear lower on the page, or sometimes, for first-time job-seekers, not at all. See Samples 12-5 and 12-6 on pages 269-270 for examples of resumes organized functionally.

Artistic Resumes

Job seekers applying to companies where creativity is highly valued may wish to apply their artistic skills to the layout of their resumes. Sample 12-7 on page 271 shows a resume that uses chronological organization but the font and page design demonstrate creativity. This type of resume is not for everyone, and will not be valued in every field. But, in careers such as advertising or video production, being demonstrating an eye for design can give you an edge.

Sample 12-3 Resume, Chronological (emphasizing job experience)

ELIZA WU

20905 SW Alice Lane
Portland, OR 97129
(503) 838-9712
eliza.wu@gmail.com

Work experience listed most recent first

PROFESSIONAL EXPERIENCE

Loan Officer, February 2007-August 2013. *OnPoint Credit Union,* Portland, OR. (formerly Portland Teachers Credit Union) Analyzed loan applications. Resolved issues relating to member accounts.

Training Specialist, May 2003-September 2007. *OnPoint Credit Union,* Portland, OR. *(formerly Portland Teachers Credit Union)* Trained employees on policies and procedures, office systems, and customer service. Revised training manuals.

Loan Processor, February 2002-May 2003. *Oregon Community Credit Union*, Eugene, OR. Communicated with loan officers and members to support application submission and loan approval decisions.

Teller, June 2000-April 2003. *Selco Credit Union*, Eugene, OR. Helped members with questions regarding their accounts; performed requested transactions.

Headings and text are contrasting fonts

VOLUNTEER SERVICE

Treasurer, November 2012-present. *Wheels for Children (nonprofit organization)* Prepare monthly financial reports using Excel. Submit tax payments to the IRS and prepare required tax reports. Prepare and mail end-of-year tax documents to contributors.

PROFICIENCIES

General, Managerial, and Payroll accounting principles
Computer accounting applications (QuickBooks, SalesForce, Zoho Books)
Microsoft Office applications (Excel/ Word)
Problem-Solving Skills
Business Communication

Indicates degree in progress

EDUCATION

B.A., Business, focus on Accounting. Degree expected June 2015.

AWARDS

Portland State University President's List 2012-2013
Seashore Foundation Scholarship 2014

REFERENCES

Available upon request.

Sample 12-4 Resume, Functional (emphasizing skills)

Gordon K. Oliver

1234 Arthur St. Beaverton, OR 97007 (503) 508-9750 gk.oliver@gmail.com

Professional Objective:

Use my significant writing and analytical background in a career as an information technology specialist.

Professional objective useful because experience and education are varied

Work Skills

All bullet points line up vertically

- Microsoft Office applications: Access, Excel, Word, Publisher, and PowerPoint.
- Windows XP/7.
- Maintain websites in SharePoint.
- Troubleshoot and resolve computer application problems.
- Write and edit documents for business communication and public readership.

Education

Certificates, Portland Community College, Portland, OR:

- Computer Information Systems, Expected June 2014
- Database Design and SQL, June 2013
- Java Application Programming, June 2012

Bachelor of Arts, 2007: Journalism. Portland State University, Portland, OR

Honors

Harvey Scott Award for Editorial Writing, PSU, 2006.

Work Experience

- Heritage Outreach Specialist, Oregon Historical Society, Portland, OR(August 2009-present) Write articles about shows and acquisitions for OHS website; write and edit letters, brochures, and other print marketing materials.
- Digital Preservation Technician, Oregon Historical Society, Portland, OR (July 2007-August 2009) Photographed and recorded materials in digital format; Processed donated materials for preservation.
- Registration Specialist, Heathman Hotel, Portland, OR (November 2005-July 2007)

Volunteer Service and Activities

- Webmaster, Portland Softball League (2011-present)
- Hood to Coast Race relay team (2009, 2010, 2012, 2013)
- Big Brother/Big Sister program (Big Brother since 2008)

Significant community service

References

Available upon request.

Sample 12-5 Resume, Functional (emphasizing skills in a new career path)

Jim Stevenson

1111 Stark St, Portland, OR 55555
jimstevenson@email.com
(333) 777 - 9999

Professional objective useful because degree not in desired area, experience limited

Career Objective

Seeking position where I can continue to advance my scripting and code development skills as part of a security operations, network monitoring, or application development team.

Work Experience

SatTech, Richmond, VA, Associate Operation Systems Support Engineer (Nov 2013 - Jan 2015)

- Provided enterprise support related to information technology threat monitoring and compliance with security patching requirements
- Developed automated script for identification of internal systems exploitable by the Heartbleed SSL vulnerability
- Created internal Wiki site for storage of standard operating procedures (SOP) documents and knowledge base for troubleshooting security monitoring systems
- Wrote SOPs documenting Network Security and Intelligence Team business processes

Skills-based work description

IT Training

- SANS SEC504 Hacker Techniques, Exploits, & Incident Handling, June 2013
- Computational Investing 1, from Georgia Tech via Coursera with Signature Track, May 2013

Certification

- GCIH - GIAC Certified Incident Handler, August 2013

Skills

Detailed skills list

- Tivoli Netcool – Network Management Framework
- Python
- Javascript/node.js
- Database Management using MySQL
- Web Development
- Linux (RHEL) and shell scripting (bash)
- Nmap
- SNMP
- Microsoft Office Suite: Visio, Sharepoint, Excel, and Word

Education important but placed last because degree not in career area

Education

- BS, Ecological Agriculture, 2012. University of British Columbia, Vancouver, B.C., Canada

References available upon request.

Sample 12-6 Resume, Artistic (emphasizing personal qualities)

PEGGYOLSEN

Intelligent. Creative. Adaptable.

EMAIL: p.olsen@gmail.com

PHONE: 555 867 5309

Contact information at top

EDUCATION

2015 — **B.A. Physical Anthropology**
Minor: Philosophy
Portland State University
GPA: 3.77

2014 — **Myakka City Field Training Program**
Lemur Conservation Foundation

2009 - 2010 — **Women's and Gender Studies**
University of British Columbia

ABOUT ME

Location: 12345 Couch Street
Portland, OR 97209

Interests: Human Evolution
Normative Ethics
Web Development
Social Justice
Creative Writing
Customer Service

Focuses on interests rather than goals

WORK EXPERIENCE

2012 - Today — **FLOOR MANAGER/SALES**
Nordstrom
- Provided customer service and basic sales training to new sales associates
- Calculated and submitted weekly sales statistics for each associate to upper management
- Built and maintained lucrative sales relationships
- Provided personalized stylist services to long-term clients

Reverse chronological organization

Jan - Aug 2012 — **SENIOR INTERN/RETAIL RECRUITER**
Classic Clothiers
- Sought out, interviewed, and contracted with local designers to create a unique retail space in a start-up Portland design shop
- Assisted in the design, patterning, and creation of new clothing styles
- Tailored and worked on the reconstruction of wedding dresses and other specialty garments
- Assisted in the execution of fashion show events

Feb - June 2011 — **ART PROGRAM COORDINATOR/INSTRUCTOR**
Madison Elementary School
- Worked with school faculty and vendors to obtain supplies and refreshments for students
- Worked 1-on-1 with students to address specific needs and individual development
- Developed and utilized original lesson plans during instruction

OBJECTIVE

"I am looking for a position that requires me to wear many hats--I am a 'Jill of all trades' by nature, and am happiest when I have a variety of tasks on my plate. I love to learn, experiment, and challenge myself every day; from CSS to tailoring to scaling 30-foot ladders, I am ready to go!"

Uses "Objective" section to note personal strengths

SKILLS

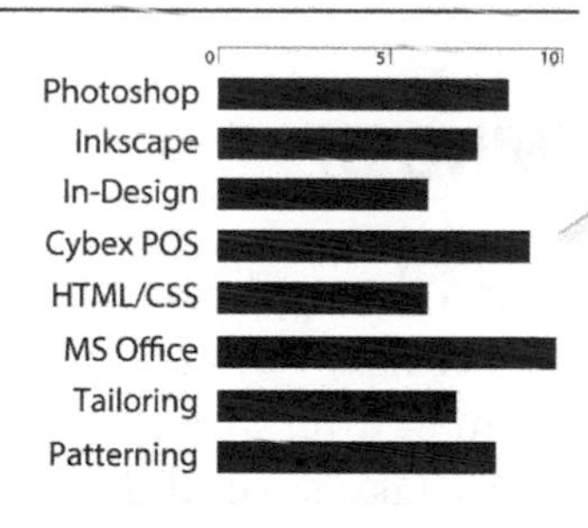

Artistic focal point

REFERENCES

Available on request

SENDING THE APPLICATION PACKAGE

Email

If you are sending your application by email, the cover letter should be in the body of the email (readable when the recipient opens the email message), and the resume should be an attachment.

When you are satisfied with your edits to the resume file, **save it in PDF format.** If you send your resume as a word processing file, there is a significant chance that your formatting may look different on the receiving end, as your reader may have different settings, even within the same word processing program. Page breaks, for example, are liable to fall in unexpected places. Sending the resume as a PDF file ensures that your careful formatting will look as good to the recipient as it does to you.

Postal Mail

If you are sending the cover letter and resume by postal mail, the letter should be in business letter format, full block style (See Figure 12-3, page 261, Sample Printed Cover Letter). Copy or print the resume on good quality bond paper. If your resume runs to a second page, print each on a separate sheet of paper, and make sure your name is at the top of the second page. (No double-sided printing—the second page may not be read.) Use a standard paper clip to keep pages of the resume together. If employers scan or copy resumes, a staple may be an obstacle. Lay the cover letter on top of the resume and insert both into a large manila envelope, roomy enough so that your documents lie flat. It is also acceptable to fold your letter and resume together in thirds and insert into a normal business-size envelope.

Before sealing the envelope, make sure you have the correct address for your recipient on the cover letter, and copy that address to the envelope, along with your own return address. Apply correct postage (oversize envelopes require extra stamps), and mail.

Use the checklists on the next two pages to make sure your application materials are the best they can be before sending.

FOLLOWING UP

After you send the application, you will be anxious to hear a reply, but try to be patient. The hiring manager may be reading a handful of applications, or perhaps even hundreds. Following up with an email after a reasonable time, however, will help the hiring manager remember you. He or she may take several days to reply (although replying immediately with a general receipt is preferable, should you ever be in the position of reviewing applications).

After a week has passed, you may inquire about the status of your application politely, with a follow-up email using the job title as subject line.

If you are interviewed, it is good manners to thank the interviewer, either with a card by postal mail, or with an email. Be sure to proofread your follow-up or thank you letter, as all correspondence, before sending.

COVER LETTER Checklist ✔

An Effective Emailed Cover Letter . . .	✔
Is written in email message (not as attachment)	
Uses the correct email address for recipient	
Is sent from your professional-sounding email address (first.lastname; no cute nicknames)	
Provides job title or ID code in subject line	
An Effective Printed Cover Letter . . .	✔
Is printed in clear black ink	
Is formatted in full block style	
Uses standard business letter format for return address, date, signature	
Includes a subject line with the job title (and code, if available)	
An Effective Cover Letter of Any Kind . . .	✔
Includes a salutation (Dear [Name, or Hiring Manager])	
Includes an introductory paragraph explaining how you found out about the job and why you are interested	
Provides details in one or two middle paragraph(s) explaining why the job appeals to you, how it fits with your career goals, and emphasizing any special qualifications or experience	
Concludes with a reference to the resume and a thank you; asks for contact/interview	
Includes a closing (Sincerely)	
Includes a signature line (your name in an email; your name + a handwritten signature in a print letter)	
Provides contact information under signature line (email address, phone number)	
Uses correct grammar, spelling, and punctuation	

RESUME *Checklist* ✔

An Effective Resume . . .	✔
Is limited to one or two pages	
Is formatted clearly and attractively	
Is sent as PDF file to maintain formatting	
Is sent as an attachment to an emailed cover letter OR an enclosure in a print letter	
Includes no irrelevant or inappropriate content	
Uses correct grammar, spelling, and punctuation	
Includes these Required Elements	✔
Name and contact information	
Education (diplomas, degrees, or certifications)	
Work experience, including military service	
Work-related skills	
May Include these Optional Elements	✔
Volunteer experience and community activities	
Awards and achievements that suggest your strengths	

DISCUSSIONS

1. You want to apply for a job in human resources, but you have not worked in that field for five years. After being laid off, you had trouble finding another position. To support yourself and your family, you have been providing daycare in your home. Now you have found an advertisement for the same job you used to have. What should you say in the cover letter? How should you shape your resume?

2. You have had two significant careers: yoga teacher and accountant. You are open to finding a job in either category, but the two fields have conflicting priorities: one values spiritual and intuitive perception; the other values precise, mathematical results. If you leave one of your careers off the resume, you will have a gap. What should you do?

3. Find a job advertisement and share it with the class. Brainstorm about the qualities the advertiser is looking for: which qualities seem to be absolute requirements, and which are preferences? What kind of person do you think might do well in this job, and why?

4. Explore at least two career-related websites such as CareerBuilder.com, Monster.com, SimplyHired.com, Indeed.com, or others that you may know of in your field. What are the advantages and disadvantages of the sites you visited? Which one is most useful to you, and which one is the least helpful? Share your observations with the class.

EXERCISES

1. **Find a job advertisement in your field. Identify key words in the job description,** and list them according to quantifiable requirements (how many), knowledge requirements (information), procedural competence (skill sets), and personality traits (strengths). Share the job ad and your lists with a classmate.

2. For the job advertisement you found in Question 1, **write a cover letter and resume.**

3. Peer review: Share job ads and rough drafts of cover letters or resumes with a small group of classmates, assigned by your instructor. **Write a response to each person in your group, including the following elements:**
    - **Identify key words in the job ad and look for them in the letter and resume.** How can the writer improve the visibility of these key elements in his or her documents?
    - **Review the cover letter** carefully. What impression does it give about the writer? Be honest. Point out parts that need to be revised, and explain why.
    - **Examine the resume** as if you were a prospective employer. What is promising? Are there any warning signs? How could it be reworked or re-organized to make it easier to find what you want to know?

Resources - Editing

A good editor can save your professional life. This person can save you from embarrassing typos (imagine the problems with a simple word like "shift"), or larger problems like writing a personal essay instead of an analysis ("Why I Love the Movies" instead of "Trends in 21st Century Cinema." A good editor is the person who reviews your carefully-crafted document and allows you to polish it until it shines. A good editor can also make sure that you are on the right track in the first place and that you haven't gone in a direction inconsistent with the document's purpose, audience, and subject matter.

Remember that *editing is not the same as revising*. Editing happens near the end of the document cycle, whereas revision is one or two steps back, depending on the needs of the document cycle. The writer always revises their own work, but the writer doesn't always edit their own work. It's preferable to have a trained editor or trusted colleague perform the editing function.

Types of Editing

Most large technical writing groups use a two-tier approach to the final stages of a document:

1. Editing, which includes two sub-phases:
   a) Substantive Editing – looking carefully at the content (substance) and structure
   b) Copy Editing – searching for page layout consistency and surface problems such as grammar and spelling
2. Proofreading – checking the page layout, and ensuring that all the surface problems have been fixed

In large writing groups, designated editors will review all external communication. They may edit hard copy drafts using specific copy editing symbols. Some of the most common are shown in Table E-1 on the next page.

Table E-1 Copy Editing Symbols

Symbol	Meaning	Example
	Delete	...as as in current practice.
^	Insert	When go...
	Close space	...time. However,...
#	Add space	...time.However, ...
	Start new paragraph	...next Thursday. On Monday, ...
≡	Upper case	internet
	Transpose	She however chose...
SP	Spelling	Apearance SP
stet	Leave as is	internet stet
⊙	Add period	...next Thursday On Monday, ...

Reviewers can also express grammar or formatting concerns with comments in the margin as shown in Figure 2.

For our purposes in this textbook, we divide the final stages into just two areas:

1. Editing – looking carefully at the content (substance) and structure as well as searching for surface problems such as grammar and spelling
2. Proofreading – checking the page layout, and ensuring that all the surface problems have been fixed

How to Approach Editing

When you are tasked with an editing project, remember that the writer may take any corrections or comments personally if you're not careful. Some people are able to accept editing much more easily than others. If you have a good sense of who the writer is, you can edit in a way that he or she will be able to appreciate.

Some guidelines to keep in mind are:

- Be kind.
- Be punctual. Your writer has a deadline. Get the edits back as soon as possible. If you're not sure when the edit is needed, ask. Then, deliver.
- Do not change/delete/or add to the writer's words or format. Make suggestions using comment boxes.

- Keep your comments focused on the text, not on the individual. Instead of writing "You've run two sentences together," you could write "This is a run-on sentence." Take the "you" out as much as possible.
- Point out what the writer does well. Give positive feedback. It's particularly good to use several positive comments if you have to give some negative ones.
- Check the writer's work against a quality checklist and style sheet, if available.
- Don't over-correct. If you're not sure that the writer has made an error, you can ask a question, or you can leave it alone. Do not suggest a correction if you're not sure there's a problem. For example, "Is this an analysis? This seems more like a summary" is better than "Wrong focus. Do an analysis."
- Add end comments, and thank the writer for allowing you to edit his or her document.

How to Edit

When you have been asked to edit someone else's document, follow this sequence:

1. Locate the editing or review tools in your application.

   Note: For some people, editing a hard copy reveals more problems than editing online. Consider printing out the document for review and then adding your comments to the electronic file.
2. Review the document as a whole and make sure you understand the major purpose it was intended to accomplish.
3. If you have access to any guidelines or criteria that the writer is supposed to be following, check the document against those standards. Then, let the writer know where the document may not be meeting them.
4. Review the structure and determine if it needs headings or paragraph breaks to make the text more understandable.
5. Review the format. Does the document look professional? Does it follow the expected pattern for the document type? Does it follow the guidelines for effective page design? Would it appeal to its audience?
6. Review the content for understandability, logic, and tone.
7. Review the content for spelling, grammar, and punctuation problems.

The example on the next page shows a well-edited workplace document.

Sample E-1 Edited Document

Gracious Good Gadgets

MEMORANDUM

Side comments

DATE: October 31, 2017

TO: Stan Wilkins, Manager

FROM: Jo Smith, Employee

SUBJECT: Summary

Comment [Office1]: Since you are a writer, maybe you could put Technical Writer here.

Comment [Office2]: Can you be a little more specific about what this memo is about? Just "Summary" doesn't really tell me a topic. I think this is a Summary for Documentation Improvements?

I have found a solution for the internal process for Gracious Good Gadgets. Through the research that I've conducted, I'd like to present this memo report. I have summarized an article, "Updating Internal Process Documentation," by Rebecca W. Walton. It was published in *Intercom*, March 2005.

Comment [Office3]: I like your upbeat approach, but I think that "documentation" should be added after "process."

Comment [Office4]: I like the way you separate the body of the report from the introduction.

Updating Internal Process Documentation

With a broad range of team members selecting, researching, writing, and submitting grants, it's important to know that they should follow a detailed internal process. Updating the process documentation will guarantee that team members use it. Documentation should be updated when there is a change to processes, changes among your users, and an increasing number of internal problems. Nevertheless, you can save time by updating the existing documents regardless if they were defective. You'll be able to stress the problems in existing documents, and extract all the good materials. However, it's important to interview your team members to get an impresion on their needs and suggestions. Creating useful documentation for your team members will pay off in the end. Once you have updated the documentation, plan a meeting to distribute the documentation. Train team members by discussing the content and its use, making sure to have team members ask questions or suggestions. User-focused documentation updates will benefit your team by improving teamwork, increasing efficiency, and inspiring confidence in the documentation. All team members will have clear responsibilities, which will guarantee that they will be doing what they're supposed to be doing. Encourage team members to use the updated documentation, while always interviewing users for suggestions to specifically suit their needs. Therefore, if the documentation is easy to use, the user will use it.

Comment [Office5]: Could you add some organization here by creating another paragraph? This sentence seems to be going into detail about when to update. Maybe you could use separate paragraphs for when, how, and why (the benefits).

Comment [Office6]: Spelling

Comment [Office7]: Move to area where you discuss benefits of updating?

Comment [Office8]: Good! These are clear benefits!

Comment [Office9]: I'm glad you included Walton's important message here.

Jo, you did a very good job on this memo. I thought that some visual organization by using paragraphs might help Stan see the different sides of your topic. However, for a short summary, it's okay to use one long paragraph. So either way, you're fine.

End comments

Thanks for letting me edit your memo, Jo. I hope this helps Stan to find the best way to improve our process!

How to Accept Edits

To have your work edited by another person can be a bit scary. After all, you worked hard on it, and maybe you believe that you've put part of yourself into the writing. This is usually where writers get into trouble—believing that somehow part of their being, their essence, is tied into those words on the screen.

In creative writing, considered "writer-based" communication (page 36 shows a graphic representation for differences between writer-based, reader-based, and topic-based), the writer is primary. Your feelings, opinions, expressions, and imaginings are all appropriate when writing creatively.

However, as you move into the realm of workplace writing, you have to distance yourself from the document. It is not your "baby," "brain-child," or "work of art." Your name may actually be nowhere on the document, especially if it's intended for external audiences. You are thinking about the reader and the topic, primarily. And, when you use an editor, you are taking advantage of an objective reader, one who will dare to tell you what you may not have seen for yourself.

Therefore, when receiving edits, think of the document as a thing you have given to the world. You don't own it. However, you are responsible for making it better. Go into your logical left-brain, accept the edits gracefully, and get to work.

Some guidelines to keep in mind are:

- Run grammar and spell check as a courtesy to your editor before you give him or her the document. However, scrutinize the changes that the spelling and grammar checker want to make to your document. Because it's automated, it can sometimes be wrong.
- Give your editor as much information as possible about the intended audience for the document and its purpose. If you have guidelines that you were supposed to follow, share them with the editor.
- Think of your editor as your supporter, not your detractor. The editor is on your side. Don't take any criticism personally. It's all about the document, not you.
- Ask the editor any questions you may have about the edits. Sometimes comments can be hard to understand, especially when cryptic language is used. (Does "space" mean add space or take it out?)
- Decide what you would like to accept and what you think is not necessary. You have the final say. However, there is an exception: If you are in a writing work group that requires formal editing (publishing house, software documentation, etc.), you can discuss the changes with the editor, but in the end, the editor has the final say.
- Thank the editor.

Resources - Grammar

APOSTROPHE

The apostrophe (') is used primarily to indicate contraction (where a letter has been left out) or possession. It is not normally used to create plurals.

Rule: To indicate contraction, insert the apostrophe where letters have been removed.

Examples we've (we have), don't (do not)

Rule: To indicate possession for most words, use apostrophe + s.

Examples Joanie's book, pitcher's throw

Rule: To indicate possession for a plural word ending in "s," place the apostrophe at the end of the word.

Examples ladies' room, players' turns

Rule: To indicate possession for a singular word ending in "s," add apostrophe + s only if the resulting letter combination is pronounceable.

Examples Gus's car, Socrates' student

BURIED VERB

Verbs often hide in phrases that dilute and defuse their impact. They may masquerade as adjectives or nouns. Buried verbs are often surrounded by weak verb forms that cushion them from a direct relationship with the subject.

Rule: Bring verbs to the active position.

Examples

WEAK: Ram and his friend made a **decision** to change the presentation.

BETTER: Ram and his friend **decided** to change the presentation.

WEAK: If we do an **analysis** of the three products, we may make important informational **discoveries** about their quality.

BETTER: If we **analyze** all three products, we may **discover** important information about their quality.

COLON

Colons—two dots, one above the other (**:**)—function to introduce what comes after the punctuation mark. They are properly used to introduce lists, quotations, and definitions. Although they frequently precede single words or phrases, they may also join independent clauses as long as there is a sense of introduction.

Rule: Use an independent clause (stand-alone sentence) before the colon.

Examples

Allen announced: "Everyone must be ready to go in the next five minutes."

Sales, as shown in the figure below, are declining:

Some of the predators in the new exhibit are very dangerous: the lions and tigers, for example, need special enclosures.

Rule: Use a colon to separate titles from subtitles or chapter from verse, and to indicate ratios or times. In correspondence, use a colon for salutations or subject lines.

Examples

French Cooking I: Sauces

Genesis 2:12

The ratio of concentrate to water is 1:3.

Dear Ms. Templeton:

Attention: Human Resources

Subject: Feb. 23 Accident

COMMA

A comma separates parts of a sentence from each other to clarify meaning. The placement of a comma can affect meaning, so it is an important consideration. Because commas create separation, they may not be placed between subject and verb, or interrupt any sequence of words that depend upon each other for meaning. They also cannot be used to connect clauses (see "Comma Splice," below).

Rule: Use a comma before a coordinating conjunction in a compound sentence.

Examples

This house is a good investment, so purchasing it is a wise choice.

The chairperson managed a difficult controversy well, but she forgot to keep everyone informed.

Rule: Use a comma on both sides of a word or phrase within a sentence to indicate an element that is not essential to the basic structure of the sentence.

Examples

The Oregon junco, a bird common to roadsides and back yards, nests on the ground.

This procedure, complex and time-consuming, is done only on Tuesdays.

COMMA SPLICE

A comma splice happens when a writer uses the comma to join independent clauses (stand-alone sentences). It is an error. A comma generally separates elements and is not strong enough to connect sentence parts without help.

Rule: Do not use a comma to connect independent clauses.

Examples

INCORRECT (COMMA SPLICE): Logan left the room, the laptop computer was on the table.

CORRECT: Logan left the room, but the laptop computer was on the table. (Conjunction added after the comma)

CORRECT: Logan left the room. The laptop computer was on the table. (Sentences separated into two sentences)

CORRECT: Logan left the room; the laptop computer was on the table. (Semicolon added and comma deleted)

CORRECT: Logan left the room, leaving the laptop computer on the table. (Rewritten sentence)

CONJUNCTION

A conjunction is a connecting word. There are two types of conjunctions in English: coordinating and subordinating.

Coordinating Conjunction

There are only seven coordinating conjunctions, and they can be remembered with the mnemonic "FANBOYS." The chart below shows the coordinating conjunctions:

Table G-1 Coordinating Conjunctions

Coordinating Conjunctions	
F	For
A	And
N	Nor
B	But
O	Or
Y	Yet
S	So

Rule: Use a **coordinating conjunction** with a comma to join complete sentences of approximately equal weight.

Examples

The inserts are not ready, and I do not feel comfortable going ahead.

Driving during rush hour will be slow, so let's get an early start.

Everything seems to be in order, but we should wait for Jamie to arrive.

Subordinating Conjunction

There are too many subordinating conjunctions to provide a comprehensive list, but sixteen common subordinating conjunctions are shown in the table below:

Table G-2 Subordinating Conjunctions

Subordinating Conjunctions (partial list)			
After	Before	Since	When
Although	Even if	Though	Whenever
As	Even though	Unless	Where
Because	If	Until	While

Unlike coordinating conjunctions, they may be placed either at the beginning or middle of the combined sentence. If the subordinating conjunction is placed at the beginning of a sentence, a comma is used between clauses; if placed between clauses (mid-sentence), no comma is necessary, although one is sometimes used for emphasis.

Rule: Use a **subordinating conjunction** to join clauses when the clause following the conjunction depends on the other clause to complete its meaning.

Examples

After we completed the testing phase, we began to revise the user materials.

I will not be able to have the presentation ready unless I can get a copy of the brochure.

Until I hear from Mr. Barnes, I will not be able to open the file.

I would like to attend the meeting, even if the rest of the staff will not be there.

DASH

A dash (-- or —) is generally used to indicate a break in thought, or an insertion. Place a second dash to mark a return to the main topic. The dash can be useful when inserting a quick definition or background within a sentence. When used too frequently, however, it can make the writing look disorganized and choppy.

In page design, an "em dash" (—) is distinguished from an "en dash" (–) in length. In the days when a typesetter inserted a metal piece to represent a dash, an "em dash" was the width of the capital letter "M" and the "en dash" was the width of the small "n." Now, an em dash is used as the punctuation mark, and an en dash is used the same way as a hyphen.

Word processors often, but not always, insert an em dash when two hyphens in a row are typed. You can insert it as a special symbol if it does not appear automatically. Check your organization's style sheet to see whether two hyphens are acceptable as a dash, or whether you must use an em dash.

Rule: Use multiple em dashes (usually 2 in a row, with a space between) to indicate information that is missing or censored.

Example The man being questioned, Mr. G — —, claims he saw nothing at all.

Rule: Use an em dash to mark the beginning and end of an insertion.

Example The snapping turtle—at least before it tried to bite my finger off—was an interesting pet.

Rule: Use one em dash to indicate a break in thought.

Example Noah plays the guitar beautifully—I don't know how he learned so quickly.

MISPLACED OR DANGLING MODIFIER

A modifier is a word, phrase, or clause that alters the meaning of another part of a sentence. Adjectives and adverbs are always modifiers; so are prepositional phrases. Clauses beginning with a subordinating conjunction can modify other clauses.

Common single-word modifiers include only, all, just, mere, and not.

Misplaced Modifier

Rule: Place the modifier next to, or very near, the word it modifies.

Examples

Only bonus packs are given to clients. (The clients get nothing but the bonus packs)

Bonus packs are given only to clients. (The clients, not anyone else, gets the bonus packs)

Rule: Do not place the modifier where it can confuse the meaning.

Examples

CONFUSING: I adopted a dog from the shelter in the car. (Is the shelter in the car?)

CLEAR: I adopted a dog from the shelter; he is in the car.

CONFUSING: We need to hire a new manager to take over desperately. (Do we want a desperate takeover?)

CLEAR: We desperately need to hire a new manager to take over.

Dangling Modifier

Rule: Make sure the modifier (usually a phrase) has a target word in the sentence.

Examples

CONFUSING: Running down the field, the game ended. (The game was running down the field?)

CLEAR: As I ran down the field, the game ended. (Target word "I" added)

CONFUSING: Walking into the market, tomatoes were piled high in the produce section. (Tomatoes were walking?)

CLEAR: Walking into the market, I saw tomatoes were piled high in the produce section. (Target word "I" added)

CONFUSING: While texting, the car hit a light pole. (The car was texting?)

CLEAR: While the driver was texting, the car hit a light pole. (Target word "driver" added)

PARAGRAPHING

A paragraph is a visual representation of a single topic. Starting a new paragraph lets the reader know that you are moving on to a new topic.

Rule: Use paragraphs to organize topics.

In general, apply these guidelines when writing paragraphs:

- State the topic of the paragraph in the first sentence. For example: "Arsenic is a very dangerous chemical." The rest of the paragraph could explain how dangerous it is and what its effects on the human body are.
- Keep your paragraphs fairly short. Most readers are turned away by long paragraphs.
- Use transition words at the beginning of the paragraph to show the relationship of the new paragraph to the last one. For example: "In contrast, …"
- Place important information in the first sentence or the last sentence, not in the middle of the paragraph. Putting important information in the middle of a paragraph "buries" it. Notice how the topic sentence in the first bullet above makes a critical statement about arsenic that can be explained in the rest of the paragraph.
- Read your paragraph aloud and listen for parts that don't seem to fit or flow logically. If there are sentences or phrases that don't fit, move them to another paragraph, rewrite them, or leave them out. Your reader should never have to reread the paragraph to understand your meaning.
- When in doubt about whether or not to start a new paragraph, go ahead and do it. Your instinct is probably correct.
- Even if a new paragraph has a very close relationship to the previous paragraph, rename every noun. Don't use "it" or "her" to refer back to a noun (For example: "yearly report" or "Susan Donovan") in the previous paragraph. You can use a shortened version of the noun if there is absolutely no doubt about which noun you're referring to ("report" or "Donovan").

PARALLEL STRUCTURE

Parallel structure is the patterned repetition of words and grammatical forms within a sentence, paragraph, or list. It is a way of adding balance, rhythm, and predictability to your writing. Items presented in numbered or bulleted lists, especially, should be in parallel grammatical form.

Rule: Use parallel structure when possible, especially in lists.

Examples

To make your own clothes, you will need to measure yourself. (Repeated pattern: infinitive verb + object)

These methods create sound on a guitar:

- Plucking
- Hammering
- Bending
- Strumming (Repeated pattern: gerund form of verb)

More examples of parallel structure can be found in "Chapter 4 - Page Design."

PASSIVE VOICE

Passive voice is a reversal of the normal subject + verb order that diminishes the role of the subject. Passive voice constructions put the actor or subject at the end of the sentence, preceded with the word "by," and sometimes leave the subject out altogether. Although technically correct, passive voice constructions tend to be wordy and awkward, so they are generally considered to be poor style.

Rule: Avoid passive voice to make sentences stronger.

Examples

PASSIVE VOICE: The machine was repaired successfully by the mechanic.

ACTIVE VOICE: The mechanic repaired the machine successfully. (Clearer, and fewer words)

PASSIVE VOICE: The card game was won by the least experienced player.

ACTIVE VOICE: The least experienced player won the card game. (Clearer, and fewer words)

Passive voice is used exclusively in some technical writing environments, such as lab reports, where the identity of the subject is irrelevant. And, if you want to emphasize the object rather than the subject for any reason, passive voice can be a useful option.

Rule: Use passive voice in special circumstances.

Example

PASSIVE VOICE: Potassium was added to the mixture slowly. (The focus is on the potassium rather than who added it)

ACTIVE VOICE: James Fisk, Jr. added potassium to the mixture slowly. (In a lab report, the technician's name is not relevant; the passive voice above is more appropriate)

PRONOUN

A pronoun is a word that stands in for a specific noun. Below is a table showing commonly-used pronouns, separated by person, number and case.

English pronouns do not currently have a satisfactory gender-neutral mode; this lack has spurred a number of creative solutions. The traditionally plural "they" is now in common practice used also to refer to a singular person. The pronoun "one" is also coming back into use, although not as frequently as "they."

Other pronouns currently being proposed as substitutes for gendered pronouns, but not in frequent or accepted use at this time (see Experimental Gender Neutral Pronouns, below).

Table G-3 Pronouns

Pronouns							
Number and Case	Singular Subject	Singular Object	Plural Subject	Plural Object	Possessive (adjectival)	Possessive (noun)	Reflexive
Traditional	I	Me	We	Us	My/Our	Mine/Ours	Myself/Ourselves
	You	You	You	You	Your	Yours	Yourself/Yourselves
	He/She/It/ One	Him/Her/It/ One	They	Them	Their	Theirs	Himself/Herself/ Themselves
Gender-Neutral in Use	They/It/One	Them/It/ One	They	Them	Theirs		Themselves
Experimental Gender-Neutral	Ze, Ey, E	Em, Zem	Zey	Em, Zem	Eirs		Emself, Emselves

Rule: Check company style sheets and standards before using experimental pronouns.

SEMICOLON

A semicolon (;) is a punctuation mark that looks a little like a comma and a little like a colon but should not be confused with either. It is a mechanical connector, used to combine two complete and related independent clauses.

Semicolons are very commonly misused. Most misuse occurs when writers insert semicolons when a comma should be used.

Rule 1: Use an independent clause (capable of standing alone as a separate sentence) on each side of the semicolon.

Rule 2: Make sure that the relationship between the two independent clauses is clear without adding extra words or explanation.

Examples

CONFUSING: Duncan reports that the packaging needs reinforcement; Wendy will get the coffee tomorrow. (Meets Rule 1, but not Rule 2)

CORRECT: Duncan reports that the packaging needs reinforcement; some boxes have broken open in transit. (Meets both Rules 1 and 2)

CONFUSING: The new stained glass in the lobby is beautiful; especially the light coming through. (Meets Rule 2, but not Rule 1)

CORRECT: The new stained glass in the lobby is beautiful; it softens the light in the waiting area. (Meets both Rules 1 and 2)

A semicolon is also commonly used to separate items in a list, especially when those items are longer than just a word or two and/or contain internal punctuation that could cause confusion.

Rule: Use a semicolon to separate items in a list, especially when those items are longer than just a word or two and/or contain internal punctuation that could cause confusion.

Examples

Tomorrow I would like you to use the hose from the shed to water the plants, even if they do not seem dry; remove small weeds from the edges of the garden beds, along the path; and make sure the gate is locked after the 6th graders leave.

To register a utility trailer, the Department of Motor Vehicles requires Form 266, signed and dated; Form 2244 completed, including the VIN number; the Bill of Sale, signed by all parties to the transaction; and $182 in cash.

SENTENCE FRAGMENTS

A sentence fragment is a group of words that cannot stand alone as a sentence and thus is considered incorrect in professional writing. Sentences in English MUST have a functional subject and verb and cannot depend for complete meaning on another clause.

There are several common reasons that people write in sentence fragments:

- Writers sometimes confuse the pauses and emphases in spoken or casual English with the way that sentences need to be written formally.
- Writers sometimes leave out a subject or verb, thinking that it is understood.
- Writers sometimes separate a dependent clause from the sentence that completes its meaning.
- Writers sometimes use an incorrect verb form.

Rule: Make sure sentences have both a subject and verb and make sense when read separately from nearby sentences.

Examples

FRAGMENTS: No tears. Moving on now. (Form is casual, not grammatical)

CORRECT: Instead of crying, let's move on. (Words added to complete the thought)

FRAGMENT: Lost my dog. (Missing subject)

CORRECT: I lost my dog. (Subject added)

FRAGMENT: George and Anna. (Missing verb)

CORRECT: George and Anna will come. (Added words to form complete sentence)

FRAGMENT: Although I didn't know them. (Dependent clause)

CORRECT: Although I didn't know them, the people around me in the airport were very understanding. (Dependent clause connected to another clause for completion)

TRANSITIONS

Transitional aids are formatting, words, and phrases that let the reader know what's coming ahead. Just as drivers depend on guidance from road signs, your readers, making their way through your document, will know there is a curve ahead because you have prepared them.

Transitional Formatting

You can use formatting "signals" to help guide your reader. For example, when you drive into a town, it's helpful to see a sign that says "Welcome to Happydale" because it confirms your location on the map.

Using the same analogy of driving a car, your titles, headings, and topic sentences are like the street signs that direct the reader to the ideas and information you want them to find.

Rules: Use **titles** to give the overall subject you are covering.

Use **headings** to signal the subject matter and changes in the subject matter.

Use **subheadings** to signal groupings of similar topics within the subject matter heading.

Use a **paragraph** to signal a topic, or a shift in the current topic.

Use a **topic sentence** (the first sentence) in the paragraph to let the reader know what the paragraph is about.

Use **numbers** to signal a sequential process or order of importance.

Use **bulleting** where sequential order or importance is not relevant.

Transitional Words and Phrases

You can also use certain words to signal your reader about connections or unexpected reversals. When you correctly use a transitional word or phrase, you are helping the reader "frame" the information and understand its relationship to the other information in the paragraph.

Rule: Use transitional words and phrases to show relationship.

Examples

UNCLEAR: The bus was late. I arrived at the luncheon on time.

CLEAR: The bus was late. However, I arrived at the luncheon on time.

Without the transitional word "however," the two sentences are just a collection of side-by-side facts. Adding the transitional word helps the reader understand the relationship of the facts to each other.

The table on the next page shows some very common transitional words and phrases, what they signal, the punctuation they require, and an example of each:

Table G-4 Transitional Words and Phrases

Transitional Words and Phrases			
Word or Phrase	**Signal**	**Punctuation Required**	**Example**
Although	Showing unexpected connection or reversal	None	I'm not going to eat much, although I'm very hungry.
And	Connecting	Comma before	I'm not going to eat much this week, and I hope to drop a few pounds.
Because	Showing logical cause	None	I'll eat a large meal because I'm really hungry.
But	Reversing, disconnecting or subtracting	Comma before	I'm not going to eat much, but I'm very hungry.
Even though	Showing unexpected connection or reversal	None	Even though I'm very hungry, I'm not going to eat much.
For example	Giving an example	Period or semicolon before Comma after	I love apples in my lunch. For example, today I had apple slices with peanut butter.
However	Showing unexpected connection or reversal	Period or semicolon before Comma after	I'm very hungry; however, I'm not going to eat much.
In addition	Adding similar information	Period or semicolon before Comma after	I ate a healthy breakfast. In addition, I'll eat a healthy lunch.
In fact	Emphasizing	Period or semicolon before Comma after	I'm hungry. In fact, I'm famished.
In spite of	Showing persistence	Period or semicolon before Comma after	In spite of my low score on the midterm, I think I can get an A out of the class.
Meanwhile	Showing concurrent time relationship	Period or semicolon before Comma after	I'm going to eat lunch now. Meanwhile, Tim is fixing the car.
Moreover	Adding similar information	Period or semicolon before Comma after	I ate a big breakfast; moreover, I plan to eat a large lunch.
On the contrary	Showing unexpected connection or reversal	Period or semicolon before Comma after	You probably thought I was hungry. On the contrary, I'm still full from lunch.
Then	Showing sequential time relationship	Period or semicolon before Comma after	I'm going to eat lunch. Then, I'll fix the car.
Therefore	Showing logical effect	Period or semicolon before Comma after	I'm really hungry; therefore, I'll eat a large meal.

Resources - Professional Vocabulary

Alignment. The position where the text lines up. The most common alignments are left-aligned, right-aligned, center, and justified (both right- and left-aligned).

APA. The American Psychological Association, an organization of psychologists, produces a style guide for research papers. The *Publication Manual of the American Psychological Association* is used widely in documents related to the social and behavioral sciences. You can find more information about APA style at http://www.apastyle.org/.

Audience. The person or group of people for whom a particular communication is intended. For example, the audience for this textbook is made up of community college students.

Bid. As a verb, this means to offer to supply goods and services within a particular price range and timeline. As a noun, this refers to the completed proposal.

Bitmap graphic. A graphic created using an arrangement of bits or pixels. A digital photo is an example of a bitmapped image.

Blog. Short for "web log," this is a serialized Internet column written from a personal point of view. Blogs are sometimes written just for the satisfaction of their authors, but can also produce income for writers through advertising on a dedicated site. Blogs can also be included in newsletters or company websites to offer the warmth and appeal of a personal perspective.

Caption. A label that accompanies a table, graphic, or example inserted into a larger document. Captions usually include a title for the inserted material and source credit. They may be numbered sequentially throughout a document or chapter.

Caution. Text and graphics advising the reader to be careful because tools, equipment, or product could be damaged if instructions are not followed carefully.

Chicago Style. A set of standard format rules developed by the University of Chicago Press and published in *The Chicago Manual of Style.* It includes rules about grammar, spelling, and hyphenation, in addition to documentation standards. For more information about Chicago Style, see the Chicago Manual of Style Online, at http://www.chicagomanualofstyle.org/tools_citationguide.html.

Chunking. A term originated by George A. Miller in 1956 to indicate grouping items together for better mental processing and memory.

Citation. An acknowledgment of the use of an outside source, usually found within the text and at the end of the document. Citations are formatted in predictable styles, governed by organizations such as MLA (Modern Language Association) or APA (American Psychological Association).

Cliché. An overused phrase, usually a figure of speech that has lost its original freshness. For example, "it went over like a lead balloon."

Closing. A separate line positioned below the content of a letter or email and before the signature, such as "Sincerely" or "Best regards."

Cognitive psychology. A branch of psychology that focuses on how human beings take in new information and remember it.

Comma splice. A type of run-on sentence in which two sentences are joined with a comma.

Communication triangle. A visual conceptualization of the technical writing situation that includes writer, reader, topic, purpose, content, tone, and format. James Kinneavy originated this idea in 1969, using the terms encoder, decoder, reality, and signal.

Content page. A page that is accessed from the home page of a web site. A content page contains information on a specific subject.

Copyright. Sometimes denoted with the symbol ©, copyright is the right to control how a work is distributed. Writers and artists sometimes hold copyright over their own work, and sometimes this right belongs to the publisher. Unless use of a work falls under "Fair Use" guidelines, permission must be sought from the copyright holder for copying.

Creative Commons. CreativeCommons.org is a nonprofit organization that has invented a style of copyright license that allows original text and art to be shared freely under certain conditions. By labeling work specifically with a Creative Commons (CC) license, writers, researchers, and artists can modify copyright terms. Work copyrighted with a Creative Commons license includes some scientific research, textbooks, graphic art, and music. For more information about Creative Commons licensing, go to *creativecommons.org*.

Cutaway drawing. A drawing in which the surface layer(s) is removed so that the interior of the subject can be seen. Cutaways are useful when it is difficult or impossible to see what is inside of the subject in its normal state.

CV or Curriculum Vitae. Latin for "course of life": a document presenting the educational and work-related experience of a job applicant. In the United States, a CV is reserved mainly for occupations involving research or teaching. It includes all the relevant experiences of the applicant, including positions held, publications, and presentations.. It may be many pages in length, as some applicants' publication or presentation experiences stretch over many years. Outside of the United States, the term "CV" is used more generally, instead of "resume."

Danger warning. Text and graphics advising the reader that bodily harm or death could occur through misuse of the equipment or product.

Deliverable. A result expected at the conclusion of a project, or at some specified stage. A deliverable may be a specific and measurable quantity of a particular item, such as *1000 lbs.* of refined sugar; or it may be an intangible quality, subject to judgment or approval, such as a *user-friendly* system or a *satisfactory* organizational plan. “Deliverables” are often mentioned as such in proposals for projects; they may also be discussed in a Results or Conclusions section.

Document cycle. The phases of document production, beginning with research and continuing with drafting, review, and proofreading, and ending with the final copy.

Documentation style. A set of standards for citing sources, both within the body of a document and at the end. Common documentation styles in use include APA (American Psychological Association) and MLA (Modern Language Association).

Doublespeak. An unethical way of writing or speaking, in which the writer or speaker presents information so as to prevent the audience from understanding its full meaning. For example, referring to deaths as "collateral damage."

DPI. Dots per inch. DPI is a measurement of the resolution of a digital photograph. The higher the number, the more information is stored in the photograph file.

Editing. The process of reading a document and making suggestions for revision. Editing should not be confused with revising. They are separate activities, often accomplished by two different individuals.

Exclusionary language. Word choices that exclude individuals based on gender or other differences. Common examples of exclusionary language include words like "mailman" to describe both male and female mail carriers.

Exploded view drawing. A drawing in which the parts of the subject are seemingly flying away from the central horizontal and vertical axes. Exploded views are useful for showing the parts of the subject and how they fit together.

Fair Use. This term refers to the acceptable use of copyrighted material without a specific request for permission. Federal copyright law allows writers to use material from print or online sources with proper acknowledgment without seeking permission from the original authors, as long as the purpose of the newly written document does not infringe on the profit or acclaim the original author might expect to receive. "Fair Use" guidelines require that writers consider the type of material being copied, the quantity being used, purpose of the use, and its effect on demand for the original. For a full discussion of Fair Use under U.S. Copyright Law, see http://www.copyright.gov/fls/fl102.html.

Font. Generally, a typeface. For example, Times New Roman and Helvetica are fonts. Some writing professionals differentiate between font and typeface, claiming that font is the practical application of a typeface design.

Gantt chart. A type of chart used to show progress. Gantt charts are frequently used in project management to show the various stages of a project, the amount of time each stage is scheduled to take, the deadlines, and progress within the stage. Gantt charts can also show *dependencies,* or how one part of a project affects another.

Gender-neutral language. Language that removes gender preference and/or assumption of either/or gender categories. Job titles can be made gender-neutral (for example, “waitress” becomes “server”), and pronoun references can be changed from “he or she” to “they.”

Grant. A sum of money awarded to an applicant through a competitive process, to support and encourage the goals of a particular granting organization, such as cultural development or medical research. Grants do not need to be repaid, but often require a detailed report about how the money is spent.

Hard-copy document. A document printed on paper.

Home page. The first page that a user sees when he or she accesses a web site. Typically, the home page acts as a table of contents for the web site. Also referred to as Landing Page.

HTML. Hypertext Markup Language. Widely-accepted software language (or code) that determines how web pages are formatted.

Hyperlink. An underlined phrase on a web site or in a document that allows the reader to click on the phrase and automatically open a web site.

IFB. Invitation for Bid. A document sent out to generate competitive pricing on a pre-planned project or product with detailed specifications. In contrast to an RFP (Request for Proposal), an IFB does not require any creative solutions from the bidder. IFB and RFQ (Request for Quotation) are used interchangeably.

Inflated language. An inadvisable writing style that puffs up ordinary statements to make them seem more important. For example, "We will remunerate you upon receipt of the invoice." Translation: We will pay you as soon as we receive a bill.

Initial capitalization. This term refers to the standard of capitalization used in titles, in which the first letter of every important word is capitalized. Generally, articles and prepositions are not capitalized.

Instructions (set of). A series of steps written to teach or show how to perform an action or procedure. Instructions include numbered steps and commands.

Justified text. A type of text alignment that lines up words at both the left and right margins, causing irregular spacing between words. Justified text is used in newspaper columns and in other documents where it is important to define borders, but is usually not used in letters or reports.

Lorem ipsum. A jumbled version of a Latin text by Cicero that is commonly used as dummy text to fill space when designing documents.

MLA. Modern Language Association. The MLA is a professional organization made up of teachers and professors in the humanities. The *MLA Handbook for Writers of Research Papers* sets rules and models for page settings and citation format.

Note. When used in a set of instructions, a note lets the reader know how to make the task easier or more efficient. It may also give extra information that is not vital to the understanding of the procedure.

Operational manual. A type of manual that allows the reader to read section by section, gaining knowledge of the subject.

Parenthetical definition. A brief definition or clarification of a term in which the definition occurs immediately after the term and is enclosed in parentheses or dashes.

PDF. Portable document format. PDF (.pdf) is commonly used for sending digital documents because the formatting and content cannot be changed. A PDF is very similar to a hard-copy document.

Plagiarism. The act of using words, ideas, or images that originated with another individual or company without acknowledging the borrowing. Plagiarism is a form of stealing. Even with acknowledgment, extensive borrowing is not permissible without permission from the author.

Plain Language. Refers to a standard established for federal documents to improve communication. Documents must be easily readable on the first try and use everyday words, avoiding inflated or bureaucratic vocabulary.

Process description. A description of a particular sequence of actions or procedures that typically occur over and over with predictable results. Process descriptions can be very helpful to maintain consistent results in the workplace, where different people may do the same task.

Ragged right text. A type of text alignment that is left-aligned only, allowing the text that flows to the right margin to end naturally.

Readability. The ease of reading a document. A readability index shows the scholastic grade level for a document's audience.

Recipe English. The type of language commonly used in recipe writing. Recipe English leaves out important parts of speech such as "the" and "a." Recipe English can introduce confusion in many circumstances and should be avoided when writing instructions.

Reference manual. A type of manual that allows readers to find what they want quickly. A reference manual is not intended to be read in a linear manner, from beginning to end.

Resume. A document presenting a jobseeker's educational and work experience. The resume is normally a one- or two- page document, accompanied by a cover letter introducing the applicant to the hiring manager.. This document may also be referred to as a CV. See "CV" above for more information about that term's usage.

Revising. The process of changing a draft. Revising is done by the writer after a self-edit of the document or in response to editing by others. Revisions may be minor, such as correcting spelling or punctuation, or they may be significant, such as rewriting large sections.

RFP. Request for Proposal. A document issued by an organization to invite proposals for completing a project or providing a service. This document normally includes details about the project, such as desired timeline and general specifications, but leaves some aspects open to interpretation or innovation. The goal of an RFP is not only to get a good price, but also to invite solutions to a need or problem.

RFQ. Request for Quotation. An invitation for companies or individuals to offer a price for supplying a specific, predetermined product or service. This document normally includes detailed specifications and does not require innovation or creativity on the part of the bidder. The goal of an RFQ is to encourage competitive pricing.

Run-on sentence. An ungrammatical joining of two complete sentences.

Salutation. A greeting that begins a letter or email. A salutation is always written on a separate line from the main content of the letter. Formal salutations usually begin with "Dear" as in "Dear Ms. Brown:". Informal salutations, especially in emails, may use "Hi" or "Hello" as in "Hi Diana". Punctuation following a salutation can be a colon or comma.

Sans serif font. A font type that uses consistent simple line weight without graphic details. For example, the letter "L" in Arial consists only of straight lines.

SEO. Search Engine Optimization. This is the practice of adjusting key words in a website to bring it closer to the top of a results list generated by a search engine, such as Google or Bing.

Serif font. A font type that has small graphic details (serifs) added to the simple letter shapes. For example, the letter "L" in Times New Roman has small lines added at the top of the letter, on the left side of the bottom, and on the right of the horizontal base.

Soft-copy document. An electronic or digital document saved as a file.

SOP. Standard Operating Procedure. An SOP document is written to describe and standardize procedures used in the workplace. Workers refer to SOPs to understand processes and replicate them according to company standards.

Style sheet. A collection of formatting choices applied to elements of the page such as headings, body paragraphs, and margins, contributing to the overall page design.

Typography. The study of text type, including when and where to effectively use particular fonts and styles, spacing between letters, spacing between lines, and spacing between paragraphs.

URL. Uniform Resource Locator. A complete web address.

User test. Also known as a field test, a user test is part of the document cycle for a set of instructions. The user is asked to use the set of instructions to perform a task while a note-taker observes. The user test is useful for finding problems with understandability or organization of a set of instructions.

Vector graphic. A graphic created using mathematical formulas. Software such as Adobe Illustrator use vector information.

Warning. Text and graphics advising the reader that injury or death is possible through use or misuse of the equipment or product.

White space. All the open space on a printed page, or computer display, that does not contain text or graphics.

Wordiness. Using many words when a few will do. Using as few words as possible usually produces the clearest communication and the best writing style, as long as all necessary parts of speech are included.

Works Cited. A list of references at the end of a document. This list is called "Works Cited" in MLA format, and "References" in APA format.

References

CHAPTER 1: PROFESSIONALISM AND ETHICS

Contreras Schwartz, L. (n.d.). Nonverbal communication with workplace interactions. *Houston Chronicle*. Retrieved from http://smallbusiness.chron.com/nonverbal-communication-workplace-interactions-844.html

Logical fallacies. (2009). Retrieved from http://www.logicalfallacies.info/

Orwell, G. (1949). *1984*. Boston: Houghton Mifflin Harcourt, 1987.

Plain Language Action and Information Network (PLAIN). (2011, May). *Plainlanguage.gov*. Retrieved from http://www.plainlanguage.gov/whatisPL/

Shakespeare, W. (2010). Hamlet, III.iv.229-230. (Originally published 1603.) In B. Mowat & P. Werstine (Eds.), *Folger Digital Library* (p. 183). New York: Simon & Schuster. Retrieved from http://www.folgerdigitaltexts.org/?chapter=5&play=Ham&loc=line-3.4.0

Smith, J. (2013, March 11). 10 Nonverbal cues that convey confidence at work. *Forbes*. Retrieved from http://www.forbes.com/sites/jacquelynsmith/2013/03/11/10-nonverbal-cues-that-convey-confidence-at-work/#7635e37f7ac5

U.S. Copyright Office. (2011, December). *Copyright Law of the United States (Circular 92)*. Retrieved from http://www.copyright.gov/title17

U.S. Copyright Office. (2012, June). *Fair Use*. Retrieved from http://www.copyright.gov/fls/fl102.html.

What Is Creative Commons? (2015). Retrieved from http://creativecommons.org/about

CHAPTER 2: THE WRITING PROCESS

Chinese proverb. as qtd. in Low P. K. C., *Leading Successfully in Asia.* (2013) New York: Springer, 2013. 88

Euripedes. (411-409 B.C.) *Phoenissae.* For full text, see *Internet Classic Archive.* Stevenson, D. (Ed.) Web Atomics. 2009. http://classics.mit.edu/Euripides/phoenissae.html

Jefferson, T. (1814, August 30). Letter to John Minor. in *The Thomas Jefferson Papers Series 1. General Correspondence. 1651-1827.* University of Virginia Library. Retrieved from http://memory.loc.gov/ammem/collections/jefferson_papers/mtjser1.html

King, M. L. (1963, August 28). *I Have a Dream*. Speech presented at March on Washington at the Lincoln Memorial, Washington, D.C. Retrieved from http://www.thekingcenter.org/archive/document/i-have-dream-1

Kinneavy, J. L. (1969). The basic aims of discourse. *College Composition and Communication, 20*(5), 297-304

Mankiewicz, Herman J. (Producer), & McCarey, L. (Director). (1933). *Duck Soup* (Motion Picture). USA: Paramount Pictures.

Pascal, B. (1656, October 23) as qtd. in PlainLanguage.gov. Retrieved from http://www.plainlanguage.gov/resources/quotes/historical.cfm. For full text, see *Provincial Letters.* Letter XVI: To the Reverend Fathers, the Jesuits. M'Crie, T. (Trans.) Retrieved from http://oregonstate.edu/instruct/phl302/ texts/pascal/letters-c.html#LETTER XVI

CHAPTER 4: PAGE DESIGN

Identifying and understanding the main idea. *Taranaki Secondary Literacy NLC.* Retrieved from http://taranakisecondaryliteracynlc.wikispaces.com/Identify+and+understand+main+ideas?showComments=1. Licensed under CC BY-SA 3.0: http://creativecommons.org/licenses/by-sa/3.0/

Johnson, N. (2013) North Sylamore Creek trail sign.

Miller, G. A. (1956). The magical number seven, plus or minus two: Some limits on our capacity for processing information. *Psychological Review, 63*(2), 81-97. doi: 10.1037/h0043158

CHAPTER 5: SUMMARIES

Aidman, E., Chadunow, C., Johnson, K., & Reece, J.. (2015). Real-time driver drowsiness feedback improves driver alertness and self-reported driving performance. *Accident Analysis and Prevention*, 81 (2015) 8-13. Retrieved from http://dx.doi.org/10.1016/j.aap.2015.03.041. Licensed under CC BY 4.0: http://creativecommons.org/licenses/by/4.0/legalcode

Gschwend, R. (2015). The development of public art and its future passive, active and interactive past, present and future. *Arts*, *4*(3), 93–100. MDPI AG. Retrieved from http://dx.doi.org/10.3390/arts4030093. Licensed under CC BY 4.0: http://creativecommons.org/licenses/by/4.0/legalcode

CHAPTER 7: GRAPHICS

Dmitry G. (2010). Low voltage doorbell wiring diagram. [Simplified Diagram] in *Wikimedia Commons.* Retrieved Oct. 4, 2015 from https://commons.wikimedia.org/wiki/File:Low_voltage_doorbell_wiring_diagram.JPG. Licensed under CC BY-SA 3.0: https://creativecommons.org/licenses/by-sa/3.0/deed.en

Draining the oil. [Photograph] (2014). Used courtesy of WikiPhoto.

Gear pump, exploded view. [Diagram]. (2005). in *Wikimedia Commons*. Retrieved November 17, 2015 from https://commons.wikimedia.org/wiki/File:Gear_pump_exploded.png Licensed under CC BY-SA 3.0: https://creativecommons.org/licenses/by-sa/3.0/deed.en

Guillem, Wereon, Hotmocha. (2009). Development family tree. [Organizational chart]. in *Wikimedia Commons*. Retrieved Feb. 20, 2017 from https://commons.wikimedia.org/wiki/File%3AUnix_timeline.en.svg. Public domain.

How to change the oil on an air-cooled Volkswagen Beetle: Step 10: Tighten the center drain plug [Line drawing]. (2014). In *Wikihow.com*. Retrieved Apr. 3, 2014, from http://www.wikihow.com/Change-the-Oil-on-an-Aircooled-Volkswagen-%28VW%29-Beetle. Used courtesy of WikiHow.

Hydrargyrum. (2013). Diagram of doorbell wiring. in *Wikimedia Commons.* Retrieved from https://commons.wikimedia.org/wiki/File%3ADoorbell_Wiring_Pictorial Diagram.svg. Licensed under CC BY-SA 3.0: https://creativecommons.org/licenses/by-sa/3.0/deed.en

Internal Revenue Service. (2014). 2013 Tax Table. In *IRS.gov*. Retrieved from http://www.irs.gov/pub/irs-pdf/i1040tt.pdf. Public domain.

Keconfer (2014). DEQ 2015 budget [Pie Chart]. in *Wikimedia Commons.* Retrieved from https://commons.wikimedia.org/wiki/File%3AMichigan_DEQ_Budget_by_Funding_Sources.jpg. Licensed under CC BY-SA 4.0: http://creativecommons.org/licenses/by-sa/4.0

Kerr, P. (2006). Swimlanes flow chart of a business process [flow chart] in *Wikimedia Commons.* Retrieved November 15, 2015 from https://commons.wikimedia.org/wiki/File:Approvals.jpg. Public Domain.

NASA. (2013) Gantt chart for Mars exploration. in *Wikimedia Commons*. Retrieved from https://commons.wikimedia.org/wiki/File%3AMarsExplorationTimeline-20130710.jpg. Public Domain.

Netalloy (2012). Buy green. [Clip Art]. in *OpenClipArt.org.* Retrieved from https://openclipart.org/detail/169400/buy-green. Public Domain.

Office of the Secretary of Defense. (2012, March). Organization of the Department of Defense (DoD)[Organizational chart]. In *Odam.defense.gov*. Retrieved from http://odam.defense.gov/Portals/43/Documents/Functions/Organizational%20Portfolios/Organizations%20and%20Functions%20Guidebook/DoD_Organization_March_2012.pdf. Public domain.

State of Working America, Economic Policy Institute. (2012). Productivity and real median family income growth 1947-2009. [Line Graph]. in *Wikimedia Commons.* Retrieved from https://commons.wikimedia.org/wiki/File% AProductivity_and_Real _Median_Family_Income_Growth_1947-2009.png. Licensed under CC BY-SA 3.0: https://creativecommons.org/licenses/by-sa/3.0/deed.en

Student work patterns vs. having college credit card debts [Bar graph]. (2007). In *Duck9.com*. Retrieved April 14, 2014, from http://www.duck9.com/College-Student-Drop-Out-Rates.htm. Used courtesy of Duck9.

Thompson, A. and Harrison, D. Gantt chart. [Template:Excel file CSE 379 Gantt Chart.xls] in *Wikimedia Commons*. Retrieved October 5, 2015 from https://commons.wikimedia.org/wiki/File%3AGantt_Chart_10-21.JPG. Public domain.

U.S. Centers for Disease Control and Prevention. [Column graph]. (2004). Percentage of persons over 18-years-old reporting severe headache or migraine in the prior 3 months grouped by age and sex. 2004-US. in *Wikimedia Commons.* Retrieved from https://commons.wikimedia.org/wiki/File%3 AHeadache-migraine_statistics-CDC_2004_US.PNG. Public domain.

U. S. Department of Labor, Bureau of Labor Statistics. (2015, Jan.). Exhibit 1. How the National Compensation Survey determines the type of medical plan employers offer. [Flow chart]. Retrieved from http://www.bls.gov/opub/btn/volume-4/understanding_health_plan_types.htm. Public domain.

U.S. National Library of Medicine. (2013). Funding levels by fiscal year [Column graph]. In *Nim.nih.gov*. Retrieved from http://www.nlm.nih.gov/about/2013CJ.html#Budget_graphs. Public domain.

Viriyincy, O. Readable bus stop schedule mockup. in *Flickr.com*. Retrieved from https://www.flickr.com/photos/viriyincy/4084549393 /in/photostream/. Licensed under CC BY-SA 2.0: https://creativecommons.org/licenses/by-sa/2.0/

Waddy, M. (2009, November 8). Oil being drained from a GMC Sport Utility Vehicle. [Photograph] in *Wikimedia.org.* Retrieved November 14, 2015 from https://commons.wikimedia.org/wiki/File:Oil_Change_oil_pan_2005_gmc_suv.JPG. Public Domain.

ZooFari. (2010). Heart Diagram. *Wikipedia.com*. Retrieved November 17, 2015 from https://commons.wikimedia.org/wiki/File:Heart_diagram-en.svg Licensed under CC BY-SA 3.0: https://creativecommons.org/licenses/by-sa/3.0/deed.en

CHAPTER 8: USER INSTRUCTIONS

Completed paper airplane. [Drawing]. (2012). In VectorGoods.Com. Retrieved from http://vectorgoods.com/wp-content/uploads/2012/04/sky-vector.jpg. Licensed under Attribution 4.0 International (CC BY 3.0).

CHAPTER 11: WRITING FOR THE WEB

EPA Recycling website [Screen Capture]. Retrieved from www2.epa.gov. Public domain.

EPA Recycling website for children [Screen Capture]. Retrieved from www3.epa.gov. Public domain.

Maggie Sottero wedding gown web site (2014). in *Maggiesottero.com*. Retrieved from http://www.maggiesottero.com/. Used courtesy of Maggie Sottero Designs.

State of Oregon website [Screen Capture]. Retrieved from www.oregon.gov. Public domain.

State of South Carolina website [Screen Capture]. Retrieved from www.sc.gov. Public domain.

Travel Portland content page (2014). in *Travelportland.com*. Retrieved from http://www.travelportland.com/. Used courtesy of Travel Portland.

Travel Portland home page (2014). in *Travelportland.com*. Retrieved from http://www.travelportland.com/article/favorite-hiking-spots/. Used courtesy of Travel Portland.

CHAPTER 12: JOB APPLICATION MATERIALS

Anonymous. (2015). Bridal Website Mock-up.

Jim Stevenson resume. (2015). Used courtesy of N. Lidell.

Peggy Olsen resume. (2015). Used courtesy of S. Sylwester.

Résumé or resume or resumé. (2014). In *The American Heritage Dictionary*. Retrieved from http://ahdictionary.com/word/search.html?q=resum%C3%A9&submit.x=43&submit.y=24

Résumé. (2014). In *Merriam-Webster Dictionary.* Retrieved from http://www.merriam-webster.com/dictionary/r%25C3%25A9sum%25C3%25A9

Resume, resumé, or résumé? (2014). In *Pain in the English.* Retrieved from http://painintheenglish.com/case/193

Index

A

B

C

D

E

F

G

H

I

J

K

L

M

N

O

P

T

U

V

W

Y

About the Authors

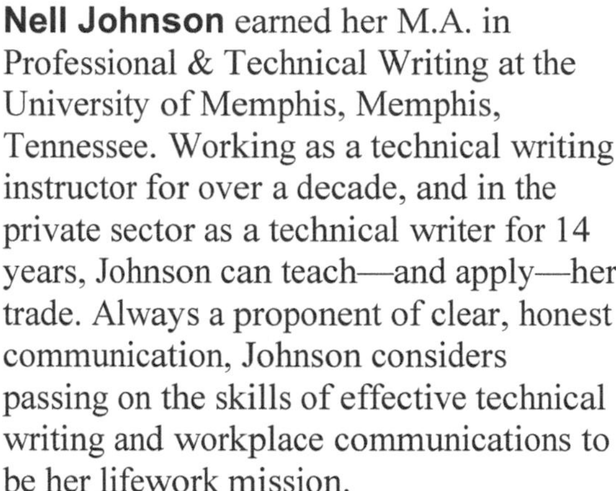

Nell Johnson earned her M.A. in Professional & Technical Writing at the University of Memphis, Memphis, Tennessee. Working as a technical writing instructor for over a decade, and in the private sector as a technical writer for 14 years, Johnson can teach—and apply—her trade. Always a proponent of clear, honest communication, Johnson considers passing on the skills of effective technical writing and workplace communications to be her lifework mission.

Johnson teaches online sections of technical writing at Portland Community College in Portland, Oregon. She has recently taken up ballet.

Mary Sylwester has taught composition and literature for over twenty years: in Iowa, Maryland, and Oregon. She has a Ph.D. in English from the University of Iowa.

Sylwester currently teaches composition and technical writing classes at Portland Community College and Portland State University in Portland, Oregon. She enjoys exploring local restaurants with her husband, leading a community garden near her home, and providing a secure home base for her four children, who keep moving in and out of the nest.

CPSIA information can be obtained
at www.ICGtesting.com
Printed in the USA
LVHW060824250123
737910LV00010B/313